Applied Psychology for Foundation Year

Applied Psychology for Foundation Year: Key Ideas for Foundation Courses introduces students to topical issues and controversies within specific areas of applied psychology, bringing together current theories and studies from a number of areas within applied psychology through a series of interesting and current debates and controversies.

Included in this book are a series of snapshots of how psychologists have tried to apply their findings to real-life problems. Using a clear structure and accessible tone, this book demonstrates how psychological research can be applied to inform current debates across a variety of the field's subdisciplines. Through examination of both established theoretical ideas and more recent empirical evidence, it enables readers to see how research is linked to practical application in occupational psychology, educational psychology, criminology, sport psychology and environmental psychology. In doing so, it explicates contemporary theories and studies and contributes a cross-cultural understanding of these topics. This book's wide coverage of topics and theories is designed to enable readers to not only immerse themselves in topical and often controversial debates but also to develop a critical awareness of alternative viewpoints, methodological weaknesses and theoretical shortcomings. Readers are encouraged to consider and question these theories and consider the implications of this research and how the findings can be applied to their own experience.

Applied Psychology for Foundation Year is a key textbook for both foundation year and introductory psychology courses and will be of interest to anyone wanting to delve into topical issues in contemporary psychology.

Wendy Garnham is a Reader in psychology and Director of Student Experience for the Central Foundation Years at the University of Sussex, UK. As co-founder of the Active Learning Network, Wendy has experience teaching across the educational spectrum from reception to postgraduate level, including leading a further education psychology department to Grade 1 status and leading a sixth form before returning to Higher Education. Dr. Garnham has won several awards for innovative teaching, including a National Teaching Fellowship in 2020 and was part of a CATE award–winning team for Foundation Year teaching in 2019.

Applied Psychology for Foundation Year

Key Ideas for Foundation Courses

Wendy Garnham

LONDON AND NEW YORK

Cover image: © Getty Images

First published 2023
by Routledge
4 Park Square, Milton Park, Abingdon, Oxon OX14 4RN

and by Routledge
605 Third Avenue, New York, NY 10158

*Routledge is an imprint of the Taylor & Francis Group,
an informa business*

© 2023 Wendy Garnham

The right of Wendy Garnham to be identified as author of this work has been asserted in accordance with sections 77 and 78 of the Copyright, Designs and Patents Act 1988.

All rights reserved. No part of this book may be reprinted or reproduced or utilised in any form or by any electronic, mechanical, or other means, now known or hereafter invented, including photocopying and recording, or in any information storage or retrieval system, without permission in writing from the publishers.

Trademark notice: Product or corporate names may be trademarks or registered trademarks, and are used only for identification and explanation without intent to infringe.

British Library Cataloguing-in-Publication Data
A catalogue record for this book is available from the British Library

Library of Congress Cataloging-in-Publication Data
Names: Garnham, Wendy, author.
Title: Applied psychology for foundation year: key ideas for
   foundation courses/Wendy Garnham.
Description: Abingdon, Oxon; New York, NY: Routledge, 2023. |
   Includes bibliographical references and index. |
Identifiers: LCCN 2022029400 (print) | LCCN 2022029401 (ebook) |
   ISBN 9781032360003 (hardback) | ISBN 9781032359977
   (paperback) | ISBN 9781003329763 (ebook)
Subjects: LCSH: Psychology, Applied. | Psychology.
Classification: LCC BF636 .G3337 2023 (print) | LCC BF636 (ebook) |
   DDC 158–dc23/eng/20220716
LC record available at https://lccn.loc.gov/2022029400
LC ebook record available at https://lccn.loc.gov/2022029401

ISBN: 978-1-032-36000-3 (hbk)
ISBN: 978-1-032-35997-7 (pbk)
ISBN: 978-1-003-32976-3 (ebk)

DOI: 10.4324/9781003329763

Typeset in Times New Roman
by Apex CoVantage, LLC

Access the companion website: www.routledge.com/cw/Garnham

Contents

Acknowledgements ix
Preface xi

CHAPTER 1 **Who is watching you?** **1**
    The power of the eyes – a brief, historical tour 2
    Are we as sensitive to the idea of being watched as has
    been suggested historically? 4
        Exploiting this sensitivity 7
    Does this sensitivity to the eyes mean we "change"
    our behaviour in response? 8
        Can watching eyes make us more pro-social? 8
        Can watching eyes reduce crime? 10
        Can watching eyes make us more COVID-safe? 11
    Is this really because we are so concerned with
    our reputation? 12
        We like to avoid risks 12
        We are concerned with maintaining a good reputation 13
        There are limits to the watching eyes effect (and that
        mainly relates to the limitations on benefits for us) 16
        On reflection 18
    References 18

CHAPTER 2 **How do you learn best?** **21**
    Learning as construction 22
        Piaget's stage theory 23
    Do we need teachers anymore? 27
    Vygotsky's peer learning 28
    Differences in active learning effects 30
    What makes a good teacher? 32
    References 35

CHAPTER 3 **Do video games have value?** **39**
    Can video games improve our cognitive skills? 40
    Reasons to be cautious? 43
    Perhaps video games just make us more pro-social 45
    Is it just pro-social games that make us behave more
    pro-socially? 47
    If pro-social games make us more pro-social, do anti-social
    video games make us behave more anti-socially? 48
    It's not that straightforward 50
    References 52

CHAPTER 4 What colour are you wearing today?......55
The Lady in Red revisited 56
Is this a universal phenomenon? 58
The catch 60
And how about the gentlemen among us?.....60
A focus on fashion 62
Taking the colour effect into the sporting arena..........................62
Is this specific to individual sports?..........64
The exceptions to the rule 65
References 67

CHAPTER 5 How to win at sport 71
Rule number 1: Make sure you take advantage of the home advantage 72
    The effect of a crowd 73
    The role of the ref...................74
Rule number 2: Keep your arousal/anxiety levels under control 76
    Explaining catastrophe 78
Rule number 3: Have self-belief 80
Rule number 4: But don't be too overconfident 82
Rule number 5: The force is within (or in technical terms, be driven by intrinsic motivation, not external rewards) 85
Rule number 6: Smile when you're winning (unless you're in a combat sport) 87
Rule number 7: High five your teammates 87
References 88

CHAPTER 6 Are you keeping your employees happy? ...93
Happy employees are more committed to the organisation 94
Happy employees work well with others......95
Happy employees are likely to perform better 96
Happy employees are more creative 98
Happy employees are safer employees 99
    Suggestion 1: Make sure there are a moderate number of plants in the office ...100
    Suggestion 2: Empower your staff 103
    Suggestion 3: Be a happy boss 105
References 106

CHAPTER 7	**Is it possible to detect deception?**	**111**
	Just how bad are we at detecting deception?	113
	Are verbal cues more reliable?	115
	Why not eliminate visual information altogether?	117
	The unconscious lie detector	118
	Are certain individuals better lie detectors than others?	121
	How can we improve deception detection?	123
	Use a group	123
	Use drawing as a detection tool	125
	Use unexpected questions	127
	References	129
CHAPTER 8	**Can you spot a criminal?**	**133**
	The "criminal type"	134
	Are there physical characteristics that relate to criminal behaviour?	136
	So what does this criminal stereotype look like?	138
	Why are honesty and dominance so important?	141
	The self-fulfilling prophecy and where our story becomes a little less clear	142
	Why does it matter?	143
	The criminal stereotype can influence us even before a case gets to court	146
	Physical appearance implications for criminals	147
	References	148
CHAPTER 9	**Where is a good place to live?**	**153**
	The Lungs of London	154
	Gender effects exist	155
	The Phytophilic Effect	156
	Specific benefits associated with green space	156
	You might just live longer	156
	You might perform better at work or school	157
	So, what happens if there are not many nature walks or parks locally?	159

You might feel better mentally 161
You might feel better physically 163
You might benefit economically too 165
The Biophilia Hypothesis 168
But not all green space has the same effect . . . 169
Experience matters. 170
Perhaps it is not the green space itself
that is important at all but what we do
in the green space. 171
Is it just our evolutionary past having
an effect? 173
Looking forward 173
References 174

CHAPTER 10 Is it good to spend time by the sea? 181
Blue space as health-enabling 182
Blue space and mental health 184
Explaining the restorative effects
of blue space 185
Mediating factors. 186
The type of blue space matters 187
Is this a Eurocentric view?. 188
Some blue space is good but not too much 188
Looking to the future 189
References 190

CHAPTER 11 The psychology of Christmas 193
How to promote happiness in the
festive season. 194
Should we give gifts at all? 195
How to choose the most appropriate gift. 196
Christmas shopping 199
The Christmas dinner. 201
The Christmas spirit. 202
Does the Christmas spirit exist? 204
Christmas as a time of relaxation. 204
References 205

Index 209

Acknowledgements

I would like to thank Adam Woods and Nivedita Menon from Routledge for their help and support in getting this book published. It has long been one of the things on my bucket list and this would not have been possible without the professionalism and support of the Routledge team.

Thankfully I am surrounded by superstars who have provided me with unlimited encouragement and support. In particular, I would like to thank Graeme Pedlingham, and my team of Foundation Year colleagues. I hope they know how much they are valued.

I would also like to thank Heather Taylor for her constant encouragement, support and supply of coffee and chocolate where needed and Tab Betts and Paolo Oprandi for their overflowing enthusiasm and belief in me. Thank you also to the incredible colleagues that I haven't yet mentioned who inspire me every day – too many to mention individually here but you know who you are.

To my parents, thank you. Not only did you set me up to believe I could achieve but you taught me the value of fun in everything. Hopefully this book will convey some of that fun and interest to its readers. Finally, for all the love, laughter and of course, their incredible patience while I wrote this book, thank you to my long-suffering husband Alan, and our boys, Harry, George, Ben, Robin and Tom to whom this book is dedicated. They are my world.

Preface

This book is intended to entice readers into the fascinating world of psychology, to inspire, enthuse and hopefully encourage readers to want to find out more and continue their exploration of this subject. If it manages to succeed in only one of these aims, that is a good thing because this is very much a foundation, a diving board into a broad and vast field of research which we only scratch the surface of here.

Included in this book are a series of snapshots of how psychologists have tried to apply their findings to real-life problems. For example, is passively listening to a lecture the best way to learn? Is there a proven way to detect deception in others? Or is there a winning formula for success in sport? You will find out why it is good to have a plant or two in the office, why you need to be cautious with people who are good at poker and why singing Christmas carols might have added benefits for our well-being. You'll find out why sportspeople such as Eric Bristow or Sally Robbins can aid our understanding of sporting success and perhaps be able to throw new light on why Tottenham Hotspur (my favourite football team) haven't won the Premier League for some time.

The aim of this book is to enable readers not only to immerse themselves in topical and often controversial debates but also to develop a critical awareness of alternative viewpoints, methodological weaknesses or theoretical short-comings. As you read the chapters, do try to link what you read to your own experience. Question the theories, think about the implications of this research and perhaps even plan how you might address these issues in your own research going forward.

Enjoy!

Chapter 1

Who is watching you?

Would you change your behaviour if you saw a picture of a pair of eyes on the wall in front of you? Historically, the suggestion has been that you would and this idea has been used in cultural products such as films and novels. This chapter explores the watching eyes effect through experimental psychological studies that show you donate more, are more honest and are likely to recycle more when a picture of a pair of eyes is present. It explores applications in the area of health such as hand-washing behaviour and crime such as reducing bike theft as well as asking how this might come in useful for politicians running for office or for marketing executives. In this chapter, theories of why we are so susceptible to this effect are explored including Reputation Management Theory and the Risk Aversion Hypothesis and limitations of the effect are considered.

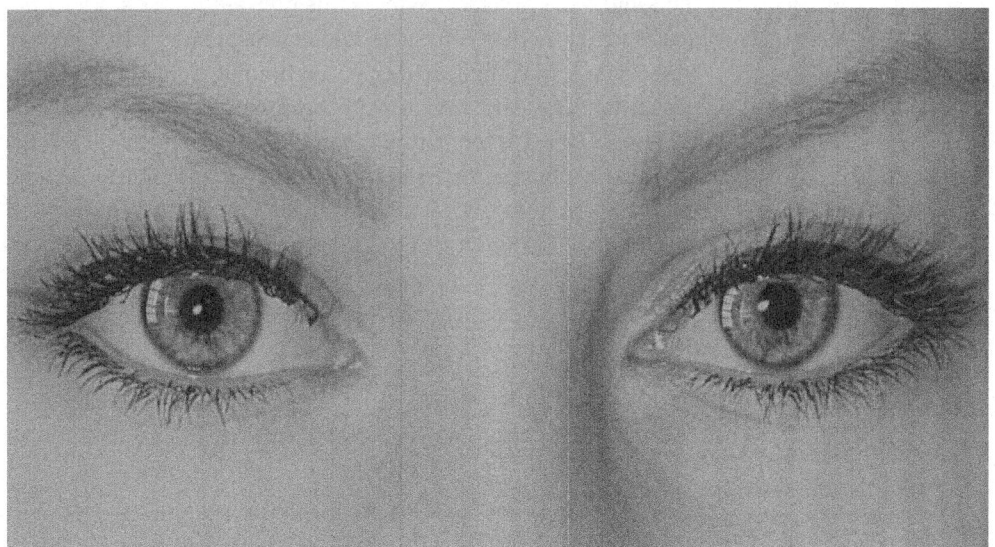

■ **Figure 1.1** Can a picture change behaviour?

Ever had the feeling that someone is watching you? Chances are that feeling led to change in your behaviour at some level or so the evidence would suggest. The "Watching Eyes" effect as it has come to be called, refers to a phenomenon whereby our behaviour becomes more altruistic and pro-social when we believe we are being watched.

THE POWER OF THE EYES – A BRIEF, HISTORICAL TOUR...

The effect has long-standing historical roots. In Ancient Egypt, for example, the Eye of Horus was used to symbolise protection and restoration. It was used as a symbol on amulets to protect the wearer or to ensure their health and was often painted onto bows of ships before they set off on long voyages to protect them from evil forces. It was considered an "eye of God" (Edwards & Oakley, 1996).

How about the Ancient Greeks? Glaucon, one of Plato's older brothers (Plato was an Ancient Greek philosopher), mentions the power of the eye in his rendition of the story of Gyges, a shepherd. Gyges found a ring in the underworld that, when worn, made him invisible. However, being rendered as such meant that Gyges could behave terribly and avoid the consequences. For example, he even seduced the queen and plotted with her to kill the king! What a terror! Why is this relevant to our story of the watching eyes effect? Because Adeimantus, Plato's other brother (they clearly liked to keep discussion running in the family) suggested that the only reason we behave ethically and morally is because we have a reputation to uphold. When others are watching us, we function co-operatively because we want to be able to benefit from all the good things that come with having a good reputation. Glaucon was not very positive about the human race, believing that even if an honest citizen received a similar ring to Gyges, they too would behave in an utterly unethical manner. Oh dear.

The idea of surveillance being a cue to morally acceptable behaviour was later revisited by Jeremy Bentham, an English philosopher living in the 18th century, who introduced the term "panopticon" to describe an application of this effect. Perhaps, just perhaps, if people were more likely to behave in a morally superior way when they thought they could be seen, this could be the key to solving the problem of poor behaviour in places such as prisons or schools. Bentham developed the concept of a circular prison where all in-mates could be observed at all times by security guards who were present in a central observation area, concealed from view of the prisoners. Whether inmates were actually being watched at any one time was impossible to tell, so they had to be on their best behaviour just in case. Millbank Prison was constructed using Bentham's panopticon principles.

The idea of the panopticon was met with hostility from some quarters. French philosopher Michel Foucault described the panopticon as a mechanism of power akin to keeping inmates in a "cruel, ingenious cage". Whilst Bentham certainly had his critics, it is not an idea that has been long buried. Open plan kitchens in

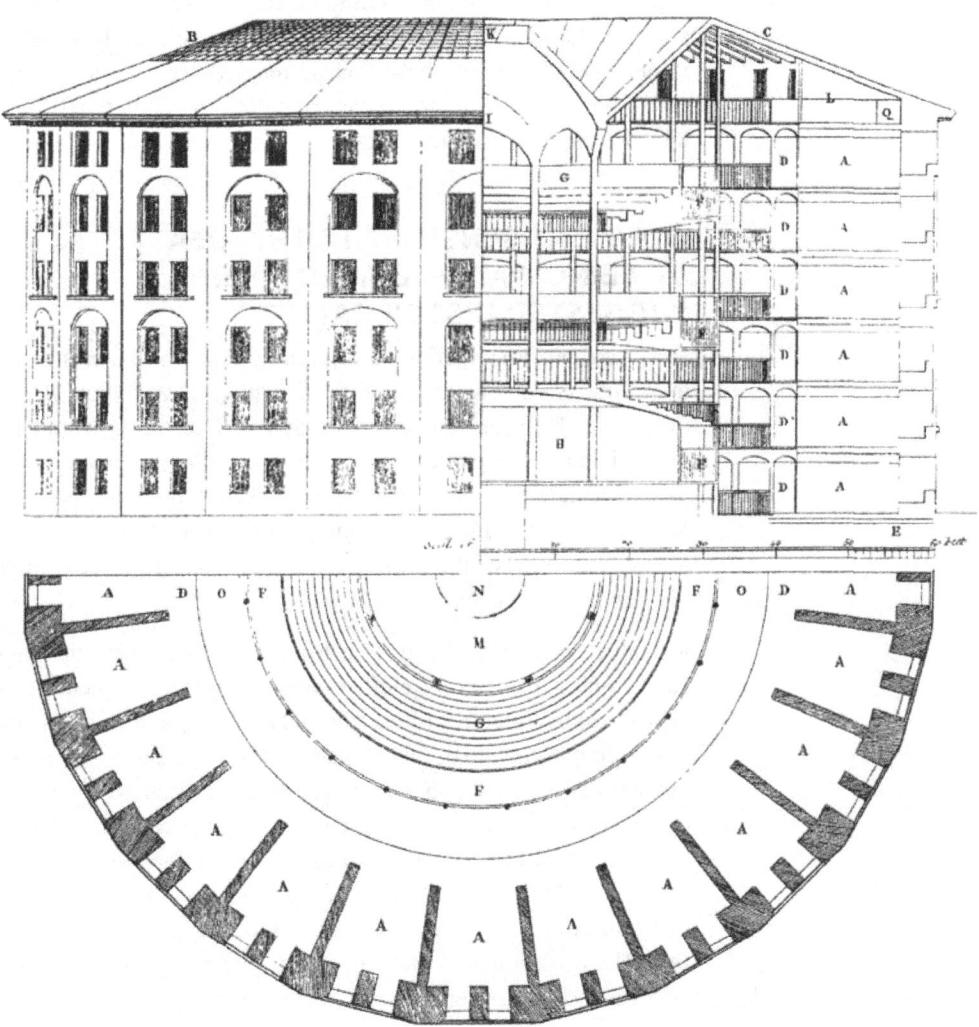

■ **Figure 1.2** A plan for a panopticon prison as suggested by Jeremy Bentham. This was drawn by Willey Reveley in 1791.

restaurants are now commonplace where you can see your food being prepared, scrutinising the process. Indeed, there is an argument that the concept of the panopticon has morphed as technology has developed (Fyfe & Bannister, 1996). Closed circuit television for example now creates the feeling of being watched in public places, even if we are not sure whether there is someone physically watching us at any point. George Orwell in his book *1984* talked about how "Big Brother is watching you" and Big Brother does a lot of that in some countries such as China where a social credit system works on the basis of rewarding citizens for observed pro-social behaviour.

Given the moralistic and ethical arguments that abound in philosophical circles, some important questions arise: Are we as sensitive to the idea of being watched as is suggested? If so, does it mean we change our behaviour in response? And if so, is this really because we are so concerned with our reputation? Let's take these questions one at a time.

ARE WE AS SENSITIVE TO THE IDEA OF BEING WATCHED AS HAS BEEN SUGGESTED HISTORICALLY?

Let's take our imagination on a journey. You are in a children's museum. As you enter, you see, at the desk, a transparent donation box which has a sign on it saying "Donations would be appreciated". Alongside this statement, you see a picture of a pair of female eyes and a pair of male eyes. Would you donate? Would it make a difference if the pictures were of noses rather than eyes? Or how about if they were mouths? These are, after all, human facial cues.

Kelsey et al. (2018) did just such a study. One week, the sign showed pictures of eyes, another week it might show pictures of noses, another, pictures of mouths and another pictures of chairs, a non-human inanimate object. The authors measured the average amount of money donated per patron in each week. Those exposed to the sign showing pictures of eyes, were more likely to donate than those exposed to the other versions of the signs. The mean donation in the eyes condition was $0.18 compared to $0.008 in the nose condition, and $0.011 in the mouth condition. The eyes, it would seem, play a special role in attracting our attention and fostering pro-social behaviour.

I know what you are thinking. That donation amount seems incredibly small. However, the authors calculated, on the basis of the number of visitors, that this increase in donations would amount to an additional $12 a week, almost the same as the average donation amount per week ($15)!

Now think about the effect this might have on getting people to vote. In the recent American Presidential election, Joe Biden and Donald Trump might have made use of a watching eyes image to ensure their followers made it to the polling station. When the 2011 Municipal Elections took place in Key West Florida, Panagopoulos was on hand to try out the watching eyes effect to see if it influenced the number of people voting. Whilst one group were not sent anything, those in the other three groups were sent postcards with a reminder that it was their civic duty to vote. For a third of these individuals, they had a postcard with a picture of a palm tree on it. The palm tree was seen to be a nonpolitical image. For a third, they had a postcard with a political image on it, an American flag. For the final third, they had a picture of forward gazing eyes on their postcard. Did the watching eyes have any effect? Well, they only went and led to the highest turnout for voting out of the four groups!

The power of the watching eyes effect has even made it into popular films. If any of you have watched a film called *Labyrinth*,

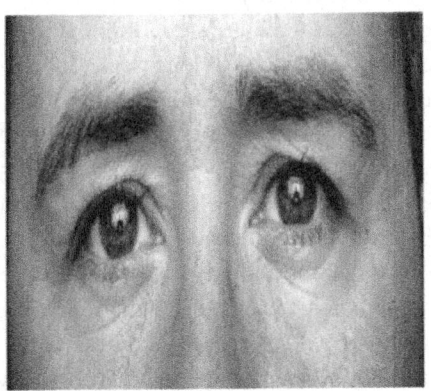

■ **Figure 1.3** One of the treatment condition mailing samples used in Panagopoulos (2014).

■ **Figure 1.4** The placebo condition mailing sample used in Panagopoulos (2014).

there is a character there called Pale Man. Pale Man is not a likeable character. In fact, if truth be told, he is a child-eating creature. The reason Pale Man is relevant for our story is that his eyes can be placed in the sockets on his hands. We are drawn to look at these even though they are not on his face! This is not altogether surprising given that our human perceptual system is known to have neurons that respond selectively to eye-like stimuli (Emery, 2000).

So, it does appear that we are especially sensitive to the eyes. Simon Baron-Cohen suggests that the eyes are in fact the most emotionally informative part of the face. Along with Therese Joliffe in 1997, he created a "Reading the mind in the eyes" task. Participants were asked to look at the eye region of several faces and make a forced choice between which of two words described how that individual might be feeling (Baron-Cohen et al., 1997a). Despite being able to accurately assess aspects such as gender from the pictures, individuals with autism were unable to accurately ascertain what the person might be feeling or thinking, unlike a nonclinical control group of adults. Baron-Cohen et al. (1997b) replicated this effect showing that complex mental states are identifiable by nonclinical adults from pictures of the eyes alone but it does not work if pictures of mouths are used.

Exploiting this sensitivity

Given the sensitivity of us all to the eyes, what applications might this have? I'm going to start by throwing a big word in here: anthropomorphism. You may have heard of it. If you haven't, what it means in simple terms, is this, assuming that non-human objects or agents have "human-like characteristics, motivations, intentions and emotions" (Epley et al., 2007).

Who wouldn't enjoy playing with a tennis ball that had a smiley face on it for example? But I'm not sure the same positive feeling extends to a pumpkin with a sinister face carved into it. Advertisers have jumped upon this in trying to market their products effectively. Knowing that we show a particular sensitivity to the eyes, and that we tend to then imbue non-human objects with human-like characteristics, opens up a world of possibilities for advertisers to appeal to different markets. Hart and Royne (2017) demonstrated this using car advertisements.

This study included 185 adults. Each was asked to respond initially to a series of eight items related to loneliness and knowledge about cars as assessed by themselves. They were then shown a single print advertisement for a car. Having looked at the advert, they were then asked about their attitude towards the brand and to the advertisement as well as their intention to purchase the product. There were four digital print advertisements used in the study:

- Direct anthropomorphism: the car was shown with a human-like mouth and eyes
- Non-anthropomorphism: the car was shown with normal features
- Contextual anthropomorphism: the car was shown with normal features but surrounded by paparazzi watching it. This was designed to give the impression of the car as a human celebrity.
- Non-anthropomorphism contextual: the car was shown with normal features in its normal context, that is, on a road.

Which advert led to the most enhanced evaluations and expressed intentions to buy the product? Why, the adverts where the cars were shown to have features resembling eyes. Participants' attitudes towards the brand and the advertisement were enhanced for anthropomorphism prints and this was so particularly for contextual advertisements. There were some important individual differences however. The effect was particularly strong for those individuals who rated themselves as high in loneliness. Ownership of a product that possessed human-like qualities had particular value for them. Conversely, individuals who already had very strong product knowledge did not respond so much to these adverts. The moral of the story would appear to be, know your audience!

DOES THIS SENSITIVITY TO THE EYES MEAN WE "CHANGE" OUR BEHAVIOUR IN RESPONSE?

Can watching eyes make us more pro-social?

To answer this question, let's imagine that we are in a staff room where we have the option to help ourselves to tea or coffee, with milk if required. Next to the kettle, we see an honesty box where we are supposed to put our money to cover the cost. On the cupboard door, just above the kettle, and at eye level, there is a sign giving instructions for payment. On the sign, you also see a picture of flowers. Do you put your money in the box? As a good, honest citizen, I have no doubt that you would pay your money. That's exactly what Bateson et al. (2006) might have thought too before they did their study.

Across ten weeks, Bateson and colleagues counted the amount of money in the honesty box and measured the total volume of milk consumed each week and calculated the ratio between the two. They also, rather slyly, changed the picture on the notice. Some days it had a picture of a forward-facing pair of eyes. Some days it had a picture of a flower. To their surprise, people paid 2.76 times more in the weeks when the eyes were present on the notice than when it was a flower. The authors suggest that the image of the eyes gave visitors to the coffee room the impression they were being watched.

This is not an isolated example of how pictures of eyes affect our behaviour. Cécile Sénémeaud and colleagues (2017) wanted to investigate whether pictures of eyes could be used to increase the number of people who came forward to give blood. At the beginning of a lecture, 454 first year undergraduate students were given a flyer promoting the need for blood donation volunteers. On some of the flyers, there was a picture of a pair of human eyes. On other flyers, there was a neutral drawing such as a flower pattern. At the bottom of the flyer, there was a pledge form that students could complete to promise to give blood, stating their name and contact details. These were placed into a box at the end of the lecture.

At first glance, it didn't look as though the picture of eyes had had much effect, certainly in terms of pledges given. However, the researchers also measured the number of students who actually turned up to donate blood. In line with Bateson's honesty box study, Sénémeaud's team found that students who had received a flyer with a pair of eyes on it were almost three times as likely to come to give blood than students who received the flyer with the neutral drawing on it! A possible explanation proposed by the authors was that the human eye picture creates a form of implicit social pressure to donate.

That social pressure to donate has also been demonstrated in a study of shoppers in Stockholm, Sweden. Ekström (2012) studied the behaviour of people who recycled cans and bottles at their

■ **Figure 1.5** The flyers used in Sénémeaud et al.'s study.

local supermarket. In doing so, shoppers can keep the money for themselves or donate it to a charity and have to register their choice by pressing a button next to the recycling machines. Placing a picture of a pair or eyes next to the buttons increased the donated amount by 30% on days when there were few other recycling customers around.

Can watching eyes reduce crime?

Given the power of the watching eyes effect, it is not surprising to know that researchers soon turned their attention to looking at how this effect might be used to reduce crime. Nettle et al. (2012) decided to study its value in terms of reducing bike theft on a university campus. They installed signs showing a black and white image of a pair of male eyes with a direct forward gaze on walls in three locations where bike theft had been particularly high at Newcastle University.

Before the study began, there had been 39 bike thefts in these locations. In the 12 months following the posting of the signs, this had decreased to just 15, a huge reduction of over 60%. What an amazing result!

Dear (2018) went one step further in a crime study conducted in Hereford with West Mercia police. Using signs not dissimilar from Nettle's, Dear erected signs at sites selected by Hereford Police including a fast-food outlet where anti-social behaviour had been reported, at Hereford Country Hospital where cycle theft had been an issue and at a High Street fashion store where shoplifting was an ongoing problem. Not only was there a significant reduction in cycle theft at the local hospital but there were also reductions in shoplifting at the High Street fashion store and in the fast-food store, a dramatic reduction in anti-social behaviour was reported. When signs were used at a local rural area where fly-tipping was commonplace, this reduced and at a local park, the number of incidents of anti-social driving reduced to almost zero. A Gamekeeper reported an 80% reduction in poaching following the introduction of the signs but as the saying goes "You can't win em all" as someone stole the signs!

Together, the work of Dear and of Nettle and colleagues suggests a powerful effect of watching eyes on crime reduction. But nothing is ever that straightforward in psychology. Unfortunately, Nettle et al. reported that although crime had reduced hugely in the three experimental areas, it had in fact increased substantially in neighbouring areas where previously bike theft had not really

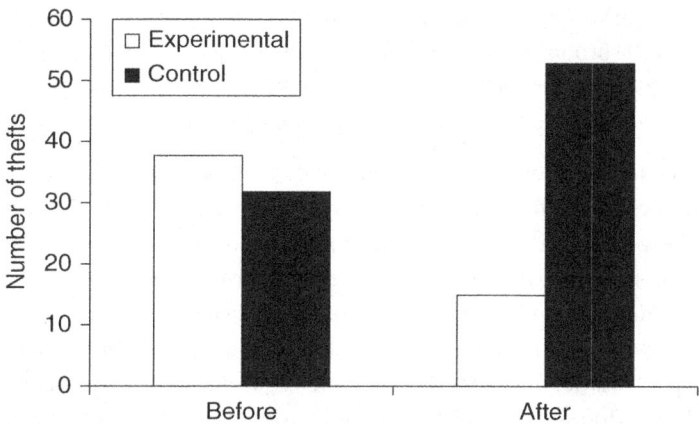

■ **Figure 1.6** Numbers of notified bicycle thefts in the 12 months before and after the intervention for the experimental locations (black bars) and the control locations (grey bars) in Nettle and Bateson's Cycle Theft study (2012).

been a problem. Across 16 different neighbouring areas, in the 12 months before the study, there had only been 31 bike thefts. Following the initiation of the study, this increased by another 30. There were even 21 thefts from 14 locations that had never experienced any bike thefts before the study. It therefore appears that the watching eyes effect had reduced crime where the signs were but displaced rather than removed the criminal activity.

Can watching eyes make us more COVID-safe?

That said, the watching eyes effect can be of great use, no less now after the COVID pandemic, than before. If images of watching eyes can reduce crime and make us more pro-social, can they also be used to improve adherence to improved hygiene measures such as hand-washing?

The work of Stefan Pfattheicher and colleagues in 2018 would suggest so. Before the COVID pandemic hit, they were already exploring whether the watching eyes effect could be used to improve hand hygiene compliance in public toilets. A sign was placed directly above the sinks, advising that hand-washing protects against the spread of germs. In one condition, the message was accompanied by a pair of stylized watching eyes. In the other condition, a picture of three stars accompanied the message. Did it have any effect? Well, I think you are going to guess this one correctly. The answer is a resounding yes. Hand-washing occurred far more often in the eyes condition than in the stars condition (83.3% compliance compared to 71.9%). Just in case you are wondering, the study did not involve people observing in the washroom itself thankfully – the magical soap dispenser set timestamps for each use and a hidden observer located 15 metres away monitored time of entry and time of leaving the restroom.

Let's not underestimate the potential of this finding in a post-COVID world. Now that gyms are once again open, there is the potential there for infection-related behaviours to increase. I'm sure you don't need me to tell you how exercise bikes and treadmills may be rather sweaty after use. Now, be honest. How many of you take the time to use the paper dispenser and cleanser spray bottles to clean the equipment? Well, good news comes from Mobekk et al. (2020) in their Norwegian gym study. Stick a picture of a pair of watching eyes above the cleanser spray bottles and hey presto. Cleaning of the exercise bikes and treadmills increases substantially.

IS THIS REALLY BECAUSE WE ARE SO CONCERNED WITH OUR REPUTATION?

It is now well established that the watching eyes effect can be a powerful influence on our behaviour. From donations to hand-washing to reductions in crime. The question that remains then is why? Why does a pair of eyes, one that is simply a photograph or drawing, have such a powerful effect on our behaviour?

We like to avoid risks

Two competing alternatives have been proposed in the literature. The first is the risk aversion hypothesis (Neilands, 2020). The premise of this theory is that humans are less likely to engage in risky behaviour when they feel they are being watched because of the risk of guilt that would result. As a result, they adhere to social norms, norms that should be reinforced and not broken. After all, there may be negative consequences if they are (Chudek & Henrich, 2011). It is not a ridiculous idea at all. We know for example that people who score highly on measures of risk aversion also tend to show greater susceptibility to the watching eyes effect (Keller & Pfattheicher, 2011) and there are many examples in the animal kingdom where eyes or eye spots are used as warnings to others. Avoid the bad outcomes! Lloyd (2015) for example suggests that herring gulls are slower to approach food if they are being watched. Could it be they sense risk?

However, the evidence does not always sit so neatly with this interpretation. Bateson et al. (2013) explored the effects of a picture of watching eyes on littering behaviour. In one condition, they ensured there was no litter around the bike racks. In the other, they increased the litter using screwed up and regular leaflets, sweet wrappers and drink cans. I wonder if there were some confused students watching on at this point. In three of the six locations, a picture of watching eyes was posted on the wall by the bike racks and in the other three locations, no watching eyes were posted. If the risk aversion theory is correct, we might expect passers-by to be more likely to litter in the latter condition than in the first and even more so in the presence of the watching eyes sign as it would increase adherence to the social norm of littering. However, the watching eyes signs actually reduced littering when large numbers of others were around. An alternative theory was needed.

We are concerned with maintaining a good reputation

The alternative theory proposed is that the watching eyes effect is due to reputation management (Alexander, 1987). If you are an individual with a good reputation (which I know you all are), then you should receive more help than those with a bad reputation (Francey & Bergmüller, 2012). How do we preserve our good reputation? By helping others in situations where we can be observed of course.

How do we decide between the two? Neilands et al. (2020) decided to put the two opposing theories to the test using a sample of dogs. Yes, dogs. If you have ever had a dog, you will know that they have a tendency to look into your eyes to assess your attentional state. Mine usually did so to see if she could bury her toy in my flowerpot. We also know that dogs will change their behaviour in response to being observed to avoid punishment. My dog was caught sitting on our kitchen table, a forbidden behaviour. But having been seen, she immediately switched her attention to the garden as if she had chosen the vantage point to admire my plants.

Neilands, in a rather ingenious study, presented dogs with two trials. In the first trial, the "Go" trial, the owner encouraged their dog to take the food that had been placed on the floor. In the "Leave" trial, they were instructed not to take the food. Once the command had been issued, the owner then turned away and a photo became visible above the food. In one condition the photo showed a pair of eyes looking directly forwards. In the other condition, the photo showed flowers. The researchers measured not only obedience but also the speed with which each dog approached the food. Would the eye picture have any effect?

The good news is they studied some very obedient dogs who demonstrated significant sensitivity to their owner's commands. But in terms of the pictures? They had no effect at all. The researchers believe this is evidence in support of the reputation management theory, suggesting that the watching eyes effect is a uniquely human phenomenon, designed to help preserve our good reputation and all the positive consequences that come with maintaining it. In other words, dogs care little for their reputation.

The suggestion that reputational concerns lie behind the watching eyes effect is also consistent with the results of studies such as Nettle et al.'s (2013) Dictator Game study. In the dictator game used by Nettle, students were shown two envelopes. One was marked as the envelope for them to take away and the other was marked as being for a random student. On the desk were four £1 coins and two 50 pence pieces. Students were asked to put whatever money from this selection they wanted, in each of the two envelopes. The envelope for the other student was then put in a cardboard box.

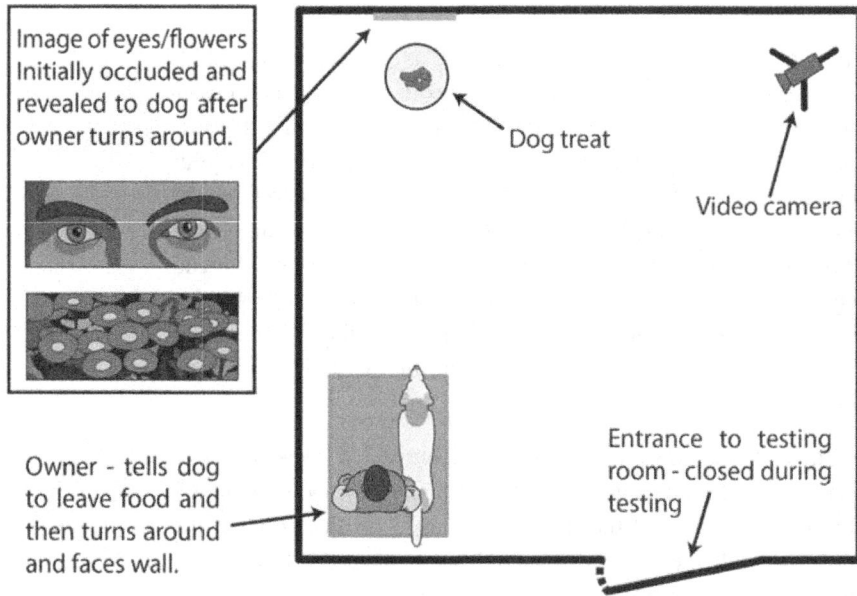

■ **Figure 1.7** The set-up used in the study by Neilands et al. (2020).

Whilst making their decision, students sat in a cubicle where a poster was displayed depicting a message ("Please do not consume any food or drink in the cubicle") and either a pair of female eyes, a pair of male eyes or the Institute of Neuroscience logo. While 80% of students donated something to the other student when exposed to the poster showing eyes, only 63% did so in the logo condition. However, there was no evidence of an increased mean donation effect.

In a further meta-analysis of seven studies of watching eyes effects in this game, involving 887 participants in total, Nettle et al. (2013) reported again that watching eyes increase the probability of donating something but do not increase the mean donation amount. Being seen to give something far outweighed consideration of how much to give.

Still not convinced? Then look what effect the watching eyes have on private as opposed to public behaviour. Thomas Van Rompay et al. (2009) asked participants to complete a large-scale survey of a well-known Dutch bank. Whilst completing the survey, the experimenter just happened to drop a bundle of questionnaires on the floor, exclaiming "Oh no, I had just ranked them in numerical order". Would participants help the experimenter? The experimenter then handed the participant one of the questionnaires. Only one question on it was of interest and that was the question that asked about willingness to donate to charity. In one condition, a security camera was visible and participants were told that the room was under constant surveillance. In the other condition, there was no security camera.

Well, as you can probably guess by this point in our story, participants were more likely to offer help when the security camera was visible than when it wasn't. However, it had no effect on their private helping behaviour as measured by the donation to charity question on the questionnaire. Only behaviour which was publicly observable was affected. This effect was particularly pronounced in individuals scoring high in need for social approval. Behaviour that isn't publicly observable is unaffected by the watching eyes. It won't affect our reputation and therefore is not susceptible in the same way as behaviour that is open to social scrutiny.

Bateson et al. (2013) obtained similar findings in their study of littering mentioned earlier, showing that watching eye images reduced littering only when there were larger numbers of people present. However, the interpretation offered by these authors is not in terms of reputation management but much more in terms of sign salience. In a large anonymous crowd, we tend to avert our gaze from others so few people may be watching us in return. The sign may therefore become more salient. In an empty café such as that studied by Ernest-Jones et al. (2011), again the signs may become more salient. However, when we are interacting with others we know in a social group, the sign may lose its salience and effect. I would argue that such findings are not out of line with the reputational model and indeed Bateson et al. (2006) have promoted the theory in their own work elsewhere.

There are limits to the watching eyes effect (and that mainly relates to the limitations on benefits for us)

So, what happens then when helping behaviour involves a cost to us and little benefit? Would the watching eyes effect still hold? Manesi and Pollet (2017) tried this out in their lost letter field experiments. In a series of three studies, they arranged for research assistants to drop letters around two neighbourhoods, differing only in size and socio-economic status, in Amsterdam. Each of the letters had the stamp and logo of Rijksuniversiteit Groningen on them and were addressed to T.V. Pollet at Vrije Universiteit Amsterdam. On one-third of the envelopes there was a picture of a pair of eyes, on another third, a picture of flowers and on the final third, there was no additional picture.

No significant effect of the eye images was found. Why not? The authors suggest that the main reason is that there are costs involved and little benefit to be gained. People who find the lost letters have to take time and effort to get to the post box to post them and in contrast to actions such as avoiding littering, there is no particular reward, in terms of reputation, to be gained.

Similarly, if eyes that are averted are used as opposed to those showing direct gaze, reputational concerns lessen and the eyes have little effect on behaviour. Manesi et al. (2016) tested this by asking participants to take part in a "typing task" which involved typing a string of random characters, that appeared on the computer screen, without error, using the keyboard. They were told that they were Partner A and would be paired with someone else, Partner B, who would have to complete any outstanding task trials that they had not already done themselves. As each string of letters appeared, a pair of eyes or flowers was shown above it. The eyes were either shown open but averted away from the participant, looking forward in direct gaze or closed. Watching eyes led to fewer trials being left for Partner B, that is, the participants were more pro-social. However, the same could not be said for averted or closed eyes or, indeed, for the flower pictures. When the results from three different studies were pooled, the authors reported a completion rate of 56.8% for the participants who saw the watching eyes but only 47.3% for those shown the other stimuli. It appears that the reminders of reputational concerns are the dominant force behind the watching eyes effect and those eyes have to be attentive and watching.

So what happens when the desire to be helpful towards others conflicts with the desire to maintain our good reputation as an honest person? Oda et al. (2015) tested just this. Imagine you are asked to roll a die to raise money to support disaster relief efforts for those affected by the Japanese earthquake and tsunami. Whatever number you report rolling will determine the contribution made and you need to record the donation amount corresponding to the number rolled on the piece of paper in front of you. As you are seated in your computer booth, you see that there is a poster displaying the work of the Japanese Red Cross Society. On the computer screen in front of you, not only are there the instructions but also a background screen featuring either an image of stylised eyes (the experimental condition) or a diffuse patten of the same elements (control condition).

This was exactly the set up used in Oda et al.'s study. Were Japanese students honest about their dice rolls? And what effect did the watching eyes have? In the control condition, where diffuse elements of the stylised eyes were presented on the screen, the actual donation was 7.5% higher than the expected amount. Over 26% of responses were that the die number rolled was 5. In other words, there was a tendency to be pro-social and lie about the actual number rolled, to increase the donation made. Surely the number 6 should have been reported more often? No, not according to the authors who have identified research that suggests extremes are more often avoided in Asian compared to Western cultures (e.g. Chen et al., 1995).

So, how about when the stylised eyes were used? Such pro-sociality decreased. Now, the desire to be seen as honest overtook. Although the authors argue that this demonstrates that the desire to avoid violating social norms is stronger than the drive to maintain a good reputation, they do agree that it is not clear-cut. The erosion of trust caused by lying can damage a bad reputation beyond repair so again reputational concerns are important.

On reflection

So, what can we conclude from our journey through the watching eyes effect? It seems that Adeimantus was really onto something in his original claims that reputational concerns fuel the watching eyes effect. It is clear that they do influence us to be more pro-social, less criminal and more generous citizens and increasingly the evidence points to the effect being linked to our desire to preserve our good reputation in the eyes (notice the pun!) of others and to attract the positive consequences that may result from such. Oh how shallow we are!

REFERENCES

Alexander, R. D. (1987). *The biology of moral systems*. Aldine de Gruyter.

Baron-Cohen, S., Jolliffe, T., Mortimore, C., & Robertson, M. (1997a). Another advanced test of theory of mind: Evidence from very high functioning adults with autism or Asperger syndrome. *Journal of Child Psychology and Psychiatry*, *38*(7), 813–822.

Baron-Cohen, S., Wheelwright, S., & Jolliffe, A. T. (1997b). Is there a "language of the eyes"? Evidence from normal adults, and adults with autism or Asperger syndrome. *Visual Cognition*, *4*(3), 311–331.

Bateson, M., Callow, L., Holmes, J. R., Redmond Roche, M. L., & Nettle, D. (2013). Do images of "watching eyes" induce behaviour that is more pro-social or more normative? A field experiment on littering. *PloS One*, *8*(12), e82055.

Bateson, M., Nettle, D., & Roberts, G. (2006). Cues of being watched enhance cooperation in a real-world setting. *Biology Letters*, *2*(3), 412–414.

Chen, C., Lee, S. Y., & Stevenson, H. W. (1995). Response style and cross-cultural comparisons of rating scales among East Asian and North American students. Psychological Science, 6(3), 170–175.

Chudek, M., & Henrich, J. (2011). Culture – gene coevolution, norm-psychology and the emergence of human prosociality. *Trends in Cognitive Sciences*, *15*(5), 218–226.

Dear, K. (2018). *Towards a psychology of surveillance: Do 'watching eyes' affect behaviour?* [Doctoral dissertation, University of Oxford].

Edwards, S., & Oakley, S. (1996). *The symbolism of the eye of Horus in the pyramid texts*. Swansea University.

Ekström, M. (2012). Do watching eyes affect charitable giving? Evidence from a field experiment. *Experimental Economics*, *15*(3), 530–546.

Emery, N. J. (2000). The eyes have it: The neuroethology, function and evolution of social gaze. *Neuroscience & Biobehavioral Reviews*, *24*(6), 581–604.

Epley, N., Waytz, A., & Cacioppo, J. T. (2007). On seeing human: A three-factor theory of anthropomorphism. *Psychological Review*, *114*(4), 864.

Ernest-Jones, M., Nettle, D., & Bateson, M. (2011). Effects of eye images on everyday cooperative behavior: a field experiment. *Evolution and Human Behavior*, *32*(3), 172–178.

Francey, D., & Bergmüller, R. (2012). Images of eyes enhance investments in a real-life public good. *PLoS One*, *7*(5), e37397.

Fyfe, N. R., & Bannister, J. (1996). City watching: Closed circuit television surveillance in public spaces. *Area*, 37–46.

Hart, P., & Royne, M. B. (2017). Being human: How anthropomorphic presentations can enhance advertising effectiveness. *Journal of Current Issues & Research in Advertising*, *38*(2), 129–145.

Keller, J., & Pfattheicher, S. (2011). Vigilant self – regulation, cues of being watched and cooperativeness. *European Journal of Personality*, *25*(5), 363–372.

Kelsey, C., Vaish, A., & Grossmann, T. (2018). Eyes, more than other facial features, enhance real-world donation behavior. *Human Nature*, *29*(4), 390–401.

Lloyd, E. A. (2015). Adaptationism and the logic of research questions: How to think clearly about evolutionary causes. *Biological Theory*, *10*(4), 343–362.

Manesi, Z., & Pollet, T. V. (2017). No support for the watching eyes effect across three" lost letter" field experiments. *Letters on Evolutionary Behavioral Science*, *8*(1), 12–15.

Manesi, Z., Van Lange, P. A., & Pollet, T. V. (2016). Eyes wide open: Only eyes that pay attention promote prosocial behavior. *Evolutionary Psychology*, *14*(2), https://doi.org/10.1177%2F1474704916640780.

Mobekk, H., Hessen, D. O., Fagerstrøm, A., & Jacobsen, H. (2020). For your eyes only: A field experiment on nudging hygienic behavior. *Frontiers in Psychology*, *11*, 3489.

Neilands, P., Hassall, R., Derks, F., Bastos, A. P., & Taylor, A. H. (2020). Watching eyes do not stop dogs stealing food: Evidence against a general risk-aversion hypothesis for the watching-eye effect. *Scientific Reports*, *10*(1), 1–8.

Nettle, D., Harper, Z., Kidson, A., Stone, R., Penton-Voak, I. S., & Bateson, M. (2013). The watching eyes effect in the Dictator Game: it's not how much you give, it's being seen to give something. *Evolution and Human Behavior*, *34*(1), 35–40.

Nettle, D., Nott, K., & Bateson, M. (2012). 'Cycle thieves, we are watching you': Impact of a simple signage intervention against bicycle theft. *PloS One*, *7*(12), e51738.

Oda, R., Kato, Y., & Hiraishi, K. (2015). The watching-eye effect on prosocial lying. *Evolutionary Psychology*, *13*(3), https://doi.org/10.1177%2F1474704915594959.

Panagopoulos, C. (2014). Watchful eyes: Implicit observability cues and voting. *Evolution and Human Behavior*, *35*(4), 279–284.

Pfattheicher, S., Strauch, C., Diefenbacher, S., & Schnuerch, R. (2018). A field study on watching eyes and hand hygiene compliance in a public restroom. *Journal of Applied Social Psychology*, *48*(4), 188–194.

Sénémeaud, C., Sanrey, C., Callé, N., Plainfossé, C., Belhaire, A., & Georget, P. (2017). The watching-eyes phenomenon and blood donation: Does exposure to pictures of eyes increase blood donation by young adults? *Transfusion and Apheresis Science*, *56*(2), 168–170.

Van Rompay, T. J., Vonk, D. J., & Fransen, M. L. (2009). The eye of the camera: Effects of security cameras on prosocial behavior. *Environment and Behavior*, *41*(1), 60–74.

Chapter **2**

How do you learn best?

Traditional approaches to learning at university have leaned towards lecture-based presentation of material which is then "absorbed" by the learner. Is this how we learn best? This chapter explores how educational psychology can help inform the way we teach (and learn!). It looks at learning as construction starting with a consideration of Piagetian theory and eventually questions whether we need teachers at all. Vygotsky's concept of the Zone of Proximal Development is explored and this leads to a consideration of active learning as an alternative to the traditional approach. However, is simply being active sufficient for learning to occur? This chapter asks whether particular types of active learning are more effective than others and questions the idea of a one size fits all approach to learning.

■ **Figure 2.1** How do you learn best?

DOI: 10.4324/9781003329763-2

When I was at school, it was frequently said on my school reports that I was too quiet. I needed to speak up more. Hard to believe for those who know me now. If the same sort of reports were still written about me now, I suspect my colleagues would be more likely to tell me the opposite. But casting my mind back to my schooldays, it always seemed rather unfair as I felt I learnt an awful lot from listening to teachers and to my peers disseminating and discussing the content of our learning. Being actively involved in my learning, for me, meant being engaged, trying things out and constructing my own understanding of the content I was learning, not constantly speaking up. I would spend many an hour creating my revision notes, drawing, and being creative with my learning, all of which helped to enrich my understanding, strengthen my learning and feed my passion for the subjects I was encountering.

Some years later, my interest in learning led to a career in teaching and a particular interest in what is now known as "active learning". Little did I know it then but all the things I was doing in my own educational journey very much fitted the definition of active learning as provided by Prince (2004):

> *active learning requires students to do meaningful learning activities and think about what they are doing.*
>
> (p. 223)

LEARNING AS CONSTRUCTION

Active learning has its roots in constructivism. Jean Piaget, a strong proponent of this theoretical approach, emphasised the importance of being able to construct knowledge in a way that makes sense to the self. The process of construction, he argued, occurs via schemas which are similar to building blocks or categories of knowledge. As we learn, Piaget believed that we not only add to and amend existing schemas but we also develop new ones via processes of assimilation and accommodation.

Let's use an example to help explain these terms. Lisa goes to the park with her mum. As they enter the park, they see a small, four-legged animal with a tail and fur. Lisa correctly names this as a dog. She has seen quite a few small dogs from previous walks in the park with her mother and has developed a schema for them as a result. That schema tells Lisa that dogs usually have four legs, fur, a tail and they bark.

As they walk further into the park, a large dog runs by. Lisa has only ever seen little dogs before but this one matches the characteristics of a dog held in her schema. It has four legs, fur and a tail. She "assimilates" this example into her existing schema. If information can be assimilated and made sense of using existing schemas, then no genuine learning has occurred.

After their walk, Lisa and her mother head back out of the park and as they cross the road, they see a cat wandering down the street. Lisa sees it has four legs, fur and a tail and incorrectly names it as a dog. Her mother corrects her, explaining that this animal is in fact a cat. It does not bark, it meows. Lisa cannot just assimilate this example into her schema anymore. She therefore has to accommodate this new example by forming a new schema and in so doing, constructs new meaning, making sense of the world around her. Learning therefore depends on "failure", in fact Burleson and Picard (2004) suggest that failure is a prerequisite for becoming an expert.

Piaget was not only a bit of a legend when it came to explaining the process of learning but he was also an interesting guy in other ways. By the time he was 15, he had already published several articles on molluscs and in his career, he was awarded no less than 16 honorary doctorates from universities globally. He taught at an all-boys school and would regularly rise at 4 a.m. to write at least four publishable pages before he began his teaching for the day (Vidal, 2007)

Piaget's stage theory

Do we always learn the same way? According to Piaget, although we always construct meaning for ourselves using these processes of assimilation or accommodation, the quality of intelligent thought differs with age. Specifically, Piaget believed we pass through a series of four stages of cognitive development. These stages are always passed through in the same order, at approximately the same age as progression through the stages is dependent on brain maturation.

For the first two years of life, children are said to be in the sensorimotor stage of development. During this stage, simple actions such as sucking or grasping enable the children to learn that their actions can influence the world around them. They develop object permanence. To understand what this means, imagine playing a game of hide and seek with a young baby, say 6 months of age. You hide their favourite toy under a cloth. They will lean forward

■ Figure 2.2 Piaget.

to uncover it, right? Actually no. Most will act as though the toy no longer exists. Out of sight, out of mind. Only later during this stage, at around 8–9 months, will children actually look for the object. It makes sense that this is also the time at which infants show separation anxiety when their caregiver leaves the room. They finally understand that the caregiver continues to exist even if they can't be physically seen.

Around the child's second birthday, they progress to the pre-operational stage of development. A major achievement in this stage is the development of language. The child can now use words to represent objects and nowhere is this symbolic thinking clearer than in their pretend play. A teddy can now stand for or symbolise something or someone else. Despite this symbolic thinking, children at this stage find it incredibly difficult to see things from another person's perspective. What they see is what they believe everyone else sees. Going back to our hide and seek example, have you ever seen examples of young children hiding behind a curtain with their legs showing beneath the curtain? They believe that because they can't see you, you can't see them!

If you ask a child at this stage to choose a present for a sibling, chances are they will choose something they like rather than something their sibling will enjoy. Recent evidence (e.g. Galak et al., 2016) suggests we often buy things for others based on our own values, so I suspect some aspects of this stage remain into adulthood!

Imagine this scenario. There are three biscuits in the biscuit barrel. You give yourself two and the pre-operational child one. Are they happy with that arrangement? Of course not. Its unfair. They have been short-changed. You then take their one biscuit and break it in half. You still have two unbroken biscuits. Are they happy now? Well, surprisingly, yes. Now, imagine they want a drink. You have one short, fat glass and one tall, thin glass. You pour the same amount of squash into each. Happy? No. The children who receives the short, fat glass will think they have been short-changed. It "looks" to them that the other child has more. These examples illustrate what are known as conservation tasks. Children at the pre-operational stage just don't understand conservation. When they do, they are said to have progressed to the concrete operational stage.

The concrete operational stage is marked by the ability to think in a more logical manner. Children at this stage are between 7 and 12 years of age. Problem solving is however limited to concrete objects and events. Thinking in abstract terms is still a step too far.

Only when children reach 12 years of age do they enter the final stage of cognitive development, the stage of formal operations. Abstract thought is now possible and that in itself enables the individual to reason about moral and ethical issues, hypothetical issues and to use deductive logic. Let's give it a try. You're in the kitchen and you have two slices of bread and four sandwich ingredients. How many different kinds of sandwich can you make?

If you think that was easy, try this. There are four cards shown in Figure 2.3. If a card has a vowel on one side, it will have an even number on the other side. Which two cards would you need to turn over to decide whether this is true?

Finally, try answering this question: If you had a third eye, were would you put it?

■ **Figure 2.3** Four cards labelled E, K, 4 and 7.

Now in the first example, the sandwich problem, children often generate some of the possible sandwiches but overlook some combinations. There have been variations of this puzzle, for example, the chemical combinations task (De Lisi & Staudt, 1980), the Candy task (Kuhn & Ho, 1980) and the Pizza Problem (Faulkner et al., 2000) but the rationale here is that to pass this, systematic reasoning about all possible combinations is required. If you managed to demonstrate that, you might well have reached the same answer as me, 15.

In the second example, knowledge of conditional relationships are tested. This is known more commonly as the Wason Selection Task. Which two did you choose? The correct answer is E and 7. If there is not an even number on the reverse side of the E card, then you know the rule is false. Similarly, if you turn the number 7 over and it has a vowel on the other side, you know the rule is false. Turning over the 4, an even number won't tell you much. The rule doesn't predict anything about what happens if an even number is on one side. Similarly, turning over the K, a consonant won't be helpful. There is no rule pertaining to consonants. How did you do?

The final example requires abstract thinking. At the stage of formal operational thinking, we can think about hypothetical situations. Before the stage of formal operational thinking, children might suggest the additional eye goes on the face because that's where our eyes are found. However, those in the formal operational stage can generate more innovative ideas such as placing the eye on the hand so that they can see around corners or on the back of the head so that they can see in both directions. Were you that inventive?

I will give you a heads up here though. Not everyone gets to this stage, even as adults. Leroux and colleagues in 2009 published a paper demonstrating child-like thinking in the brains of adult participants and Keating (1979) reported that up to 60% of college students fail these tasks. Martorano (1977) reported that even the oldest age group in his study (12th grade so 17–18 years) could not pass some of the formal operations tasks he presented them with and Tyler (2020) suggests that in some tribal villages, formal operational thinking is not seen at all. One of the reasons proposed is that the type of tasks used to assess this level of thinking hold little relevance (Kuhn, 1979) but whatever the reason, it seems this is not a universal stage as Piaget originally suggested.

DO WE NEED TEACHERS ANYMORE?

So, according to Piaget, learning occurs through a process of assimilation and accommodation. We actively construct our understanding of the world in a way that makes sense to us. You might be wondering do we even need a teacher to learn? Discovery learning is a method of learning where a student might receive a problem to solve with little to no guidance from the teacher on how to solve it.

However, Mayer (2004) argued that pure discovery makes it very difficult for learners to identify relevant material to help them. Simply working on a puzzle or problem is not sufficient to ensure a solution is found. Fay and Mayer (1994) compared a pure discovery approach to a guided discovery approach to teaching LOGO programming. Both groups were given the LOGO manual and projects to complete. However, the guided discovery group were able to see certain design concepts being modelled along with feedback. Students in the guided discovery group fared much better in terms of their use of good design principles and ultimately solved more of the problem tasks set. When permitted to learn using pure discovery methods, some students fail to learn the underlying principle or rule and may not even come into contact with it (Shulman & Keisler, 1966).

It seems as though learning in isolation is not really the key to educational success then. Perhaps, learning alongside more knowledgeable others is? That brings us, conveniently, to another eminent psychologist, Vygotsky. Vygotsky believed, like Piaget, that learning was constructed but differed in that he thought learning could be accelerated as a result of dynamic interactions between individuals and others in their environment. Vygotsky was a Russian psychologist who wrote his dissertation on the psychology of art. However, he never formally obtained his degree, due to the Bolshevik uprising in 1917. He wrote and published no less than six books over the course of 10 years but unfortunately met an early end at the age of just 37 years when he died of TB. To add to this sad story, Vygotsky's work didn't achieve eminence until after his death as the Communist Party made his work largely inaccessible to the West thanks in large part to the mention of Leon Trotsky in his work, a person named an enemy of the state (Fraser & Yasnitsky, 2015) but also due to the mismatch between the claims Vygotsky was making and the political ideology of the Soviet state at the time (Vasileva & Balyasnikova, 2019).

VYGOTSKY'S PEER LEARNING

Vygotsky believed that learning could be extended and facilitated by working alongside others who are more knowledgeable and who could guide that individual's understanding, hence why Vygotsky's theory has often been described as a social constructionist approach (Weegar & Pacis, 2012). The difference between what a learner understands and can do themselves and what that learner understands or can do with the guidance and support of others he termed the Zone of Proximal Development. Scaffolding activities and learning experiences, to enable the student to obtain support to move through the Zone of Proximal Development, were seen as ideal.

According to this approach, the role of the teacher is to provide guided instruction for students to be able to engage in active problem solving, inquiry and collaborative activities. More recently, Prince (2004) referred to such activities as "active learning". Rather than being a unitary concept, active learning is taken to refer to a range of activities and learning exercises, for example, problem-based learning, games-based learning or object-based learning to name a few examples.

In problem-based learning for example students are encouraged to engage in self-study and then to use the knowledge gained to collaborate with peers to solve problems set by a tutor. Schmidt and colleagues decided to explore the effectiveness of problem-based learning (PBL) in 2009, by homing in on one medical school in Maastrict in the Netherlands which utilised a problem-based learning curriculum. They wanted to compare the outcomes of this approach with that from other medical schools that did not use the same approach. What they found was strong support for the active learning PBL approach. Students from the Maastrict school outperformed their peers at other medical institutions on a number of measures. For example, in terms of interpersonal skills, they outperformed those from conventional medical schools 92% of the time. In terms of practical medical skills, it was 79%. Students reported feeling more supported and less stressed and 70% of them graduated sooner than those in conventional schools.

Problems and puzzles presented to learners can evoke curiosity according to the authors and can enable the learner to see any gaps in their understanding. The activities that follow then enable that gap to be filled (Loewenstein, 1994). The role of the tutor in these contexts is simply to point learners to what it is important to learn, something that Schmidt et al. referred to as "instructional scaffolding".

The effectiveness of such instructional scaffolding can be seen in the work of Roberts (2018). Roberts presented PowerPoint slides which had an image and minimal text on them. Some of the images were paradoxical images, that is, images that appeared to be self-contradictory and some were metaphorical, using one image as an analogy of another. To work out the relevance of these images, students need to try and think at a deep level to reconcile the meaning. Roberts conducted focus group discussions with undergraduate students after a mini lecture using these images in a PowerPoint presentation. A common theme was that the paradoxical images stimulated them to problem solve and both metaphorical and paradoxical images forced them to make links with previous learning. Roberts argues that this is not just an example of an active learning strategy but an attempt to transform the whole lecture space.

Luc Budé and colleagues also used a form of scaffolding in their study of undergraduate students' attitudes to statistics. For half

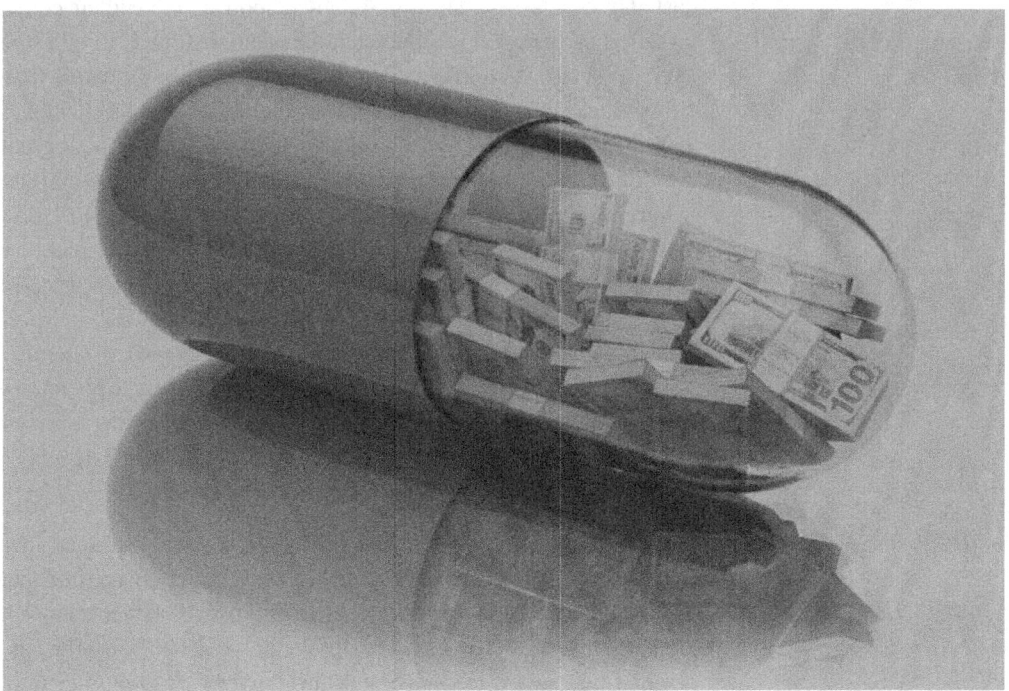

■ **Figure 2.4** A metaphorical image – what message do you think this image is trying to convey?

of the students in this study, they had access to guiding questions that could be used to direct their thinking. For the other half, they simply were asked to write down their thinking around the problem. Both groups of students were then asked to answer some achievement questions. Lo and behold, the group that had received the guiding questions showed enhanced performance on the achievement questions. Not only that, but they also outperformed students in the other group in terms of their ability to transfer their learning to new problems.

DIFFERENCES IN ACTIVE LEARNING EFFECTS

So, as long as guided questions are used to direct student's learning, then that's all we need for our story of how we learn. Right? Not quite. As you might have come to expect now, nothing is ever that straightforward in psychology. You see, there is a suggestion that the effectiveness of active learning may be different for those who are just starting out on their journey of learning in particular disciplines and those who are at a more advanced level. Cherney (2008) asked students to write down ten things they remembered from either an introductory psychology course, an introductory statistics course or a cognitive psychology course, on the last day of classes. The free-recall responses were then coded in terms of the level of understanding demonstrated. In all three courses, class activities generated higher levels of recall than other teaching approaches. Activities included forming a chain to demonstrate the speed of the human nervous system, acting out Freud's defence mechanisms or a classical conditioning activity where students learnt to salivate to the sound of a bell! In a second study, Cherney compared students studying an introductory course versus those studying upper level courses aimed at more advanced learners. Deeper learning occurred for concepts presented through activities for the latter group; however, Cherney found that deeper levels of understanding in introductory courses were demonstrated when concepts were relayed in the form of video clips. It is important therefore to assess existing levels of knowledge to tailor the active learning appropriately.

Even when active learning does have a noticeable effect, students may not be aware of this. Bjork et al. (2013) suggested that students seem to understand what is good for their learning but despite this, they don't like or appreciate it. Lobo (2017) transformed a standard lecture-based introductory class by introducing aspects such as replacing essays with cultural analyses, using collaborative platforms to complete the class readings, using reading frames to structure note-taking and using blended learning approaches. Almost 80% of students agreed that teamwork was important for their learning at the end of the first semester and 68.5% agreed that the reading frames had helped their learning. Also, 56.2% strongly agreed that collaborative reading helped and 55.3% that doing cultural analyses contributed to their learning. Although the majority of students felt that the transformation had helped their learning, their evaluations of the course overall dropped from 93/100 to 83/100 and in the second semester from 91.5/100 to 86/100.

This is not an isolated finding. Deslauriers and colleagues reported a similar outcome in their comparison of actual learning achieved versus what they called "feeling of learning" in Harvard University students. They divided students into two groups. One group experienced an active learning environment in their lessons. They were encouraged to try to solve physics problems with peers whilst the instructor circulated round the groups to answer questions. In the other group, students received passive lectures where they were shown worked examples. Most students found active learning experiences to be disjointed and lacking in flow. Many reported feeling confused and concerned that any errors would remain uncorrected. Despite these worries, students in the active learning classroom scored significantly higher in a test of learning compared to those in a passive learning classroom. Deslauriers et al. propose that this discrepancy is largely due to the experience of passive lectures as having fluency. The additional effort required in the active learning classroom was perceived as disfluency and consequently as a sign of impaired learning. However, such effort can be the very hallmark of deeper learning.

It is not just the students who may be less than keen on active learning methodology. In a study of games-based approaches to learning multiplication tables, Razak (2012) reported little enthusiasm for active learning from the tutor, who preferred a more traditional approach. Although one group of children relished the opportunity to engage in the games and made good progress, a second consisted of students who had some difficulty understanding the game or the instructions. They would often switch between different games without completing them.

One of the issues appeared to be the role the tutor played. According to the researchers, the tutor did not play as active a role herself in the learning when games-based approaches were used and reasons of anxiety and unfamiliarity were proposed to

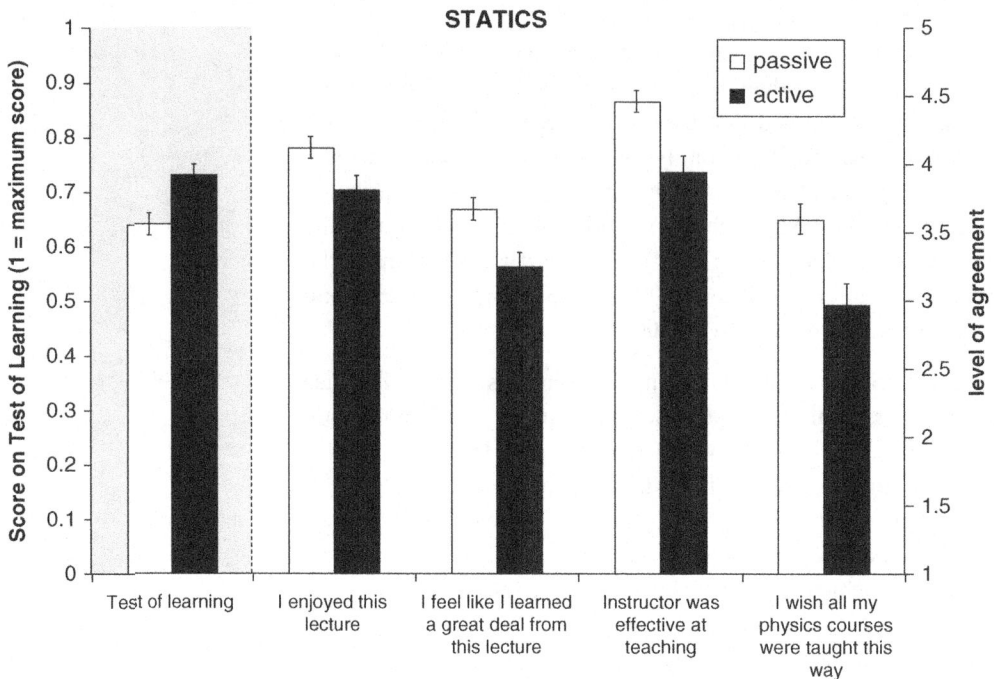

Figure 2.5 Taken from Deslauriers et al. (2011) showing the comparison of performance on the TOL and FOL responses between students taught with a traditional and active method.

underlie this. From the tutor's perspective, monitoring the children became challenging when they were engaging in computer-based tasks. Active learning clearly requires a different type of pedagogical approach from the tutor compared to traditional didactic teaching and tutors need time to adjust to this. Moreover, traditional classrooms encourage tutors to stand at the podium rather than circulate amongst student groups (Brooks, 2012). Umbach and Wawrzynski (2005) have already illustrated how the level of challenge and engagement experienced by students is dependent on the amount of time faculty interact with them, emphasising the role of the tutor, albeit in an active, participatory context rather than as a passive disseminator of knowledge. Reassuring news for those of us in the teaching industry!

WHAT MAKES A GOOD TEACHER?

So, the evidence would suggest that teachers are needed, to provide structure and guidance at a minimum. What else is required to be a "good" teacher in the eyes of students? Ayers (2001) suggests that good teachers bring a vision and a sense of commitment to the learning situation and instill in learners a sense of imagination, invention and risk-taking to learning situations. Brighouse and Woods (1999) go so far as to talk of good teachers as "energy creators". They have the ability to release what Handy (1990) referred to as the "E" factor: excitement, enthusiasm, effort, effervescence and enterprise. Learning should be fun. But didn't we already know that?

Rather than an "E" factor, Fried (2001) proposes what we might want to call a "P" factor! Good teachers, according to Fried, imbue the teaching environment with passion, something which infects those they teach with enthusiasm. This is not, however, simply about someone who disseminates information in an enthusiastic manner. Consistent with our story so far, Fried argues that teachers who bring this element of passion to the learning environment are those who participate in a learning partnership with those they teach. They do not present themselves as the characteristic "sage on the stage" (McLean & Attardi, 2018) but rather present themselves as participants alongside the students in knowledge construction.

Before we leave our factors approach, how about the "W" factor? *Who* are my learners? Ramsden (2003) points to the significance of concern and respect for our students in becoming effective teachers. Being able to identify where our students are starting from, what difficulties they may face and how they as learners might progress best is key.

Su and Wood (2012) decided to investigate further by drawing on secondary data that was obtained as a result of an essay competition for undergraduate students. The competition required students to write a 900–1,000 word essay on the topic of what makes a good university lecturer. The four winning essays and the six runner-up essays were used for their analysis. Eleven themes were identified demonstrating the range of factors that are considered to be important:

1. Being authoritative and expert in knowledge. One of the key indicators of a good lecturer was considered to be their ability to link theoretical knowledge to real-world situations but it also embraces the need for passion and inspiration. Walker (2008) suggests that good preparation of lessons is paramount.
2. Being a good communicator. This was not just about being able to communicate with clarity but also embraced aspects such as bringing a sense of humour to the learning situation.
3. Being good at using educational technologies.

4. Having a sense of humour. Laughter was seen as a valuable aspect of good teaching in as much as it provided an interlude, reduced pressure and even enhanced learning.
5. Being able to interact with students. Being able to engage with students, address their questions and share the love they feel for their subjects was seen as vital.
6. Being a reflective practitioner. This is not just about looking at what worked and what didn't in their practice but it is also considered to be as much about remembering the difficulties that they themselves might have faced as learners and what helped them to overcome these difficulties.

> "A good lecturer is a good student".
>
> (Su & Wood, 2012, p. 149)

7. Being passionate and inspiring. In comparing good and bad lecturers, one participant in Su and Wood's study contrasted the actions of both as either "light the match" (p. 149) which inspires students to go off and explore more on their own or "fill the bucket" (p. 149) and just load students with information. The ability to trigger enthusiasm in our students does appear to be of primary importance.
8. Being supportive. Being encouraging of the need to make mistakes in learning and allowing students to do so safely was a key theme mentioned.
9. Being able to facilitate student's independent learning. Giving guidance, presenting challenges and promoting creativity in thinking are all seen to be characteristics of good lecturers.
10. Being approachable. Time is precious. We all know that. But making sure we find time for our students and ensuring we are available when needed is key to positive views of lecturers.
11. Being able to provide timely feedback. Students are keen to know how they are progressing. Being able to give them feedback in a way that is timely and allows them to make good progress is seen as key. Explaining how improvements can be made or receiving constructive criticism is seen as a valuable asset in the learning process.

How do we make sense of all eleven factors? Su and Wood point to the underlying current of teaching as a "profoundly emotional practice" (p. 151). It is not just about the method of teaching used or which mode it is delivered in. It is much more about the connections made with students. Communicating content in a way that enthuses those we teach alongside an awareness of the needs and capacity of these students enables us to establish a learning environment that is enjoyable and fun to be in, that inspires and makes students feel valued in themselves. This relates to Bain's (2004) claim that good teaching is not just a matter of what technique we might use and the 11 themes show a striking similarity to those identified by Ramsden et al. (1995) which also embrace being aware and responsive to student need as well as being enthusiastic, reflective and providing feedback.

We started this chapter with the question: How do we learn best? What we have learnt appears to be that we learn best when we have an enthusiastic lecturer to guide us and support us as we construct our learning and make sense of this for ourselves. The more we are able to be active in doing this, the more likely it is we can develop a deeper understanding, and who knows, perhaps, even a passion for, our subject.

REFERENCES

Ayers, W. (2001). *To teach. The journey of a teacher* (2nd ed.). Teachers College Press.

Bain, K. (2004). *What the best college teachers do*. Harvard University Press.

Bjork, R. A., Dunlosky, J., & Kornell, N. (2013). Self-regulated learning: Beliefs, techniques, and illusions. *Annual Review of Psychology, 64*, 417–444.

Brighouse, T., & Woods, D. (1999). *How to improve your school*. Routledge.

Brooks, D. C. (2012). Space and consequences: The impact of different formal learning spaces on instructor and student behavior. *Journal of Learning Spaces, 1*(2), n2.

Burleson, W., & Picard, R. W. (2004, August). Affective agents: Sustaining motivation to learn through failure and a state of stuck. In *Workshop on social and emotional intelligence in learning environments*. MIT Media Lab.

Cherney, I. D. (2008). The effects of active learning on students' memories for course content. *Active Learning in Higher Education, 9*(2), 152–171.

De Lisi, R., & Staudt, J. (1980). Individual differences in college students' performance on formal operations tasks. *Journal of Applied Developmental Psychology, 1*(3), 201–208.

Deslauriers, L., Schelew, E., & Wieman, C. (2011). Improved learning in a large-enrollment physics class. *Science, 332*(6031), 862–864.

Faulkner, D., Joiner, R., Littleton, K., Miell, D., & Thompson, L. (2000). The mediating effect of task presentation on collaboration and children's acquisition of scientific reasoning. *European Journal of Psychology of Education, 15*(4), 417–430.

Fay, A. L., & Mayer, R. E. (1994). Benefits of teaching design skills before teaching logo computer programming: Evidence for syntax-independent learning. *Journal of Educational Computing Research*, *11*(3), 187–210.

Fraser, J., & Yasnitsky, A. (2015). Deconstructing Vygotsky's victimization narrative: A re-examination of the 'Stalinist suppression' of Vygotskian theory. *History of the Human Sciences*, *28*(2), 128–153.

Fried, R. I. (2001). *The passionate teacher*. Beacon Press.

Galak, J., Givi, J., & Williams, E. F. (2016). Why certain gifts are great to give but not to get: A framework for understanding errors in gift giving. *Current Directions in Psychological Science*, *25*(6), 380–385.

Handy, C. (1990). *Inside organizations*. Penguin Books.

Keating, D. P. (1979). Toward a multivariate life-span theory of intelligence. *New Directions for Child and Adolescent Development*, *1979*(5), 69–84.

Kuhn, D. (1979). The significance of Piaget's formal operations stage in education. *Journal of Education*, *161*(1), 34–50.

Kuhn, D., & Ho, V. (1980). Self-directed activity and cognitive development. *Journal of Applied Developmental Psychology*, *1*(2), 119–133.

Lobo, G. J. (2017). Active learning interventions and student perceptions. *Journal of Applied Research in Higher Education*, *9*(3), 465–473.

Loewenstein, G. (1994). The psychology of curiosity: A review and reinterpretation. *Psychological Bulletin*, *116*(1), 75.

Martorano, S. C. (1977). A developmental analysis of performance on Piaget's formal operations tasks. *Developmental Psychology*, *13*(6), 666.

Mayer, R. E. (2004). Should there be a three-strikes rule against pure discovery learning? *American Psychologist*, *59*(1), 14.

McLean, S., & Attardi, S. M. (2018). Sage or guide? Student perceptions of the role of the instructor in a flipped classroom. *Active Learning in Higher Education*. https://doi.org/10.1177/1469787418793725.

Prince, M. (2004). Does active learning work? A review of the research. *Journal of Engineering Education*, *93*(3), 223–231.

Ramsden, P. (2003). *Learning to teach in higher education*. Routledge.

Ramsden, P., Margetson, D., Martin, E., & Clark, S. (1995). *Recognising and rewarding good teaching in Australian higher education* (Final Report). Australian Government Publishing Service.

Razak, A. A., Connolly, T., & Hainey, T. (2012). Teachers' views on the approach of digital games-based learning within the curriculum for excellence. *International Journal of Game-Based Learning (IJGBL)*, *2*(1), 33–51.

Roberts, D. (2018). The engagement agenda, multimedia learning and the use of images in higher education lecturing: Or, how to end death by PowerPoint. *Journal of Further and Higher Education*, *42*(7), 969–985.

Shulman, L., & Keisler, E. (Eds.). (1966). *Learning by discovery: A critical appraisal*. Rand McNally.

Su, F., & Wood, M. (2012). What makes a good university lecturer? Students' perceptions of teaching excellence. *Journal of Applied Research in Higher Education*, *4*(2), 142–155.

Tyler, S. (2020). Cognitive development in adolescence. *Human Behavior and the Social Environment*, *1*.

Umbach, P. D., & Wawrzynski, M. R. (2005). Faculty do matter: The role of college faculty in student learning and engagement. *Research in Higher Education, 46*(2), 153–184.

Vasileva, O., & Balyasnikova, N. (2019). (Re) Introducing Vygotsky's thought: From historical overview to contemporary psychology. *Frontiers in Psychology, 10*, 1515.

Vidal, F. (2007). *Jean Piaget, 'friend of nature'* (pp. 91–104). Psychology Press.

Walker, R. J. (2008). Twelve characteristics of an effective teacher: A longitudinal, qualitative, quasi-research study of in-service and pre-service teachers' opinions. *Educational Horizons*, 61–68.

Weegar, M. A., & Pacis, D. (2012, January). A Comparison of two theories of learning-behaviorism and constructivism as applied to face-to-face and online learning. In *Proceedings e-leader conference, Manila*.

Chapter 3

Do video games have value?

Brain-training games have grown in popularity alongside increasing concern at the violence present in many action video games. What does the psychological evidence suggest? This chapter explores whether video games improve our cognitive abilities, whether they make us more pro-social and what role aspects such as co-operative play and competition make to the story. Could playing video games combat loneliness? Can they be used to halt the cognitive effects of aging? This chapter tries to find answers to these questions using experimental evidence from psychology but important methodological issues that plague this area of research are identified. It isn't just the positive effects that are explored, however. With reference to the General Aggression Model, the potential negative effects of video-game play are also considered. The role of arousal, identification and desensitisation in this debate lead to a more nuanced picture of the value of video games than perhaps the media give credit for.

■ **Figure 3.1** Can playing video games be good for us?

DOI: 10.4324/9781003329763-3

I know its hard to believe for those who know me☺but I am indeed old enough to remember the advent of home computers and with them the introduction of video games. Our first computer was a Vic-20 which had just one game. With the help of the space bar, you had to drop a bomb from a plane that flew from the left to the right of the screen, each time getting a little lower and a little closer to the buildings underneath. If you pressed the space bar at the right time, it would demolish the building and the plane would continue to fly. My, how video games have developed since those early days. Now you can play the role of an army officer, take on a cartoon character in a kart race or even battle your way through fantasy worlds, all at the touch of a button.

As video games have become more realistic, so the argument about the effects on individuals playing them has escalated. Does playing a shoot-em-up game make us more violent? Does playing a puzzle game online make us more intelligent? In our journey through this chapter, we will encounter these questions and some answers that psychologists have thrown our way. Warning: This is a chapter without a clear conclusion. By the time you get to the end, you will hopefully have a good idea of why.

CAN VIDEO GAMES IMPROVE OUR COGNITIVE SKILLS?

The video game market is now flooded with games that offer to do wonderous things such as improve our memory function or capacity, increase our attentional resources or even to ensure we use more of our brain that we otherwise would. Brain-training games have proliferated in recent years with the premise that practice on these tasks can have beneficial effects on our cognitive abilities (attention, memory, perception) which can facilitate our performance on simple tasks in everyday life (Simons et al., 2016). What truth lies behind these claims?

Miller and Robertson (2010) gave us reason to be optimistic in their study of 71 primary school children aged 10–11 years old. In School 1, children were asked to use a games console for 20 minutes each day. The game that they played was a standard brain-training game called Dr Kawashima's Brain Training Game, available for use with the Nintendo DS Lite system. The game requires players to complete a series of puzzles which might require them to engage in reasoning or mental calculations. In School 2, they used "Brain Gym" techniques for the same period. Brain gym techniques refer to a series of physical movements that are designed to ensure "whole-brain learning" (Dennison & Dennison, 1986). Children in School 3 really drew the short straw in this study. They were the no-treatment controls. Not sure if they had to do maths instead or engage in a bit of physical education but suffice to say they were not required to engage in any brain-training or brain gym intervention.

After 10 weeks, those playing the brain-training game were able to conduct faster and more accurate calculations and showed significant gains in self-esteem. Those engaging with Brain Gym or with no intervention showed no comparable gains in any area of self-perception.

This might suggest that brain-training games are indeed good for us and it is not a stand-alone finding. Ventura et al. (2013) investigated the effect of playing such games on persistence, a facet of conscientiousness. Video games such as the brain-training genre, introduce a certain level of challenge to players. The challenge presented to undergraduate students in Ventura et al.'s study was an anagram-riddle task. The participant had to try to solve the anagram or riddle by typing their answer into a text box and pressing a "guess" button to submit their responses within 120 seconds. They could of course, choose to skip the challenge and move to a different trial. In addition, participants were asked to state how many hours a week they played video games and to assess their own persistence using four self-report items. What did they find? The self-report measures of persistence correlated with the time spent on the unsolved problems. What does this mean? It means the higher they rated their own patience with difficult problems or time and effort spent on work, for example, the longer they persevered with the problems. For our purposes, perhaps the most interesting finding was that playing video games was also positively associated with greater persistence in the task.

Pallavicini et al. (2018) conducted a review of 35 different studies exploring the effects of video game training on healthy adults. The studies reviewed used both action games and puzzle games. In terms of cognitive skills, both reaction time measures and processing speed were positively enhanced by playing these games. Improvements were also identified in both visual and spatial working memory but only as a result of playing action video games, not puzzle games. As if that wasn't enough, the review highlighted the way that positive emotions could be induced and levels of stress reduced as a result of playing video games, suggesting a positive emotional benefit.

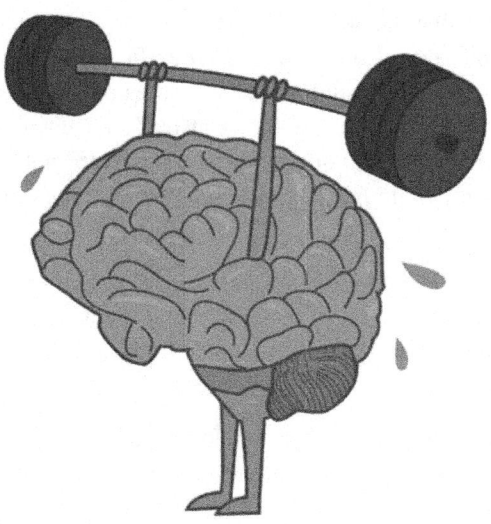

■ **Figure 3.2** Is it possible to train the brain through the use of video game play?

So it would seem that playing video games does have some potential benefits for attentional capacity, but particularly action games. Puzzles games it would appear, get bad press. But is this true? Well no. Not exactly. They appear to be useful for a different purpose. Granic et al. (2014) present a case in question. For over 10 years, researchers had been pondering over a problem. Viruses form crystals in living cells and they had yet to discover the crystal structure for a monkey virus related to the AIDS virus. Alongside this ongoing problem, a group of researchers at the University of Washington devised a video game called Foldit which enabled players to engage in puzzles requiring them to model the genetic makeup of proteins. In 2010, a competition was held and the performance of the top-scoring players was explored. Well, there was a breakthrough! Thanks to the responses of the players on this game, researchers were able to identify a solution to the monkey virus problem! The creativity fostered by the video game was sufficient to help solve a problem that had evaded scientists for years.

It is interesting to note that since then, further studies have also pointed to a link between playing puzzle video games and creativity. Crombie et al. (2016) presented 18–30-year-old students with one of three games to play: Minecraft (an exploratory "sandbox" game), Portal 2 (a puzzle game) or Serious Sam (a first person "shooter" action game). Before playing these games, all participants completed the first half of the test of creativity called the Torrance Test of Divergent Thinking. This test measures flexibility (e.g. list as many items as you can that contain wheels), originality (e.g. what would happen if we no longer needed sleep?) and fluency (e.g. how many possible uses can you think of for a box?). They then played one of the games for 30 minutes before completing the second half of the Torrance test. What did they find? Playing the puzzle game significantly improved creativity but only in terms of flexibility. Minecraft was perhaps difficult to make progress with if the player was new to this game the authors suggested.

One area where such positive findings have had a significant impact is in the field of aging research where cognitive decline is something that researchers are keen to address. With this in mind, Tennstedt and Unverzagt (2013) conducted the ACTIVE clinical trials with older adults. ACTIVE stands for Advance Cognitive Training for Independent and Vital Elderly. What did it involve? Training in memory, reasoning or speed-of-processing tasks. Straight away, improvements were noticed, specific to the type of training received.

So, playing video games, can it seems, improves self-esteem, persistence, memory and even calculation ability, dependent on the type of game played. It probably won't be surprising to know then that psychologists also believe that they can offer opportunities to support individuals with specific learning difficulties. Franceschini et al. (2013) believe that action video games can improve attention which can directly impact and improve reading abilities (specifically reading speed) in individuals diagnosed with dyslexia. This is particularly impressive given that the action video games participants were asked to play in this study did not involve any phonological or orthographic training and were only played for 12 hours (not all in one go of course!). The benefits gained were so good that they even exceeded the improvements expected from spontaneous reading development or from demanding reading treatments.

REASONS TO BE CAUTIOUS?

Before we all rush out to buy the latest video game console, you might want to read on. Simons et al. (2016) explored the effectiveness (or otherwise!) of brain-training interventions and reported that they did seem to have positive effects. However, such benefits were unlikely to transfer to new tasks that were only distantly related to the original tasks and little evidence was found to suggest that everyday cognitive performance was improved. Only given similar tasks to the original, was performance likely to improve. In other words, the benefits of such games only extend to similar, related tasks. Looking back at the ACTIVE intervention (Tennstedt & Unverzagt, 2013) which looked to be so successful initially, again, the benefits appeared to be specific to the tasks trained on. No improvements on everyday tasks was found either immediately or during the 1 or 2 years following.

Moreover, recent evidence suggests that the earlier studies exploring the effects of video games may have been overly optimistic. Makin (2016) for example pointed to the methodological difficulties inherent in many of the early studies claiming positive effects. Makin points to the work of Engle et al. who suggested that in many of these studies there is a commonly occurring "Hawthorne Effect". This is the phenomenon whereby people will change their behaviour in response to being observed. In these situations, participants may be showing something of a placebo effect (Boot & Kramer, 2014) where any improvement in performance is due to the expectation that it should have positive effects. To counter this, Melby-Lervåg and Hulme (2013) advocate the use of active control groups that engage in similar activities with the same expectations that they will be beneficial. Unfortunately, many early studies compared a group that were asked to play video games with a group that were not asked to do this but were not given a parallel, similar task.

To get an idea of the size of the problem, consider this: a staggering 68.2% of all the studies reviewed by Rossignoli-Palomeque et al. (2018) exploring brain-training effects on children and adolescents were not randomised and only 18.6% of those that were used active controls in their trials. When active control groups are used, many studies have struggled to identify even weak benefits and according to Au et al. (2015) in some cases, any effect at all. Owen et al. (2010) tested over 11,000 participants online and required them to engage in training of either reasoning skills, visuo-spatial/attentional skills or training to answer trivia questions (the control group). No evidence of any neuropsychological benefit was identified.

Stojanoski et al. (2021) controlled for the effects of expectations and recruited over 1,000 participants in their study to try to explore the effects of brain training in people who had engaged with this for up to 5 years. No association between playing these games and any measure of cognitive functioning was identified and duration of training similarly showed little relationship with cognitive performance measures. This was the case even when age was also controlled for as well as which brain-training games they had played.

Studies that claimed to find a positive impact of brain training on fluid intelligence, that is, the ability to solve novel problems and reason (Jaeggi et al., 2008) have proved difficult to replicate (Harrison et al., 2013). Putting the methodological concerns aside, even those studies that initially purported to show benefits of video games, later threw caution on their original claims. For example, Ballesteros et al. (2015) wanted to see what effect playing 20 1-hour non-action video games would have on cognitive function and well-being in an older participant group. Finding ways to maintain cognitive performance and avoid declines associated with aging is increasingly of interest to psychologists (Hertzog et al., 2009). Participants were not aware if they were in the experimental group or the control group. The experimental group were asked to practice twice, 10 different video games selected from Lumosity (www.lumosity.com). The control group were asked to discuss with members of the research group matters related to aging. All participants were asked to complete a battery of tasks that were designed to test cognitive skills both before and after the intervention. Processing speed, attention and visual recognition memory were all found to improve as a result of the luminosity training alongside two measures of well-being: Affection and Assertivity. Affection is the confidence and satisfaction with people around and assertivity refers to the self-perception of having done the right thing from another's perspective. But 3 months later, all these benefits had been lost.

PERHAPS VIDEO GAMES JUST MAKE US MORE PRO-SOCIAL

The evidence for the effects of video games on our intelligence and cognitive skills more generally is looking a tad more shaky. Perhaps there is a more hopeful picture when it comes to the effects of video games on our willingness to help others. Can playing video games make us more helpful?

Greitemeyer and Osswald (2010) certainly think so. In the first of four experiments, they asked participants to play 8 minutes of either Tetris, considered a neutral game, Lemmings, considered a pro-social game or Lamers, a violent video game. Once the 8 minutes were up, the experimenter reached across to pass a questionnaire to participants but in so doing, knocked a cup of pencils over, spilling them on the floor. Would participants help? Well, it depended on what game they had played. Those who played the pro-social Lemmings game were more likely to help (67% did so) than those playing either of the other two games (only 33% did so if they had played Tetris and 28% if they had played Lamers). In a second study, using a similar methodology, participants were asked, after the game play had finished, if they would be willing to take part in a further study and if so, how much of their time they would be prepared to allocate to this. Everyone playing Lemmings offered to help compared to 68% of those playing Tetris. Not only that but those playing the pro-social Lemmings game were willing to donate more of their time to do so.

Now imagine this scenario. You are sitting in the laboratory and have just finished playing Tetris. The male experimenter announces he has to leave the room for a couple of minutes and asks a confederate (a friend of his who knows what the study is about) to go into the room. As the confederate comes in, he approaches a female experimenter and starts to harass her, shouting, kicking a rubbish bin and pulling the experimenter's arm in an effort to get her to leave with him. The experimenter remains calm and reserved and asks the confederate to quiet down. Would you get up and intervene?

■ **Figure 3.3** A similar game to that used in Greitemeyer and Osswald's study.

Greitemeyer and Osswald tried this out in their own laboratory. What happened? Well, as you might have come to expect by now, those who played a pro-social game (this time a game called Crisis City) were more likely to intervene (56% did so) than those who played Tetris (only 22% did so). According to the authors, playing the pro-social game made pro-social thoughts more accessible.

For any teachers or would-be teachers out there, it might be worth ensuring your students play a pro-social video game before they read feedback on their essays, at least if you think there is a chance they haven't done as well as they hoped. Greitemeyer and colleagues (2012) asked undergraduate students to write an essay. They were told this would be evaluated and they would receive feedback from another person. In a rather mean twist to this story, Greitemeyer made sure that all of the feedback received by the participants was negative with a comment that suggested the essay was boring. Imagine getting that. Participants were then asked to spend 15 minutes playing a video game. This was either a neutral game (Pinball), a pro-social game (Firefighters: Saving Lives) or a violent game (Mortal Kombat). Once this time was up, the participants were asked to take part in one last study that was designed to test the effect of hearing an aversive noise on memory. Participants were informed that the person who had given them the negative feedback was to be paid according to how well they did on the memory tasks. The job of each participant was to decide on the level of noise that was to be delivered. In line with earlier findings, those playing the pro-social game in the 15 minutes before this part of the study were more pro-social. They chose significantly lower levels of the aversive noise to blast the other individual with.

IS IT JUST PRO-SOCIAL GAMES THAT MAKE US BEHAVE MORE PRO-SOCIALLY?

Not necessarily. Ask undergraduates to play a relaxing video game and they will be more likely to stay and sharpen some pencils for you in readiness for a future study. It's true. Whitaker and Bushman (2012) compared the effects of neutral games (e.g. Super Mario Galaxy) with relaxing games (e.g. Endless Ocean) with violent games (e.g. Resident Evil 4). Those playing the relaxing games were not only more likely to help but also reported feeling more positive.

IF PRO-SOCIAL GAMES MAKE US MORE PRO-SOCIAL, DO ANTI-SOCIAL VIDEO GAMES MAKE US BEHAVE MORE ANTI-SOCIALLY?

Welcome to an ongoing debate in the literature. There are multiple reasons to be concerned about this. A theoretical framework known as the GAM or General Aggression Model would suggest that playing violent video games increases aggressive thoughts, feelings and behaviours. In the short term, it may be that violent video games can prime or activate related thoughts, leading to heightened aggression. On the other hand, catharsis, originally proposed by Breuer and Freud in 1893, might suggest that playing such games offers a release from pent-up negative energy accrued through the day. So, who is right?

Let's begin by taking a look at a study conducted by Kühn et al. (2019). Kühn wanted to explore the long-term effects of violent video game play. Participants played either Grand Theft Auto V, The Sims 3 or no game at all every day for 2 months. Grand Theft Auto V was considered the violent video game and The Sims 3 was considered the neutral game. A whole battery of tasks measuring everything from aggression to lexical decisions to boredom propensity were given before and after the game playing intervention. The results suggested no effect of playing violent video games at all.

Similar conclusions were reached in a study of teenagers who spend time playing video games (Przybylski & Weinstein, 2019). In fact, back in 1985, Kestenbaum and Weinstein even reported a calming effect from playing violent video games in adolescents although more recent research shows little support for this.

In contrast to these findings, others have found very different outcomes. For example, Arevalo and Balodi (2019) believe the correlation between playing violent video games and aggression is a positive one. They compared gamers who play pro-social games with those who play violent games on a 20-item questionnaire, The Nickell Helping Attitude Scale. Consistent with previous findings, those who played pro-social games were more likely to co-operate and help others according to their responses on the questionnaire. But, in contrast, violent video games, it was claimed, encourage aggressive and impulsive behaviour among individuals.

Arevalo and Balodi are not alone in thinking this. Greitemeyer and Mügge (2014) conducted a huge meta-analysis involving no less than 98 different studies with just short of 37,000 participants.

Again, whilst pro-social video games increased pro-social outcomes, violent video games increased aggression and anti-social outcomes. In fact Anderson (2004) estimated the effect of violent video games on aggressive behaviour to be larger than the reduction in risk of HIV caused by condom use, the effect of passive smoking on lung cancer and the effects of calcium on bone mass!

Bushman and Anderson (2009) go so far as to claim that violent video games may even make us numb to the suffering and pain experienced by others. Let's illustrate with a scenario. Bob is playing a video game in the laboratory. When he has played for 20 mins, he is asked to complete a questionnaire. However, while he is completing this, he hears a loud fight taking place outside the lab and is led to believe that someone has been injured after hearing a loud crash and a groan. Would Bob get up to help?

Perhaps we should let you in on a secret here. The loud fight is actually an audio recording of two actors being played by the experimenter. Oh, and the loud crash? That was the experimenter throwing a chair on the floor to make a loud noise. And the questionnaire? That was just a lengthy bogus questionnaire designed to keep the participants busy. Well, what did they find? There was no difference in the number who offered help between violent and non-violent game players. However, those who had played the violent game took 450% longer to offer it and thought the fight was less serious. It was almost as if the video game had desensitised the individuals to violence.

Ok, I hear what you are saying – this was in a laboratory. There may be something about the situation of being in a laboratory that led to these results. Ok, well, Bushman and Anderson (2009) thought about that also and followed up this study with a second, this time done in a real-world scenario, outside a cinema. Those attending the cinema had not played video games but had watched either a violent movie or a non-violent movie. As they came out of the cinema, they encountered a confederate who had her ankle bandaged and had dropped her crutches. Would someone help her to retrieve them? It depends on which film they saw. Those watching a violent movie took over 26% longer to help!

This desensitisation effect has also been demonstrated in a study requiring participants to give jail sentences to criminals. Vignettes describing incidents of rape, physical assault, stabbings, armed robbery and murder were presented to participants after they had played violent video games for 30 minutes. Participants could choose a jail term for the character in each vignette, from a list of four possibilities ranging from no time at all to more than 20 years. If you are wondering what effect the video games had, wonder no more. Men were more likely to give shorter jail terms to the individuals as a result. For women, there was no corresponding effect. The idea of desensitisation was therefore supported only for men. If anything, women became more sensitised to violence after!

And what's more, this effect could be contagious! Greitemeyer (2019) conducted a longitudinal study exploring the level of aggression, amount of violent video game play and how individuals perceived their friends. Strikingly, an individual's whole social network can be affected by an individual's playing of violent video games. A friend's amount of violent video game play at time 1 was strongly associated with aggression at time 2. Such contagion is a concern given the moral disengagement that may result from playing such games (Gabbiadini et al., 2012).

IT'S NOT THAT STRAIGHTFORWARD

The finding of gender differences points to one of the complicating issues in this debate. There are various mediating variables that might explain the findings. For example, is it really violence per se that is important? Dowsett and Jackson (2019) found it was competition rather than violence that increased aggression. Lose in a competitive game and the effects are strengthened further.

This hints at arousal being an important aspect of the story and this would certainly sit comfortably with the study conducted by Fischer et al. (2010). Fischer and colleagues compared aggressive behaviour of those who used a personalised character with those who used a non-personalised character. When playing an aggressive game, those using a personalised character showed significantly more aggressive behaviour. Its almost as though the more similar the character is to us, the more aroused we become when playing the game and consequently the more easily this tips into aggressive tendencies.

But even here, arousal is not the whole story. Compare an individual from a "good" family environment with those from a "poor" family environment and you will find differential effects. Only those from a poor environment show both direct and indirect effects of playing violent video games on aggression which Shao and Wang (2019) believe is mediated by the normative

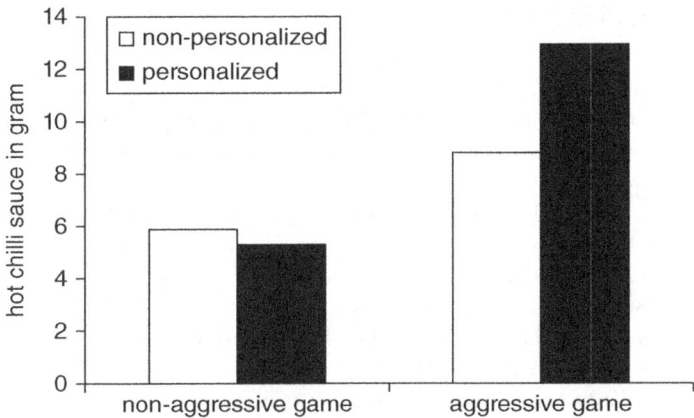

■ **Figure 3.4** Taken from Fischer et al. (2010). Playing an aggressive video game using your own personalised character increases aggressive behaviour as measured by the amount of chilli sauce we are prepared to administer to another person.

beliefs about aggression held by the family. Individuals become accustomed to violence which gives them the impression that it is a good way of problem solving. This approach is consistent with the "catalyst model" that predicts harsh early environments combined with genetic predispositions underlie the link between aggressive behaviour and playing of violent video games (Ferguson et al., 2008).

Arousal cannot be the whole story for another reason also. In cases where violent video games require co-operation, pro-social behaviour later, outside of the game, increases (Ewoldsen et al., 2012) and even just playing these games with others rather than alone is sufficient to reduce hostility and aggression (Eastin, 2007).

Whatever your view, what is clear is that the time spent playing these games is perhaps the key factor to consider. Weis and Cerankosky (2010), in a very generous study, offered to give children a video games console as reward for participation in a study. For one group, they received the console immediately and for the second group they only received this at a follow up assessment 4 months later. Well, surprise, surprise – what did those children do who received the console immediately? They used it! But unfortunately so much so that they engaged less in after school academic activities and ended up with lower reading and writing scores and greater teacher-reported academic problems at follow up.

REFERENCES

Anderson, C. A. (2004). An update on the effects of playing violent video games. *Journal of Adolescence, 27*(1), 113–122.

Arevalo, J. P. M., & Balodi, A. B. (2019). The impact of pro-social and violent video games on helping attitude a comparative study. *Journal of Content, Community and Communication, 9,* 1–5.

Au, J., Sheehan, E., Tsai, N., Duncan, G. J., Buschkuehl, M., & Jaeggi, S. M. (2015). Improving fluid intelligence with training on working memory: A meta-analysis. *Psychonomic Bulletin & Review, 22*(2), 366–377.

Ballesteros, S., Kraft, E., Santana, S., & Tziraki, C. (2015). Maintaining older brain functionality: A targeted review. *Neuroscience & Biobehavioral Reviews, 55,* 453–477.

Boot, W. R., & Kramer, A. F. (2014, November). The brain-games conundrum: Does cognitive training really sharpen the mind? In *Cerebrum: The Dana forum on brain science* (Vol. 2014). Dana Foundation.

Breuer, J., & Freud, S. (1893). Studies on hysteria. In J. Strachey (Ed.), *The standard edition of the complete psychological works of Sigmund Freud.* Hogarth Press.

Bushman, B. J., & Anderson, C. A. (2009). Comfortably numb: Desensitizing effects of violent media on helping others. *Psychological Science, 20*(3), 273–277.

Crombie, W., Moffat, D. C., & Shabalina, O. (2016, October). Video games can temporarily increase creativity; especially puzzle games. In *European conference on games based learning. Academic conferences international limited* (pp. 152–158). Academic Conferences and Publishing International Ltd.

Dennison, P. E., & Dennison, G. E. (1986). *Brain gym: Simple activities for whole brain learning.* Institute of Education Sciences.

Dowsett, A., & Jackson, M. (2019). The effect of violence and competition within video games on aggression. *Computers in Human Behavior, 99,* 22–27.

Eastin, M. S. (2007). The influence of competitive and cooperative group game play on state hostility. *Human Communication Research, 33*(4), 450–466.

Ewoldsen, D. R., Eno, C. A., Okdie, B. M., Velez, J. A., Guadagno, R. E., & DeCoster, J. (2012). Effect of playing violent video games cooperatively or competitively on subsequent cooperative behavior. *Cyberpsychology, Behavior, and Social Networking, 15*(5), 277–280.

Ferguson, C. J., Rueda, S. M., Cruz, A. M., Ferguson, D. E., Fritz, S., & Smith, S. M. (2008). Violent video games and aggression: Causal relationship or byproduct of family violence and intrinsic violence motivation? *Criminal Justice and Behavior, 35*(3), 311–332.

Fischer, P., Kastenmüller, A., & Greitemeyer, T. (2010). Media violence and the self: The impact of personalized gaming characters in aggressive video games on aggressive behavior. *Journal of Experimental Social Psychology, 46*(1), 192–195.

Franceschini, S., Gori, S., Ruffino, M., Viola, S., Molteni, M., & Facoetti, A. (2013). Action video games make dyslexic children read better. *Current Biology, 23*(6), 462–466.

Gabbiadini, A., Andrighetto, L., & Volpato, C. (2012). Brief report: Does exposure to violent video games increase moral disengagement among adolescents? *Journal of Adolescence*, *35*(5), 1403–1406.

Granic, I., Lobel, A., & Engels, R. C. (2014). The benefits of playing video games. *American Psychologist*, *69*(1), 66.

Greitemeyer, T. (2019). The contagious impact of playing violent video games on aggression: Longitudinal evidence. *Aggressive Behavior*, *45*(6), 635–642.

Greitemeyer, T., & Mügge, D. O. (2014). Video games do affect social outcomes: A meta-analytic review of the effects of violent and prosocial video game play. *Personality and Social Psychology Bulletin*, *40*(5), 578–589.

Greitemeyer, T., & Osswald, S. (2010). Effects of prosocial video games on prosocial behavior. *Journal of Personality and Social Psychology*, *98*(2), 211.

Greitemeyer, T., Traut-Mattausch, E., & Osswald, S. (2012). How to ameliorate negative effects of violent video games on cooperation: Play it cooperatively in a team. *Computers in Human Behavior*, *28*(4), 1465–1470.

Harrison, T. L., Shipstead, Z., Hicks, K. L., Hambrick, D. Z., Redick, T. S., & Engle, R. W. (2013). Working memory training may increase working memory capacity but not fluid intelligence. *Psychological Science*, *24*(12), 2409–2419.

Hertzog, C., Kramer, A. F., Wilson, R. S., & Lindenberger, U. (2009). Fit body, fit mind?. *Scientific American Mind*, *20*(3), 24–31.

Jaeggi, S. M., Buschkuehl, M., Jonides, J., & Perrig, W. J. (2008). Improving fluid intelligence with training on working memory. *Proceedings of the National Academy of Sciences*, *105*(19), 6829–6833.

Kühn, S., Kugler, D. T., Schmalen, K., Weichenberger, M., Witt, C., & Gallinat, J. (2019). Does playing violent video games cause aggression? A longitudinal intervention study. *Molecular Psychiatry*, *24*(8), 1220–1234.

Makin, S. (2016). Brain training: Memory games. *Nature*, *531*(7592), S10–S11.

Melby-Lervåg, M., & Hulme, C. (2013). Is working memory training effective? A meta-analytic review. *Developmental Psychology*, *49*(2), 270.

Miller, D. J., & Robertson, D. P. (2010). Using a games console in the primary classroom: Effects of 'Brain Training' programme on computation and self-esteem. *British Journal of Educational Technology*, *41*(2), 242–255.

Owen, A. M., Hampshire, A., Grahn, J. A., Stenton, R., Dajani, S., Burns, A. S., . . . Ballard, C. G. (2010). Putting brain training to the test. *Nature*, *465*(7299), 775–778.

Pallavicini, F., Ferrari, A., & Mantovani, F. (2018). Video games for well-being: A systematic review on the application of computer games for cognitive and emotional training in the adult population. *Frontiers in Psychology*, 2127.

Przybylski, A. K., & Weinstein, N. (2019). Violent video game engagement is not associated with adolescents' aggressive behaviour: Evidence from a registered report. *Royal Society Open Science*, *6*(2), 171474.

Rossignoli-Palomeque, T., Perez-Hernandez, E., & Gonzalez-Marques, J. (2018). Brain training in children and adolescents: Is it scientifically valid? *Frontiers in Psychology, 9*, 565.

Shao, R., & Wang, Y. (2019). The relation of violent video games to adolescent aggression: An examination of moderated mediation effect. *Frontiers in Psychology, 10*, 384.

Simons, D. J., Boot, W. R., Charness, N., Gathercole, S. E., Chabris, C. F., Hambrick, D. Z., & Stine-Morrow, E. A. (2016). Do "brain-training" programs work? *Psychological Science in the Public Interest, 17*(3), 103–186.

Stojanoski, B., Wild, C. J., Battista, M. E., Nichols, E. S., & Owen, A. M. (2021). Brain training habits are not associated with generalized benefits to cognition: An online study of over 1000 "brain trainers". *Journal of Experimental Psychology: General, 150*(4), 729.

Tennstedt, S. L., & Unverzagt, F. W. (2013). The ACTIVE study: Study overview and major findings. *Journal of Aging and Health, 25*(8_suppl), 3S–20S.

Ventura, M., Shute, V., & Zhao, W. (2013). The relationship between video game use and a performance-based measure of persistence. *Computers & Education, 60*(1), 52–58.

Weis, R., & Cerankosky, B. C. (2010). Effects of video-game ownership on young boys' academic and behavioral functioning: A randomized, controlled study. *Psychological Science, 21*(4), 463–470.

Whitaker, J. L., & Bushman, B. J. (2012). "Remain calm. Be kind." Effects of relaxing video games on aggressive and prosocial behavior. *Social Psychological and Personality Science, 3*(1), 88–92.

Chapter **4**

What colour are you wearing today?

This chapter focuses on the psychology of fashion, specifically exploring the effect of colour on the behaviour of ourselves and those around us. Chris de Burgh wrote about the lady in red in his song lyrics and this chapter takes this as its starting point. Does wearing the colour red influence those around us in matters of romance? If so, how and is this universal? In addressing these questions, issues of culture and gender are examined and the evolutionary origins of the "romantic red effect" are discussed. In addition to its effect in the search for love, colour is examined in terms of the sports arena. Does the colour of a sports kit have any bearing on the outcome of a sports match? And why is it advisable not to wear black to court? The chapter explores how the psychological evidence has been applied in real-world situations as diverse as TV shows, the courtroom, and the exam hall.

■ **Figure 4.1** Can the colour of what we wear affect our behaviour or other's behaviour towards us?

DOI: 10.4324/9781003329763-4

In 1986, Chris De Burgh topped the UK charts singing about "The Lady in Red". Yes, I will admit, it's one of my favourite tunes but since then there have been a number of other musicians and pop artists who have also sung about red dresses and red shoes. What's with the obsession with red? And does what we wear really influence our behaviour? A little delve into the psychological literature might tell us a bit more about what is going on here.

THE LADY IN RED REVISITED

I'm going to start by asking you to think back to Valentine's Day. What colour appears on most Valentine's Day cards and if you were lucky enough to be the recipient of roses, what colour were they? Chances are the answer is red. This is no coincidence if we look back in history at the use of the colour red to symbolise fertility (Knight et al., 1995) or to heighten attractiveness. Regas and Kozlowski (1998) for example suggest that as far back as the Ancient Egyptians, red lipstick and rouge were used by women to enhance their attractiveness. I suspect many of us have heard of the term "red-light district" also to refer to areas where prostitution is touted and if you haven't read it, do take a look at the *Scarlet Letter* by Nathaniel Hawthorne to see how red has been linked to passion in literature.

So in human societies, old and new, there is an association between the colour red and the idea of love, passion and sexuality. Is it just a learned association or is there something more biological underpinning this? Next time you visit a zoo or wildlife park, take a peek at the baboon enclosure, the chimpanzees or macaques. Chances are, in these communities, you will see some animals with rather large red genitalia. In fact, it may well be difficult *not* to notice. In many species, such red "ornamentation" as Elliot and Pazda (2012) call it, is designed to act as a sexual cue for potential mates that that animal is at a fertile point of their reproductive cycle. And, as Dixson (1998) has pointed out, the response of the mate is to increase their mounting behaviour and copulation attempts.

What relevance does this have for human populations? Andrew Elliot and Daniela Niesta wanted to find out. In a series of studies conducted in 2008, they asked male undergraduates to take part in a study that they described as being about the first impressions of the opposite sex. They were asked to look at a black and white photograph of a woman and to complete a questionnaire after. Where does the colour red come into this? Well the photograph was presented with either a red or a white background. Did it make a difference? It certainly did. Participants who viewed the black and white photograph against a red background rated the woman as significantly more attractive than those who saw the photograph against a white background. Similarly, show male participants a woman in a red shirt and they will express a greater willingness to take her on a date and to spend money on her compared to if she is wearing a blue shirt. Such effects are not, Elliot and Niesta demonstrated, observable in female participants and for the authors, this suggests that the "romantic red" effect points to a role for the biological, sexual signal theory. Men are, after all, operating on the basis of primitive preferences.

Not only do men rate the attractiveness of women wearing red higher, but such clothing also affects their behaviour in other ways too. Niesta Kayser et al. (2010) asked male undergraduates to participate in a study aimed to imitate an online conversation. They were shown a photo of the other person for 5 seconds and were asked to choose 5 questions from a possible 24 that they wanted to ask the other person. Unbeknownst to the participant, the questions ranged in terms of degree of intimacy. For example, a low intimacy question might be "Where are you from?" but a high intimacy question might be "How could a guy get your attention at a bar?". The photo that the participants were presented with showed a woman wearing either a red or green shirt. In line with previous findings, those who saw the woman wearing the red shirt chose to ask the woman more intimate questions than those who saw her wearing the green shirt.

How about physical behaviour? In a second study, Niesta Kayser and colleagues gave participants a photo to look at and –

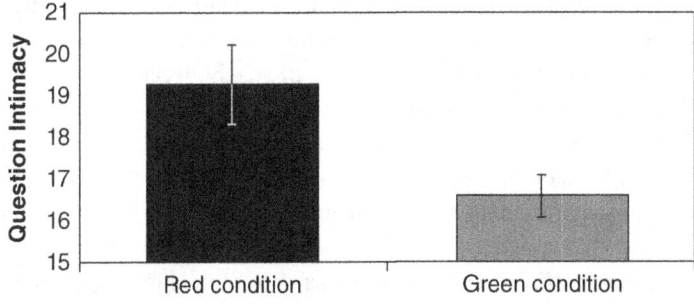

■ **Figure 4.2** Niesta Kayser et al. report that question intimacy choice of men increases when women wear red.

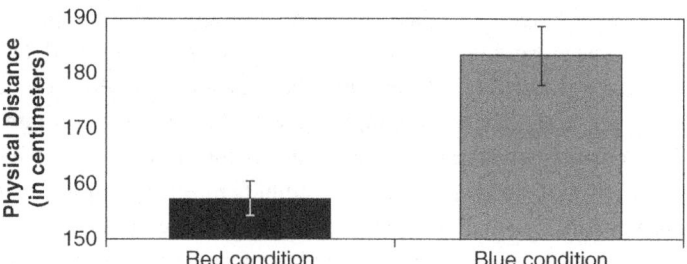

■ **Figure 4.3** Niesta Kayser et al. discovered that men will place their chair closer to that of a female who has been seen to wear red.

informed them that they would be going to another room to have a conversation with her. Again, the colour of the shirt worn by the woman was changed – for some participants, they saw her wearing a red shirt, and for others they saw her wearing a blue shirt. The participants were escorted to a room where two chairs were positioned, one on the left side of the room (where they were told the woman would sit) and another on the right side facing a table which they were instructed to bring over. The distance between the participant's chair and the woman's chair was measured. Lo and behold, those who saw the woman wearing the red shirt sat closer to her chair than those who saw her wearing the blue shirt. The men in this study were again particularly drawn to the lady in red.

IS THIS A UNIVERSAL PHENOMENON?

If the power of red in attracting a mate does have biological origins, we might well expect this effect to be universal. And, in fact, the evidence so far does indeed suggest this is the case. Elliot, Tracy, et al. (2013) examined the romantic red phenomenon with a group of males living in Burkina Faso. Their homes were in a remote village, a small rural settlement. The reason for choosing this participant group was precisely because they were "culturally isolated" (Elliot, Tracy, et al., 2013) and moreover, in this group, red is often associated with negative events such as bad luck or illness. As in earlier studies, a black and white photo was presented to each participant showing a West African woman with either a red or blue background. Despite the cultural isolation, participants showed the same romantic red effect, with ratings of attractiveness being higher when a red background was shown. Not only that but participants were more likely to volunteer to meet her and more interested in courting her. It was particularly interesting to note that the reaction to the red background did not extend to desire to have sexual intercourse with the woman shown in the photo. Red appeared to be related to romantic rather than sexual attraction. The age of romance is not dead. Yet.

In fact the colour red may come in handy. Guéguen (2012) asked confederates to act as hitchhikers. Each confederate was instructed to wear the same clothes, other than the colour of their T-shirt was varied. With various control measures built in, such as all confederates being of the same height, all having been rated similarly for attractiveness and all wearing the same clothing items, the hitchhikers took it in turns to test 960 drivers each. After 80 motorists had passed, the confederate would change the T-shirt to another coloured T-shirt. After 240 drivers had passed, the confederates swapped over. The conclusion of this story is a simple one – as far as male drivers were concerned, they were more likely to stop when the hitchhiking confederate was wearing a red T-shirt than when they were wearing yellow, green, black, white, or blue. Female drivers showed no such effect.

If you work in hospitality, there may be more interesting news for you too. Wear red and you are likely to get more tips and greater amounts of tips too. Guéguen paired up with Jacob in 2011 to study the tipping behaviour of 722 restaurant customers, all of whom sat alone. The colour of the T-shirt worn by the waitresses was varied over a 6-week period. Consistent with our story so far, men gave significantly more money in tips and gave tips more often when the waitress wore red. No effect of colour was found amongst women patrons. And no, you don't need to rush out and buy a red T-shirt either. There is a reason that the most successful lipstick colour is red – Guéguen and Jacob (2011) reported that the tipping effect also works for waitresses who wear red lipstick. Compared to waitresses wearing brown, pink or no lipstick, those wearing red received both more tips and greater amounts of tips from male patrons of a restaurant.

Lipstick and T-shirts aside, think about the accessories, ladies. If you are still not convinced, take a look at the work of Hanyu Lin (2014). When asked to rate photographs of women carrying laptops, male participants perceived women carrying a red laptop as significantly more attractive than the same women carrying a silver, blue or black laptop. However, this did not translate into a desire to engage in sexual activity. The effect was again specific to the perception of men.

THE CATCH

Before the ladies amongst us rush out to buy the latest red laptop, shirt or dress, I should point out that the story is a little more nuanced than we are letting on. We know, for example, that wearing red has no effect on how likeable others rate us (e.g. Elliot, Tracy et al., 2013) Neither does it affect ratings of intelligence or friendliness (Roberts et al., 2010) or ratings of assertiveness or health (Lin, 2014) and it may only be applicable to young, but not menopausal women (Schwarz & Singer, 2013). Perhaps older women are seen as less sexually receptive it has been argued (Pazda et al., 2012). There are limits to the romantic red effect after all.

AND HOW ABOUT THE GENTLEMEN AMONG US?

And for the gentlemen among us, don't think for one minute that wearing red has no effect on the ladies. It just seems to work in a different way. As Elliot and colleagues (2010) point out, there are many species in which females are attracted to males displaying red including species such as stickleback fish (Milinski & Bakker, 1990), finches (Burley, 1982) and macaques (Waitt et al., 2003). Red colouration in these species is often a signal of rank and importance and is believed to be linked to levels of testosterone (Setchell et al., 2008).

■ **Figure 4.4** Male finches have been shown to be particularly alluring to females when they have red colouration on their chests.

In human societies, we often associate red with status and authority. In many cultures, it is used to symbolise prosperity (Ewing, 2006) and as Elliot and colleagues discuss, historically it was reserved for the clothing of the upper class. When asked what they value in potential dates, women will often refer to status indicators in their responses (Buss, 1989) and, as Ellis (1992) points out in a review of the literature, high status is associated with positive predictors of reproductive success.

So what does this mean in terms of our romantic red effect? Elliot et al. (2010) wanted to find out. In a method reminiscent of some of their earlier work, a black and white photograph of a man was shown to participants, all of whom, this time, were women. In half of the cases, the photograph had a red background and in the other half, a white background. Women were asked to rate the attractiveness of the man in the photo, how pleasant the man was to look at and whether they were likely to find him attractive if they met him face to face. Attractiveness ratings soared when the red background was used. This effect did not work when men were asked to do a similar task.

It is possible that this effect is heightened when women are at the most fertile point of their cycle. Certainly in some species, the sensitivity of females to red in males is highest when they are at their most fertile (Boulcott & Braithwaite, 2007). We also know that females are more likely to choose to wear red themselves when they are at their most fertile (Beall & Tracy, 2013). Eisenbruch et al. (2015) used daily hormone sampling via saliva samples to estimate where women were in their reproductive cycle. They invited participants to come into the laboratory on four occasions during one or two menstrual cycles. On these visits, not only did they provide another saliva sample but they were also photographed. No surprise to know that women who were in the most fertile part of their cycle chose to wear red more often then than in the other phases of their cycle.

The same red preference is shown when women are expected to meet an attractive man. When asked to select a standardised T-shirt to wear, women were more likely to select a red rather than green one compared to when they believe they are going meet an unattractive man or an averagely attractive woman (Elliot, Greitemeyer, et al., 2013). So ladies, its not just the men's sensitivity to red that is important but our decision to use red to relay signals too. Still not convinced? Then do what Elliot and Pazda (2012) did and take a look at the web profile picture people post on dating websites. According to these authors, women interested in casual sex are more likely to be wearing red in their profile picture. And more so than women on dating websites which facilitate marital relationships.

A FOCUS ON FASHION

So, does this spell the end for the "little black dress"? We have now made a strong case for replacing it with the little red dress after all. Well, not quite. If red is just not your colour, big up the fashionista status by walking out in black. Kramer and Mulgrew (2018) studied participants in a British reality TV show "First Dates". You may well have seen this yourself. People meet on a blind date to have a meal together. What a perfect opportunity Kramer and Mulgrew thought, to look at the colour of clothing worn when meeting what could potentially be a possible future mate. So, in they dived. 546 daters were asked to complete an interview before the date and during the date. These two occasions allowed Kramer and Mulgrew to compare the colour of clothing worn at two time-points. Consistent with previous studies, the amount of red worn did increase from pre-date to date for both men and women. BUT, (wait for it), the effect was even stronger for black clothes. What is going on here I hear you wonder. Well, Pazda et al. (2014) believe that whilst red signals sexual receptivity, black signals something quite different – perceived fashionableness and both are seen as equally attractive (Roberts et al., 2010).

TAKING THE COLOUR EFFECT INTO THE SPORTING ARENA

That is, attractive in the relationship domain. Both black and red can serve a very different function in the sports arena. You may well have heard of the New Zealand "All Blacks". It isn't just their ritual dance that is designed to intimidateate their opponents. Frank and Gilovich (1988) suggest black kits are often assessed as indicating more aggression. In a study of US National Hockey League and National Football League players, they found that those wearing black kits were punished for aggressive behaviour more than players wearing other colours. Moreover, when teams that usually wear non-black uniforms switched to black uniforms, they experienced a dramatic increase in penalties being awarded against them.

As for red, as we have seen, this is often linked to levels of testosterone and dominance. Being seen as dominant in a sporting competition could be to the competitor's advantage. Hill and Barton (2005) studied the effect of colour of kit (red or blue) on success at the 2004 Olympic Games in Athens. They looked at four combat sports: Tae-Kwon-Do, Boxing, Greco-Roman Wrestling and Freestyle Wrestling. Guess who won more fights? Yes, those wearing red. This finding was even more impressive when we consider that this pattern was found in 16 of 21 rounds and 19 of 29 weight classes. This effect is, however, only consistent when the two competitors are of similar ability.

So does wearing red instill the wearer with greater confidence? Sorokowski and colleagues (2014) suggest not. Instead, they argue for an observer effect. Students from both Poland and from China were asked to watch a 2-minute video showing a semi-professional boxing match. The match chosen was one where it almost ended in a tie. In other words, it was a close match. Six different versions of the fight were viewed with the only difference being the colour of the competitors' shorts (red, black or blue). Whilst watching the video, participants were asked to imagine themselves in the role of referee. In this role, their job was to estimate the number of effective blows made by each boxer. When one competitor wore blue trunks, the other competitor (wearing black or red) was always considered to be superior. However, there was no effect when both competitors were wearing red or black. Wearing red or black was sufficient for that competitor to be seen as aggressive, stronger and dominant to the observer. This finding was particularly important in highlighting the universality of these colour effects. In China, red is often associated with courage and loyalty, success and fortune (Cullen, 2000) whereas in western cultures, it is often associated with danger, anger or strength (Adams & Osgood, 1973). These cultural associations aside, the effect identified in the boxer study showed that colour can have similar emotional consequences in a sporting arena.

Sorokowski et al.'s finding is not a standalone finding. When asked to judge Tae-Kwon-Do matches where the only thing that differed was the colour of the kit worn, 13% more points were awarded to those wearing red than to those wearing blue (Hagemann et al., 2008). It does appear to be the effect on the observer that counts. Certainly we know that in achievement-based tasks such as an IQ test, brief exposure to the colour red can impair performance (Elliot et al., 2007) so the perception of red is indeed important.

CHAPTER 4 What colour are you wearing today?

■ **Figure 4.5** Red protective equipment can potentially give a sporting advantage in martial arts.

However, not everyone agrees. Dreiskaemper and colleagues decided to measure strength and heart rate of athletes during a combat situation. Participants were asked to take part in a combat competition once wearing a blue jersey and once wearing a red jersey. The combat involved using "smash sticks" to hit each other with, with the aim being to hit their opponent's upper body more than they were hit themselves. Heart rate during the fight and strength before the fight (as measured by a leg dynamometer which measured the maximum tractive force exerted while pulling a 40cm iron chain on a platform) were significantly greater for those wearing red. It isn't just the referees that are influenced by kit colour – the competitors themselves were too.

IS THIS SPECIFIC TO INDIVIDUAL SPORTS?

These studies explore individual sports. Surely it wouldn't work in team sports. Would it? Hill and Barton (2005) decided to look at footballing competitions and picked on the Euros as their focus. Hill and Barton compared the performance of five teams when wearing red shirts with their performance when wearing shirts that were white or blue. They performed best when wearing red. This is painful news for a loyal Tottenham Hotspur supporter like me (they play in white and blue). Even more so when the findings of Attrill and colleagues in 2008 are considered. They analysed the relative league positions of teams wearing different coloured kits. It didn't matter which league division they looked at, red teams always had the best home record as measured both by position in the league table and the percentage of maximum points achieved. Perhaps that explains why Spurs lost against Liverpool in the Champion League final.

On the note of football, I am going to get you to cast your mind back to the painful memory of England's loss in the Euro's final in 2021. Yes, the penalties. It was painful but it could have been worse. If the Italian goalkeeper had worn a red shirt to be precise. Greenlees et al. (2013) asked 40 experienced footballers to take 10 penalty kicks. Before they did so, they were asked to rate their expectancy of success. The first time they took their penalties, the goalkeeper wore a black shirt. The second time, he wore either a red, yellow, green or blue shirt. All the footballers were expectant of success and shirt colour didn't affect this. But in terms of the actual penalties scored, significantly fewer were scored when the goalie wore red.

THE EXCEPTIONS TO THE RULE

So black and red work in our favour. Much of the time. But as you may be expecting in the wonderful world of psychology, there are some exceptions. If you want my advice, don't wear black if you are a suspect in a crime. (Better still, don't commit crime in the first place.) In any situation where aggression is concerned, black can evoke negative reactions and while this might lead to more success in a sports arena, it may backfire if for any reason, you end up in a criminal court. In a study by Vrij (1997), participants were asked to watch a videotaped scenario and try to imagine themselves in the situation before answering a questionnaire. The scenario shown was one in which a man, sitting with friends at a table, drinking beer, becomes annoyed at being watched, pulls out a knife and lunges towards the participant with insults and threats. In an analogous control scenario, the scenario involved a man using a screwdriver to tamper with a bike. He turns round and walks towards the participant holding the screwdriver out. Participants were asked how threatened they felt and were asked to rate the extent to which the man made an aggressive or dangerous impression.

In each scenario, for half of the participants, the man in question was dressed in black. For the other half, he was dressed in light-coloured clothing. Did this make any difference? As you can probably guess by now, yes, it did. The man dressed in black was rated as more aggressive and left participants feeling more irritated than the man in the light-coloured clothing.

In a second study, partcipants were asked to look at a photograph of a suspect that they were told had been taken into police custody. It was clearly stated to participants that it had not yet been proven whether the woman was guilty. For half of the participants, the woman wore a light-coloured outfit. For the rest, they saw a photo of a woman wearing black. All participants were asked to make judgements about how physically aggressive the suspect was likely to be, the extent to which she was likely to have a criminal record and how likely it was that she had been arrested for a violent crime. They were also asked to make judgements about how likely it was that she would reoffend and how argumentative she was likely to be. As in their first experiment, the black clothed suspect was rated as being more aggressive and made the most guilty impression.

There may also be situations where wearing red doesn't work in our favour. Consider a job interview for example. Wearing a red shirt then wouldn't help you too much. At least not if we believe Maier et al. (2013). In their study, participants were asked to do one of three things: to play the role of a staff manager evaluating applicants for a job, to evaluate a person in a photograph in terms of whether they would make a good candidate for a dating website or to evaluate the person in the photo with no additional information given. A photograph of a male wearing either a red or a green shirt was presented. In all conditions, participants were asked to evaluate the intelligence of the person in the photograph and in the job scenario, competence was also emphasised. Those who saw the photograph of the man in the red shirt rated him as significantly less intelligent than those seeing him in the green shirt and this was strongest in the job scenario condition where competence was emphasised. When the colour of a tie was manipulated, similar patterns were obtained. Those seeing the man wearing a red tie considered him to have less earning potential and less leadership appeal. The context in which we find ourselves therefore does make a big difference to how we are perceived.

So where does that leave our story of clothing and colour? As with many things in life, the recommendation would be to dress authentically. I mean this quite literally too. Gino et al. (2010) gave participants a paper and pencil matrix task and a perceptual task to complete whilst wearing either genuine or fake designer sunglasses. Those wearing the fake sunglasses were more likely to cheat across the tasks given! Not only that but those wearing the fake sunglasses were significantly more likely to report people they knew as likely to behave dishonestly and considered common behaviours to be less truthful.

REFERENCES

Adams, F. M., & Osgood, C. E. (1973). A cross-cultural study of the affective meanings of color. *Journal of Cross-cultural Psychology*, *4*(2), 135–156.

Attrill, M. J., Gresty, K. A., Hill, R. A., & Barton, R. A. (2008). Red shirt colour is associated with long-term team success in English football. *Journal of Sports Sciences*, *26*(6), 577–582.

Beall, A. T., & Tracy, J. L. (2013). Women are more likely to wear red or pink at peak fertility. *Psychological Science*, *24*(9), 1837–1841.

Boulcott, P., & Braithwaite, V. A. (2007). Colour perception in three-spined sticklebacks: Sexes are not so different after all. *Evolutionary Ecology*, *21*(5), 601–611.

Burley, N., Krantzberg, G., & Radman, P. (1982). Influence of colour-banding on the conspecific preferences of zebra finches. *Animal Behaviour*, *30*(2), 444–455.

Buss, D. M. (1989). Sex differences in human mate preferences: Evolutionary hypotheses tested in 37 cultures. *Behavioral and Brain Sciences*, *12*(1), 1–14.

Cullen, C. (2000). *Global graphics*. Rockport Publishers

Dixson, A. F. (1998). *Primate sexuality: Comparative studies of the prosimians, monkeys, apes and human beings*. Oxford University Press.

Eisenbruch, A. B., Simmons, Z. L., & Roney, J. R. (2015). Lady in red: Hormonal predictors of women's clothing choices. *Psychological Science*, *26*(8), 1332–1338.

Elliot, A. J., Greitemeyer, T., & Pazda, A. D. (2013). Women's use of red clothing as a sexual signal in intersexual interaction. *Journal of Experimental Social Psychology*, *49*(3), 599–602.

Elliot, A. J., Maier, M. A., Moller, A. C., Friedman, R., & Meinhardt, J. (2007). Color and psychological functioning: The effect of red on performance attainment. *Journal of Experimental Psychology: General*, *136*(1), 154.

Elliot, A. J., & Niesta Kayser, D. (2008). Romantic red: Red enhances men's attraction to women. *Journal of Personality and Social Psychology*, *95*(5), 1150.

Elliot, A. J., Niesta Kayser, D., Greitemeyer, T., Lichtenfeld, S., Gramzow, R. H., Maier, M. A., & Liu, H. (2010). Red, rank, and romance in women viewing men. *Journal of Experimental Psychology: General*, *139*(3), 399.

Elliot, A. J., & Pazda, A. D. (2012). Dressed for sex: Red as a female sexual signal in humans. *PLoS One*, *7*(4), e34607.

Elliot, A. J., Tracy, J. L., Pazda, A. D., & Beall, A. T. (2013). Red enhances women's attractiveness to men: First evidence suggesting universality. *Journal of Experimental Social Psychology*, *49*(1), 165–168.

Ellis, B. J. (1992). The evolution of sexual attraction: Evaluative mechanisms in women. In J. Barkow, L. Cosmides, & J. Tooby (Eds.), *The adapted mind* (pp. 267–288). Oxford University Press.

Ewing, T. (2006, August). 'í litklæðum'–coloured clothes in medieval Scandinavian literature and archaeology. In *Thirteenth annual international saga conference, Durham and York*. Academia.

Frank, M. G., & Gilovich, T. (1988). The dark side of self-and social perception: Black uniforms and aggression in professional sports. *Journal of Personality and Social Psychology*, *54*(1), 74.

Gino, F., Norton, M. I., & Ariely, D. (2010). The counterfeit self: The deceptive costs of faking it. *Psychological Science*, *21*(5), 712–720.

Greenlees, I. A., Eynon, M., & Thelwell, R. C. (2013). Color of soccer goalkeepers' uniforms influences the outcome of penalty kicks. *Perceptual and Motor Skills*, *117*(1), 1–10.

Guéguen*, N. (2012). Color and women hitchhikers' attractiveness: Gentlemen drivers prefer red. *Color Research & Application*, *37*(1), 76–78.

Guéguen, N., & Jacob, C. (2011). Enhanced female attractiveness with use of cosmetics and male tipping behavior in restaurants. *Journal of Cosmetic Science*, *62*(3), 283–290.

Hagemann, N., Strauss, B., & Leißing, J. (2008). When the referee sees red . . . *Psychological Science*, *19*(8), 769–771.

Hill, R. A., & Barton, R. A. (2005). Red enhances human performance in contests. *Nature*, *435*(7040), 293–293.

Knight, C., Power, C., & Watts, I. (1995). The human symbolic revolution: A Darwinian account. *Cambridge Archaeological Journal*, *5*(1), 75–114.

Kramer, R. S., & Mulgrew, J. (2018). Displaying red and black on a first date: A field study using the "first dates" television series. *Evolutionary Psychology*, *16*(2). https://doi.org/10.1177/1474704918769417.

Lin, H. (2014). Red-colored products enhance the attractiveness of women. *Displays*, *35*(4), 202–205.

Maier, M. A., Elliot, A. J., Lee, B., Lichtenfeld, S., Barchfeld, P., & Pekrun, R. (2013). The influence of red on impression formation in a job application context. *Motivation and Emotion*, *37*(3), 389–401.

Milinski, M., & Bakker, T. (1990). Female sticklebacks use male coloration in mate choice and hence avoid parasitized males. *Nature*, *344*(6264), 330–333.

Niesta Kayser, D., Elliot, A. J., & Feltman, R. (2010). Red and romantic behavior in men viewing women. *European Journal of Social Psychology*, *40*(6), 901–908.

Pazda, A. D., Elliot, A. J., & Greitemeyer, T. (2012). Sexy red: Perceived sexual receptivity mediates the red-attraction relation in men viewing woman. *Journal of Experimental Social Psychology*, *48*(3), 787–790.

Pazda, A. D., Elliot, A. J., & Greitemeyer, T. (2014). Perceived sexual receptivity and fashionableness: Separate paths linking red and black to perceived attractiveness. *Color Research & Application*, *39*(2), 208–212.

Regas, J. C., & Kozlowski, K. (1998). *Red my lips: A cultural history of lipstick*. Chronicle Books.

Roberts, S. C., Owen, R. C., & Havlicek, J. (2010). Distinguishing between perceiver and wearer effects in clothing color-associated attributions. *Evolutionary Psychology*, *8*(3), 147470491000800304.

Schwarz, S., & Singer, M. (2013). Romantic red revisited: Red enhances men's attraction to young, but not menopausal women. *Journal of Experimental Social Psychology*, *49*(1), 161–164.

Setchell, J. M., Smith, T., Wickings, E. J., & Knapp, L. A. (2008). Social correlates of testosterone and ornamentation in male mandrills. *Hormones and Behavior*, *54*(3), 365–372.

Sorokowski, P., Szmajke, A., Hamamura, T., Jiang, F., & Sorokowska, A. (2014). "Red wins", "black wins" and "blue loses" effects are in the eye of beholder, but they are culturally universal: A cross-cultural analysis of the influence of outfit colours on sports performance. *Polish Psychological Bulletin*, *45*(3), 318–325.

Vrij, A. (1997). Wearing black clothes: The impact of offenders' and suspects' clothing on impression formation. *Applied Cognitive Psychology: The Official Journal of the Society for Applied Research in Memory and Cognition*, *11*(1), 47–53.

Waitt, C., Little, A. C., Wolfensohn, S., Honess, P., Brown, A. P., Buchanan-Smith, H. M., & Perrett, D. I. (2003). Evidence from rhesus macaques suggests that male coloration plays a role in female primate mate choice. *Proceedings of the Royal Society of London. Series B: Biological Sciences*, *270*(suppl_2), S144–S146.

Chapter 5

How to win at sport

How can we maximise success for the GB Olympic Team? Psychology may be able to help. This chapter presents seven "rules" for success based on psychological research. It covers everything from the role of the crowd (and what happens without one as in the COVID pandemic), to confidence in our ability, to the use of body language. Why do teams tend to perform better when playing at their home than when playing away? What role does self-belief play in success? And is it possible to be too confident? This chapter searches for answers to these questions and draws on research from sport and exercise psychology to look at how theories of motivation and arousal such as Catastrophe Theory and Processing

■ **Figure 5.1** Is there such a thing as a winning formula for sporting success?

DOI: 10.4324/9781003329763-5

Efficiency Theory may be useful in developing competence in the sporting arena, why sport scholarships need to be handled carefully and why high-fiving your teammates is positive in more ways than one.

As I write this, the Olympic Games are in full swing in Tokyo, Japan. Without spectators. It is the first time in the history of the Olympic Games that athletes will be competing without a crowd to cheer them on. How will it affect the performance of the athletes? Will Japanese athletes experience greater success?

RULE NUMBER 1: MAKE SURE YOU TAKE ADVANTAGE OF THE HOME ADVANTAGE

If we delve into the psychology of sport, we might be able to answer some of these questions. Let's start with the home advantage. Chances are, if you are going to watch your team play in a competition, you are more likely to see them romp home with a win if they are playing at home than if they are playing away. It has been demonstrated in sports as diverse as hockey (Agnew & Carron, 1994), basketball (Jones, 2007) and football (Pollard & Gómez, 2009). Indeed, in 2012, Team GB's medal haul exceeded any of their previous Olympic hauls (although they did go on to exceed that too in 2016).

The reason why a home advantage exists is less clear. Fatigue caused through travel to away games has certainly been suggested but an intriguing study conducted by Boudreaux, Sanders and Walia in 2017, demonstrated that this could not explain much of the home advantage phenomenon. Their study centred on the Staples Centre in Los Angeles for the simple reason that it acts as a home stadium for two National Basketball Association Teams: the Los Angeles Lakers and the Los Angeles Clippers. When playing a game together, neither team has any substantial travel to undertake and both teams are equally familiar with the environment they are playing in. However, the designated home team is likely to experience a more sympathetic home crowd due to advanced season ticket sales. What Boudreaux and colleagues discovered was a whopping 21–22.8 percentage point advantage for the team designated as the home team. For Boudreaux, this was convincing evidence that the home advantage was not due simply to travel fatigue. Instead they suggest it is largely due to crowd effects.

The effect of a crowd

What crowd effects might be significant here? Baumeister and Steinhilber (1984) argue that the effect of a crowd can be positive in benefiting the home team but also negative for both teams, for example, to harm the opposition through hostility and consequent disorientation or even to harm the home team through excessive pressure or arousal due to distraction and stress. Perhaps this comes down to differences in experience as suggested by Cox (2008) cited by Jiménez Sánchez and Lavín (2021). Players who have more experience are likely to feed off of the crowd and perform better but novices are more likely to err and succumb to the pressure.

An interesting question that arises from this research is what happens when the crowd is just not there. Does the home advantage disappear? Little did we know it but 2020 would bring along an opportunity to test this thanks to the COVID-19 pandemic. On 13 March 2020, the *Guardian* newspaper led with the headline "Premier League and British Football shuts down until April due to coronavirus" and we were plunged into a world of lockdowns. However, on 1 June, and following in the footsteps of Germany's Bundesliga, matches were re-started, albeit without spectators. Well, it wasn't long before psychologists interested in the home advantage saw an opportunity. Jiménez Sánchez and Lavín (2021) were just such a pair. They examined the results from eight football leagues across Germany, Spain, Italy, Austria and the UK, exploring not only goals scored but also points obtained and position in the rankings. Without an audience, at least in the case of the German Bundesliga and Spain's La Liga, teams achieved fewer points and scored fewer goals at home and more away. In the Austrian and Italian Serie B leagues, there was a trend towards this also.

Similar findings were obtained by Fischer and Haucap (2021) in a study of German so-called "Ghost Games" during the COVID-19 pandemic. They examined results for teams in the top three divisions of German professional football and identified a distinct reduction in the home advantage but only for teams in the first division. On closer inspection, they discovered that the reduction had been greatest for teams that were used to usually packed stadiums. The greater the stadium capacity, the more noticeable the drop in home advantage. For teams where the crowd size was typically small anyway, the absence of a crowd has less effect. Good news for teams in the first division I guess. Fischer and

CHAPTER 5 How to win at sport

■ **Figure 5.2** COVID-19 meant the lack of spectators at many sporting fixtures.

Haucap termed this the "Ghost game effect" but argued that as a team gets used to having no spectators, its potency diminishes.

The role of the ref

So far our story has focused on the athletes themselves. In the cases discussed, professional football players have been our focus. But, as you can probably guess, the picture becomes even more complicated when we look at the effect of the crowd on referee decision-making. Nevill, Balmer and Williams, in 2002, invited 40 football referees into the laboratory to watch videos showing no less than 47 disputes that occurred during matches of the English championship. Half of the referees watched the clips in silence. That is, they were unable to hear the noise of the crowd. For the remaining half, they were able to hear the noise of the crowd. The task for the referees was to make a judgement about each of the disputes. Was it a foul by the home team? Was it a foul by the away team? Or was it no foul? If they were unsure, they were also given an opportunity to say so.

Let's see what happened to those who watched the clips in conditions of silence. Confidence soared amongst this group. The unsure option was used much less frequently, no foul was used more frequently and fouls were attributed to the home team more often than those who watched the clips with the accompanying crowd noise. I know what you are thinking – yes, but this is a study done in a laboratory. How artificial. They wouldn't be affected by crowd noise on the pitch surely?

Sorry folks to disappoint but refereeing decisions are not as objective as we might like to think. The decisions made by the group who heard the crowd noise whilst watching the clips were very similar to those made by referees on the pitch in the real football matches themselves. So, having a noisy supportive home crowd watching can, it would seem, reduce the chance of the home team being seen to commit a foul.

It isn't just the identification and calling out of fouls per se that is influenced. Buraimo, Forrest and Simmons reported that fewer yellow and red cards were given to the home team (2010) and Dohmen, in 2008, reported that a greater number of penalties were awarded to the home team. Not only that but evidence suggests that if the home team is losing, more minutes of extra time are allocated at the end of normal play, giving the home team more time to equalize (Dohmen, 2008).

So, we know that the team themselves are affected by the lack of a crowd but does this mean that such referee bias is also reduced when no spectators are present? Sors et al. (2021) set out to find an answer. They investigated matches that took place in the first and second divisions of Spain, England, Germany and Italy (feel pity, for this added up to a grand total of 841 matches!), measuring the number of fouls, red and yellow cards and penalty kicks awarded. Lo and behold, with no crowd present, the referee bias was eliminated. A home advantage was still present but significantly reduced with more away wins and fewer home wins shown.

This finding confirms that of Downward and Jones (2007) in their analysis of FA Cup performance. Whilst there were supporters in attendance at these matches, the crowd size varied significantly. Like Sors et al., Downward and Jones examined a colossal number of games (857) from over six seasons of the FA Cup. As the size of the crowd increased, so the chance of a yellow card being awarded to the home team decreased. So, what does this tell us about the effect of a crowd on a referee? If we believe Nevill and Holder (1999), the noise made by the crowd acts as a decision-making heuristic. The louder the noise, the more likely a foul was committed. Given the noise made by a home crowd is likely to be louder than that by an away crowd (usually because there are more of the home supporters), this may act to influence the decision-making of the referee. An alternative possibility has been proposed by Sutter and Kocher (2004). Referees need to be seen to be impartial to their employers but they also want to appease the crowd. On the pitch, the monitoring from their employers is less immediate than the roar of the crowd so they tend to be influenced more by the supporters.

There are some exceptions to the rule of course. This is psychology after all. In very large stadiums, where the crowds are at their maximum level, the effect of the crowd becomes more balanced and may have less effect. Similarly, it matters who you are playing against. If you are playing a superior or higher-ranking team, then you are more likely to get a yellow card awarded, even if you are the home team. Status matters it seems, even in matters of refereeing.

RULE NUMBER 2: KEEP YOUR AROUSAL/ ANXIETY LEVELS UNDER CONTROL

So far we have established that the home advantage is largely due to the effect of the crowd, both on the team and the officials. Does this mean that we will have a fair Olympics but a minimised home advantage for the Japanese athletes? Only time will tell. However, one thing is for sure. For any athlete competing in an event such as the Olympics, there will be a good deal of anxiety and arousal associated with the lead up to their event. We have already mentioned earlier in this chapter that novices are perhaps more susceptible to the arousal caused by a crowd. Is this because they experience more anxiety? Perhaps they are less likely to block out the pressure than elite athletes.

Research into the effects of anxiety and arousal on sporting performance dates right back to the 1940s (and possibly further back still!) when Hull (1943) proposed his drive theory. According to Hull, as arousal increases, so does performance. The relationship between the two is linear and limited only by how good you are at a task. In fact, Graydon (2002) summarises this approach using an equation:

Performance = drive x habit strength

Take Andy Murray for example. Cast your minds back to 2013. Andy was facing the world number 1, Novak Djokovic, in the Wimbledon final. It had been 77 years since Britain had had a men's champion in the competition. It was the final and the crowd were out in force to support the home player. Andy had taken the first set but Novak wasn't going down without a fight and came back to take the second. The arousal and anxiety must have been extremely high at this point for both players. However,

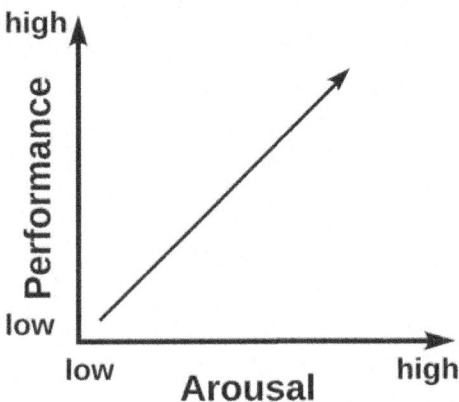

■ **Figure 5.3** Drive theory predicts that arousal will have a beneficial linear relationship with performance.

Andy increased his effort and powered through to win. So perhaps high levels of arousal are necessary for success?

Well, that certainly didn't work for tennis star David Nalbandian when he played Marin Cilic in the final at Queens in 2012. He was ranked 39 in the world. The crowd were 6,000 in number. He had been in a final before of course. He had won against Roger Federer in the Masters Cup in 2005 and reached the Wimbledon final in 2002 where he was not so lucky, losing to Lleyton Hewitt in straight sets. The pressure was on. He wanted to perform well. As Nalbandian's arousal level increased, unfortunately so did his temper. He kicked an advertising hoarding which then ricocheted off of a linesman's leg, causing it to bleed heavily. Nalbandian was disqualified and the match awarded to Cilic.

Rather than seeing the relationship between arousal and performance as linear, Yerkes and Dodson in 1908 proposed an inverted U-shape relationship between the two. Arousal, they claimed, only increases up to a certain point (the peak), and thereafter, performance deteriorates. This is certainly a better fit for what happened to Nalbandian. Or is it?

The inverted U-shape curve predicts a gradual worsening of performance as arousal continues to increase after the peak. Looking at what happened to Nalbandian, it was more of a catastrophe that happened rather than a gradual decline! As luck would have it, there is indeed a catastrophe model. Hardy and Fazey (1987) described the relationship in more detailed terms, focusing on a distinction between cognitive anxiety (worry) and a somatic component (the physical feeling experienced). As physiological

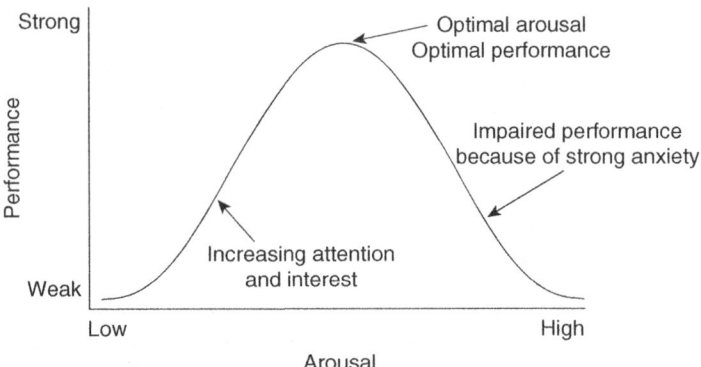

Figure 5.4 Is this graphical depiction a better fit for what happened to Nalbandian?

arousal increases, performance will be relatively unaffected, as long as we feel we have the ability to cope, that is, cognitive anxiety is low. If, on the other hand, our levels of worry are similarly high, there is a danger of a catastrophic decline in performance.

Take Eric Bristow for example. White (2001), cited in Graydon (2002), revealed how Eric Bristow, a number one world ranking darts player five times over, suddenly found one day that he could not throw a dart. Graydon suggests it took 10 years for him to overcome this. Or how about Sally Robbins, an Olympic rower. In the middle of a race, the final in the 2004 Olympics in Athens, she suddenly stopped rowing (Sparks et al., 2021). It can happen to the best of us.

Explaining catastrophe

Why does high cognitive anxiety paired with high somatic anxiety lead to catastrophe? Arguments remain but one idea, presented by Eysenck and Calvo in 1992, is the Processing Efficiency Theory. Imagine having to deal with all the task-relevant information needed for good performance as well as all the thoughts of anxiety impinging on our mental processing. It is possible to get overwhelmed unless we do one thing: increase our effort. This may slow us down (affect performance efficiency) but it shouldn't affect performance. Only if we get to the stage where we have no ability to increase effort further, catastrophe occurs.

Wilson et al. (2007) demonstrated this in a study of 18 golfers aged between 19 and 60 years. The golfers were asked to make a series of putts to target holes either when under low pressure or when under high pressure. If in the low pressure condition, they would be asked to get the ball as close to the hole as possible. They were told the study was designed to test the characteristics of the putting carpet and that their scores would be combined with those of others. In the high pressure condition, in contrast, they were told they would be videoed and their individual performance would be analysed by a golf professional to check for swing faults. Their scores would be compared, rather than combined, with those of others.

Not surprisingly, in the high pressure condition, participants reported making more effort but were less efficient in their performance. They took longer to take their putts and checked the target more often. Performance effectiveness, however, was maintained for those who showed low cognitive anxiety. Only those experiencing high cognitive anxiety showed a worse performance.

Not everyone agrees, however, and many argue an alternative explanation may be equally valid. Baumeister (1984) proposed an explanation based on the three-stage model of skill development (Fitts & Posner, 1967). Remember when you learnt to ride a bike? Or drive a car? Chances are that initially you may well have talked your way through the different elements of the skill. As you gained more practice, this need to verbalise each component part of the skill was reduced as the skill became more automatic. Eventually, at the autonomous stage, the skill can be executed without conscious thought at all. If you are an experienced driver for example, how often do you consciously think about having to change gear, when to check the mirrors, when to release the clutch. Chances are you execute these actions without giving it much thought.

So how does this apply to sport performance? According to Baumeister, the arousal and anxiety experienced lead to the athlete becoming more and more self-conscious. They attempt to exert conscious control over the action, turning their attention inwardly. In other words, it is a bit like working backwards through the three-stage model. Something that is typically automatic gradually becomes less so as we try to focus our conscious attention on the component parts of that skill. Hopefully you can imagine the effect that might have on performance. The flow of the action becomes impaired and deautomatisation occurs (Hardy, 1996). This has been called the Consciousness Processing Hypothesis (Masters, 1992) and suggests that the attempt to consciously control the action leads to a downturn in performance.

Does this idea have any value? Why yes. Ask an elite golfer to call stop at the end of their golf swing, drawing attention to the component parts of the put and their own conscious actions and performance will deteriorate (Beilock et al., 2002). However, ask them to respond to audible tones while putting and performance remains intact. Beilock also showed a similar pattern of performance in football players who were asked to participate in a dribbling exercise. When asked to focus on the performance itself, their speed of completion declined.

It isn't just golfers and footballers that show this pattern either. Sparks et al. (2021) demonstrated the same effect of conscious monitoring in a group of rowers. In this experiment, 147 rowers were watched while they rowed and were then asked how they perceived their performance amongst other things. Poor race outcome was associated with movement self-consciousness and catastrophic outcomes were predicted by extremely high conscious motor processing.

Not everyone may be affected to the same extent however. A novice athlete may actually benefit from thinking through each step of the skill execution and attempting to consciously control these. But experienced athletes might well experience "choking", the name given to the catastrophic decline in performance often seen when under pressure (Hill et al., 2010).

RULE NUMBER 3: HAVE SELF-BELIEF

We've learnt that it's good to keep arousal and anxiety levels low. How can we do that? Increasingly it seems as though self-belief plays a role here. Let's look at the example of Roger Bannister. Roger is famous for breaking the 4-minute mile. On 6 May 1954, he achieved what the *Daily Telegraph* had described as an achievement that was "as elusive as Everest" and what doctors had said could kill a man. Nonetheless, Roger had the self-belief necessary to pursue this goal and finally did so in Oxford, England. This in itself is remarkable. What is perhaps even more remarkable is that following on from Roger's achievement, 12 others also managed the same thing, all within one year of Roger's ground-breaking record. What Roger had done was to make this goal achievable and his self-belief had inspired others to give it a try.

Imagine you are going to take part in an arm wrestling competition. Your strength is measured before the competition using a hand grip and rope and pulley system. You are then given a sheet of paper and asked to list your peers according to whether you think they are stronger or weaker than you. Now the competition begins. What will predict your performance? Well, not as you might imagine, your strength! The best predictor of success is in fact likely to be your expectation of winning. If you see your partner as being superior in strength to you, they are likely to win. In Nelson and Furst's study, this was the case in 10 out of 12 contests (1972). What is even more surprising is that the partner in question was often considered weaker in the pre-test. A positive attitude trumped actual strength.

Nelson and Furst's arm wrestlers are not alone in this by any means. Members of the 1996 Atlanta and 1998 Nagano Olympic Games US team reported that confidence in their own abilities had a major effect on their performance (Gould et al., 1999) and Marsh et al. (2006) demonstrated a strong link between a positive self-concept and level of gymnastic performance in French adolescent children. George (1994) found that strong self-belief or "self-efficacy" predicted greater effort and higher hitting performance in games of baseball.

The word belief is critical here. Even if we are not actually more able than our opponent, it is the belief that we are that seems to power us through. Take Maganaris, Collins and Sharp's power lifters for example in 2000. The power lifters were given a placebo (a fake pill) and told that this was an anabolic steroid which would facilitate their performance. It was in fact a saccharine pill which would have no effect on performance. If performance showed a notable improvement, it would have to be due to the belief of the power lifter, not the pill they had taken. Remarkably, however, improvements were shown. They lifted heavier weights. Now take those same power lifters and halfway through the study, reveal to them the deception. Tell them the pill they took was just a placebo. Performance declines! The simple belief that the pill should have a positive effect was enough to actually affect their performance.

Kalasountas et al. (2007) demonstrated a similar effect with a group of college students who had just begun a fitness and conditioning course at university. Participants were asked to lift weights on a bench press and a seated leg press. Some of the students were given a placebo pill at time 1, some were given one at time 1 and time 2 and others were not given any. Those given the placebo pill were told that it contained a strong combination of amino acids which would give them immediate advantages in terms of strength. Those students who received a placebo pill

■ **Figure 5.5** What we believe about our performance has a powerful effect.

at time 1 showed significant improvements in their performance and this improvement continued at time 2 for those given a placebo then also. Those given a placebo pill only on the first time of testing showed a decline in performance at time 2.

In international sporting arenas, there have been cases documented of placebo effects facilitating performance. Christopher Beedie (2006) for example points to the examples of French cyclist Richard Virenque who was tricked by Vogt (1999) into thinking he had taken a stimulant. He went on to finish second in his time trial. Similarly, Beedie points to the 1954 World Cup final, in which the German Football Federation doctor Professor Loogen claimed to have injected the players with vitamin C. The players believed it would raise their stamina but the true effects were not even measureable. Belief in one's abilities, whether that is belief that they have been enhanced or the simple belief that we can achieve is an essential ingredient in the drive to win.

RULE NUMBER 4: BUT DON'T BE TOO OVERCONFIDENT

Whilst self-belief carries us a long way to success, being overconfident can be detrimental. It's September 20th, 1973. At the Houston Astrodome in the United States, 30,000 spectators await the "Battle of the Sexes" tennis match. Bobby Riggs, a former number 1 ranked male tennis player, is playing Billie Jean King.

Bobby, aged 55 years, has been boasting of women's inferiority and has been oozing with confidence over his ability to beat any female player. Unfortunately, Bobby's overconfidence did not serve him well. Whether through complacency (Jones et al., 1993) or whether through risk-taking (Campbell et al., 2004), he lost in straight sets to Billie.

What Bobby's example tells us is that overconfidence is sometimes detrimental. Gould et al. (1987) reported similar results in a study of police officers who took part in a shooting competition. Confidence was negatively related to performance and Hardy et al. (2004) reported an association between high confidence and lower golf scores such that individuals performed poorly when they felt confident, worried but relaxed (what he refers to as low somatic but high cognitive anxiety). Perhaps a little self-doubt is helpful? Bandura and Locke (2003) certainly think so. A reduction in self-confidence may, they suggest, force us to increase the effort we expend which may be beneficial for performance.

Woodman et al. (2010) decided to put this idea to the test. They asked 28 participants to take part in a skipping exercise. To begin, all participants were asked to skip with a grey rope for a period of 1 minute and the number of skips they managed in that time was recorded. As they skipped, they were asked to shout out "now!" each time they heard an auditory tone. This enabled Woodman et al. to get an idea of processing capacity. After completing this practice exercise, participants were asked to complete the competition task. This time, they would be doing the same task but there would be a prize for the person who performed the most skips in the time period given and the quickest mean reaction time on the auditory task. The only difference for those in the experimental group was that they were now given a white rope to use. A white rope, which they were told, would be more difficult to use than the one the other group had, because it had different qualities from the grey rope. This of course, was all a lie. The rope was exactly the same in terms of its qualities. A questionnaire measuring confidence was given both before the practice and before the competition trial.

Those in the experimental group, not unsurprisingly, showed a decline in confidence before the competition trial began. So would you if you were told the next part of the exercise was going to be more difficult? What Woodman et al. were more interested in though was the effect this had on performance. Amazingly, the slight dip in confidence was sufficient for those in the experimental group to increase the effort they put in and

■ **Figure 5.6** Don't be too over-confident. Sometimes a slight dip in confidence can help us increase our effort.

their performance outstripped those in the control group. Woodman argues that this effect is largely explained due to the lack of complacency that a dip in confidence causes. More effort is expended to close the gap between current performance the goal they want to achieve.

This explanation is supported by the work of Ede et al.(2017) using an endurance task. Participants were asked to complete a series of five plank exercises. For example, one required participants to hold themselves in a horizontal position on a mat, with their legs extended straight behind them and their body weight supported by their elbows, forearms and toes only. There were two trials of these exercises. Participants who initially underestimated their performance on the first trial tended to raise their self-belief and associated effort in trial 2 compared to those who overestimated their ability in trial 1.

In fact, the literature is replete with similar examples. Hutchinson et al. (2008) demonstrated similar effects in a study of 72 university students trying out a handgrip task. The students were asked to squeeze a dynamometer handbar for as long as they could sustain it. Who had the lowest levels of perceived exertion? You've guessed it. Those in the high self-efficacy group. Overconfidence it would seem reduces the concentration and motivation necessary to produce a good performance (Weinberg & Gould, 2007).

RULE NUMBER 5: THE FORCE IS WITHIN (OR IN TECHNICAL TERMS, BE DRIVEN BY INTRINSIC MOTIVATION, NOT EXTERNAL REWARDS)

So far we have journeyed through the valley of self-belief, the peaks and troughs of home advantage, and the path of arousal and anxiety. One thing we haven't touched on yet is the effect of rewards on performance. As I write, the breaking news is that Tom Daly and Matty Lee, Tom Pidcock and Adam Peaty have all won gold medals at the Tokyo Olympics. Fantastic! The medal itself has six grams of gold plating on it but is priceless to the winner. So, how important are extrinsic rewards to sporting performance?

Athletes who compete in sport simply to win a trophy, medal or other accolade have been described as "extrinsically motivated". (Deci & Ryan, 1985). One way in which extrinsic motivation may be enhanced is through the award of sports scholarships. These are now commonly used in university settings to enable athletic students to pursue their training and development in their sporting endeavours. Their performance is rewarded.

Historically, these scholarships have had a bad press. Ryan (1980) studied the effect of scholarships on college football players in the United States. Did it make a difference if they were effectively being paid to take part in an activity they already enjoyed? The answer was categorically yes and the effect was not pleasant. Receiving a scholarship led to a decrease in intrinsic motivation, that is the feeling that you are performing an activity for the sole purpose of the pleasure and satisfaction obtained.

Unfortunately this was a pattern played out (quite literally) in different sports too. Wagner et al. (1989) found a similar decline in intrinsic motivation in basketball players who had received scholarships at high school and Cremades et al. (2012) reported that as the amount of scholarship increased, intrinsic motivation decreased proportionally. Most recently, Moller and Sheldon (2020) demonstrated that this decline in intrinsic motivation for sport has lasting repercussions with athletes who left college even decades earlier still showing a slump in intrinsic motivation. Scholarship status was negatively related to their current enjoyment of their sport.

Why are scholarships getting a hard time? One idea is that once a scholarship has been received, the athlete comes to see their performance as being needed to justify the scholarship rather than as something satisfying in itself (Vallerand, 2007). As Deci et al. (1999) explain, when we are rewarded for doing something that we already believe is interesting, we begin to attribute our engagement with that activity as being due to the reward offered, not to our inherent interest in it. In children, Lepper and Cordova (1992) argue, they may well assume that the reason they are being offered a reward is because the behaviour itself is boring. Indeed, Wagner et al. (1989) found that scholarship athletes saw their basketball participation as work rather than leisure.

Before we reject any offers of scholarship or sponsorship, however, let's pull on the reins as not everyone agrees with this pessimistic view. Moreover, a more tailored approach can offer us a different perspective. Eisenberger and Cameron (1996) argued that the detrimental effect of rewards was a "myth". The negative effects of rewards on behaviour and engagement they argued, is rare. Perhaps what is more relevant here is the perception of the athlete towards the reward. Hagger and Chatzisarantis (2011) suggest that athletes who have a tendency to see their actions as originating from themselves are more likely to see external rewards as informative and supportive rather than controlling, as opportunities to demonstrate competence rather than as controlling and pressured. As Festinger (1961) suggested, it is not the reward itself that determines the effect of the reward; it is the meaning it carries for the recipient. Readdy et al. (2014) demonstrated just this in their study of extrinsic rewards in college football. In interviews with the footballers, it was clear that if the majority of players viewed the rewards as a way for coaches to control behaviour, motivation would decrease.

Similarly, the type of reward offered has an impact. Harackiewicz in 1979 had already demonstrated that performance-contingent rewards, that is rewards given for performing an activity well, have more of an impact than task-contingent rewards, given for participating in or completing an activity. Perhaps this is why wages and performance are related in professional football (Gasparetto, 2012).

Maybe we are just missing the point slightly here though because so far we have only focused on the effect of financial incentives. The bottom line seems to be that verbal reward in the sense of positive feedback seems to be the best reward of all. Choi (1996) reports that feedback is not only related to performance but also predicted how interesting, exciting and enjoyable participation in that sport was.

RULE NUMBER 6: SMILE WHEN YOU'RE WINNING (UNLESS YOU'RE IN A COMBAT SPORT)

Even better, give verbal feedback whilst smiling. I'm not joking. Smiling has a positive impact on sports performance. Don't believe me? Then take a look at the work of Philippen et al. (2012). They asked 34 Dutch students to either smile or frown whilst riding a stationary bike at 50–60% of their maximal heart rate reserve. Not only did the smilers feel better, they perceived themselves as exerting less effort than the frowners. Or how about Brick et al. (2018)? They explored the effect of smiling versus frowning on running. The message was clear. If you frown you are likely to feel you are having to put in more effort but if you smile, you are likely to feel more relaxed. This in turn reduces muscle tension which means you run more efficiently. It's also worth remembering at this juncture, that Abel and Kruger (2010) reported lower mortality rates in US professional baseball players by 2009, for those who showed a full (Duchenne) smile in the photographs taken of them in 1952.

But yes, you've guessed it. There is an exception. If you want to exert an exceptional muscular force such as in weight lifting, you would be well advised to show expressions of anger (Woodman et al., 2009) and if you are taking part in a combat sport, its best advised to avoid smiling at all. Kraus and Chen (2013) discovered that smiles in these situations may unintentionally signal to your opponent that you have a weaker intention to engage in hostile behaviour. Indeed, fighters who smiled more intensely in the pre-fight confrontation with their opponent were less likely to win and performed worse. Perhaps their opponent's confidence was boosted as a result of seeing the smile. It's not just the fighters that matter though. Even naïve observers judged the smilers to be less physically dominant.

RULE NUMBER 7: HIGH FIVE YOUR TEAMMATES

Our last rule relates to the power of touch, a sense that has the claim to fame of being the most well developed at birth (Kraus et al., 2010). Touch carries with it a sense of trust and co-operation and this can have a positive effect in sporting performance. Kraus and colleagues analysed the touch behaviour of 294 National Basketball Association players in a game played within the first

2 months of the 2008–2009 season. Fist bumps, high fives, chest bumps, chest punches, head slaps (the mind boggles) and hugs were just some of the measures taken. Not only did touch predict increased player performance but it predicted season performance for the team, even when aspects such as player status, pre-sea, son expectations and early season performance were accounted for. Did touch strengthen bonds between the team members? Did it help to build co-operation? It certainly seemed that way.

REFERENCES

Abel, E. L., & Kruger, M. L. (2010). Smile intensity in photographs predicts longevity. *Psychological Science*, *21*(4), 542–544.

Agnew, G. A., & Carron, A. V. (1994). Crowd effects and the home advantage. *International Journal of Sport Psychology*, *25*(1), 53–62.

Bandura, A., & Locke, E. A. (2003). Negative self-efficacy and goal effects revisited. *Journal of Applied Psychology*, *88*(1), 87.

Baumeister, R. F. (1984). Choking under pressure: Self-consciousness and paradoxical effects of incentives on skillful performance. *Journal of Personality and Social Psychology*, *46*(3), 610.

Baumeister, R. F., & Steinhilber, A. (1984). Paradoxical effects of supportive audiences on performance under pressure: The home field disadvantage in sports championships. *Journal of Personality and Social Psychology*, *47*(1), 85.

Beedie, C., Stuart, E., Coleman, D., & Foad, A. (2006). Placebo effects of caffeine on cycling performance. *Medicine & Science in Sports & Exercise*, *38*(12), 2159–2164.

Beilock, S. L., Carr, T. H., MacMahon, C., & Starkes, J. L. (2002). When paying attention becomes counterproductive: Impact of divided versus skill-focused attention on novice and experienced performance of sensorimotor skills. *Journal of Experimental Psychology: Applied*, *8*(1), 6.

Boudreaux, C. J., Sanders, S. D., & Walia, B. (2017). A natural experiment to determine the crowd effect upon home court advantage. *Journal of Sports Economics*, *18*(7), 737–749.

Brick, N. E., McElhinney, M. J., & Metcalfe, R. S. (2018). The effects of facial expression and relaxation cues on movement economy, physiological, and perceptual responses during running. *Psychology of Sport and Exercise*, *34*, 20–28.

Buraimo, B., Forrest, D., & Simmons, R. (2010). The 12th man? Refereeing bias in English and German soccer. *Journal of the Royal Statistical Society: Series A (Statistics in Society)*, *173*(2), 431–449.

Campbell, W. K., Goodie, A. S., & Foster, J. D. (2004). Narcissism, confidence, and risk attitude. *Journal of Behavioral Decision Making*, *17*(4), 297–311.

Choi, W. B. (1996). *The effect of extrinsic reward on sport performance, perceived competence and intrinsic motivation* [Doctoral dissertation, Victoria University of Technology].

Cox, R. (2008). *Psicología del deporte: Conceptos y sus aplicaciones*. Trad: A. Latrónico and L. Mesher. Médica Panamericana.

Cremades, J. G., Flournoy, B., & Gomez, C. B. (2012). Scholarship status and gender differences in motivation among US collegiate track and field athletes. *International Journal of Sports Science & Coaching, 7*(2), 333–344.

Deci, E. L., Koestner, R., & Ryan, R. M. (1999). A meta-analytic review of experiments examining the effects of extrinsic rewards on intrinsic motivation. *Psychological Bulletin, 125*(6), 627.

Deci, E. L., & Ryan, R. M. (1985). Cognitive evaluation theory. In *Intrinsic motivation and self-determination in human behavior* (pp. 43–85). Springer.

Dohmen, T. J. (2008). The influence of social forces: Evidence from the behavior of football referees. *Economic Inquiry, 46*(3), 411–424.

Downward, P., & Jones, M. (2007). Effects of crowd size on referee decisions: Analysis of the FA Cup. *Journal of Sports Sciences, 25*(14), 1541–1545.

Ede, A., Sullivan, P. J., & Feltz, D. L. (2017). Self-doubt: Uncertainty as a motivating factor on effort in an exercise endurance task. *Psychology of Sport and Exercise, 28*, 31–36.

Eisenberger, R., & Cameron, J. (1996). Detrimental effects of reward: Reality or myth? *American Psychologist, 51*(11), 1153.

Eysenck, M. W., & Calvo, M. G. (1992). Anxiety and performance: The processing efficiency theory. *Cognition & Emotion, 6*(6), 409–434.

Festinger, L. (1961). The psychological effects of insufficient rewards. *American Psychologist, 16*(1), 1.

Fischer, K., & Haucap, J. (2021). Does crowd support drive the home advantage in professional football? Evidence from German ghost games during the COVID-19 pandemic. *Journal of Sports Economics, 22*(8), 982–1008.

Fitts, P. M., & Posner, M. I. (1967). Human performance. brooks. *Cole, Belmont, CA, 5*, 7–16.

Gasparetto, T. M. (2012). Relationship between wages and sports performance. *The Empirical Economics Letters, 11*(9), 943–949.

George, T. R. (1994). Self-confidence and baseball performance: A causal examination of self-efficacy theory. *Journal of Sport and Exercise Psychology, 16*(4), 381–399.

Gould, D., Guinan, D., Greenleaf, C., Medbery, R., & Peterson, K. (1999). Factors affecting Olympic performance: Perceptions of athletes and coaches from more and less successful teams. *The Sport Psychologist, 13*(4), 371–394.

Gould, D., Petlichkoff, L., Simons, J., & Vevera, M. (1987). Relationship between Competitive State Anxiety Inventory-2 subscale scores and pistol shooting performance. *Journal of Sport and Exercise Psychology, 9*(1), 33–42.

Graydon, J. (2002). Stress and anxiety in sport. *Psychologist-Leicester, 15*(8), 408–410.

Hagger, M. S., & Chatzisarantis, N. L. (2011). Causality orientations moderate the undermining effect of rewards on intrinsic motivation. *Journal of Experimental Social Psychology, 47*(2), 485–489.

Harackiewicz, J. M. (1979). The effects of reward contingency and performance feedback on intrinsic motivation. *Journal of Personality and Social Psychology, 37*(8), 1352.

Hardy, L. (1996). A test of catastrophe models of anxiety and sports performance against multidimensional anxiety theory models using the method of dynamic differences. *Anxiety, Stress, and Coping, 9*(1), 69–86.

Hardy, L., & Fazey, J. (1987, June). *The inverted-U hypothesis: A catastrophe for sport psychology?* Paper presented at the Annual Conference of the North American Society for the Psychology of Sport and Physical Activity, Vancouver.

Hardy, L., Woodman, T., & Carrington, S. (2004). Is self-confidence a bias factor in higher-order catastrophe models? An exploratory analysis. *Journal of Sport and Exercise Psychology, 26*(3), 359–368.

Hill, D. M., Hanton, S., Matthews, N., & Fleming, S. (2010). Choking in sport: A review. *International Review of Sport and Exercise Psychology, 3*(1), 24–39.

Hull, C. L. (1943). *Principles of behaviour*. Appleton-Century-Crofts.

Hutchinson, J. C., Sherman, T., Martinovic, N., & Tenenbaum, G. (2008). The effect of manipulated self-efficacy on perceived and sustained effort. *Journal of Applied Sport Psychology, 20*(4), 457–472.

Jiménez Sánchez, Á., & Lavín, J. M. (2021). Home advantage in European soccer without crowd. *Soccer & Society, 22*(1–2), 152–165.

Jones, M. B. (2007). Home advantage in the NBA as a game-long process. *Journal of Quantitative Analysis in Sports, 3*(4).

Jones, G., Swain, A., & Hardy, L. (1993). Intensity and direction dimensions of competitive state anxiety and relationships with performance. *Journal of Sports Sciences, 11*(6), 525–532.

Kalasountas, V., Reed, J., & Fitzpatrick, J. (2007). The effect of placebo-induced changes in expectancies on maximal force production in college students. *Journal of Applied Sport Psychology, 19*(1), 116–124.

Kraus, M. W., & Chen, T. W. D. (2013). A winning smile? Smile intensity, physical dominance, and fighter performance. *Emotion, 13*(2), 270.

Kraus, M. W., Huang, C., & Keltner, D. (2010). Tactile communication, cooperation, and performance: An ethological study of the NBA. *Emotion, 10*(5), 745.

Lepper, M. R., & Cordova, D. I. (1992). A desire to be taught: Instructional consequences of intrinsic motivation. *Motivation and Emotion, 16*(3), 187–208.

Maganaris, C. N., Collins, D., & Sharp, M. (2000). Expectancy effects and strength training: Do steroids make a difference? *The Sport Psychologist, 14*(3), 272–278.

Marsh, H. W., Chanal, J. P., & Sarrazin, P. G. (2006). Self-belief does make a difference: A reciprocal effects model of the causal ordering of physical self-concept and gymnastics performance. *Journal of Sports Sciences, 24*(1), 101–111.

Masters, R. S. (1992). Knowledge, knerves and know-how: The role of explicit versus implicit knowledge in the breakdown of a complex motor skill under pressure. *British Journal of Psychology, 83*(3), 343–358.

Moller, A. C., & Sheldon, K. M. (2020). Athletic scholarships are negatively associated with intrinsic motivation for sports, even decades later: Evidence for long-term undermining. *Motivation Science*, *6*(1), 43.

Nelson, L. R., & Furst, M. L. (1972). An objective study of the effects of expectation on competitive performance. *The Journal of Psychology*, *81*(1), 69–72.

Nevill, A. M., Balmer, N. J., & Williams, A. M. (2002). The influence of crowd noise and experience upon refereeing decisions in football. *Psychology of Sport and Exercise*, *3*(4), 261–272.

Nevill, A. M., & Holder, R. L. (1999). Home advantage in sport. *Sports Medicine*, *28*(4), 221–236.

Philippen, P. B., Bakker, F. C., Oudejans, R. R., & Canal-Bruland, R. (2012). The effects of smiling and frowning on perceived affect and exertion while physically active. *Journal of Sport Behavior*, *35*(3).

Pollard, R., & Gómez, M. A. (2009). Home advantage in football in South-West Europe: Long-term trends, regional variation, and team differences. *European Journal of Sport Science*, *9*(6), 341–352.

Readdy, T., Raabe, J., & Harding, J. S. (2014). Student-athletes' perceptions of an extrinsic reward program: A mixed-methods exploration of self-determination theory in the context of college football. *Journal of Applied Sport Psychology*, *26*(2), 157–171.

Ryan, E. D. (1980). Attribution, intrinsic motivation, and athletics: A replication and extension. *Psychology of Motor Behavior and Sport*, 19–26.

Sors, F., Grassi, M., Agostini, T., & Murgia, M. (2021). The sound of silence in association football: Home advantage and referee bias decrease in matches played without spectators. *European Journal of Sport Science*, *21*(12), 1597–1605.

Sparks, K. V., Kavussanu, M., Masters, R. S., & Ring, C. (2021). Conscious processing and rowing: A field study. *International Journal of Sport and Exercise Psychology*, 1–17.

Sutter, M., & Kocher, M. G. (2004). Favoritism of agents – the case of referees' home bias. *Journal of Economic Psychology*, *25*(4), 461–469.

Vallerand, R. J. (2007). Intrinsic and extrinsic motivation in sport and physical activity: A review and a look at the future. In G. Tenenbaum & R. C. Eklund (Eds.), *Handbook of sport psychology* (pp. 59–83). John Wiley & Sons, Inc.

Vogt, W. (1999). *Breaking the chain: Drugs and cycling, The true story* (W. Fotheringham, Trans.). Random House/Yellow Jersey Press

Wagner, S. L., Lounsbury, J. W., & Fitzgerald, L. G. (1989). Attribute factors associated with work/leisure perceptions. *Journal of Leisure Research*, *21*(2), 155–166.

Weinberg, R. S., & Gould, D. (2007). *Foundations of sport and exercise psychology* (4th ed.). Human Kinetics.

White, J. (2001, 6 January). White's week: Top tips for dealing with the yips. *The Guardian Sport*, 9.

Wilson, M., Smith, N. C., & Holmes, P. S. (2007). The role of effort in influencing the effect of anxiety on performance: Testing the conflicting predictions of processing efficiency theory and the conscious processing hypothesis. *British Journal of Psychology*, *98*(3), 411–428.

Woodman, T., Akehurst, S., Hardy, L., & Beattie, S. (2010). Self-confidence and performance: A little self-doubt helps. *Psychology of Sport and Exercise, 11*(6), 467–470.

Woodman, T., Davis, P. A., Hardy, L., Callow, N., Glasscock, I., & Yuill-Proctor, J. (2009). Emotions and sport performance: An exploration of happiness, hope, and anger. *Journal of Sport and Exercise Psychology, 31*(2), 169–188.

Yerkes, R. M., & Dodson, J. D. (1908). The relation of strength of stimulus to rapidity of habit-formation. *Journal of Comparative Neurology and Psychology, 18*, 459–482.

Chapter 6

Are you keeping your employees happy?

Occupational psychology is the key theme for this chapter. The issue under consideration is how to keep your employees happy. Why should we want to? What are the benefits? And how might we go about doing so? In this chapter, five reasons for promoting happiness in employees are outlined. The effect of happiness on performance, pro-social behaviour, and even aspects such as commitment to the organisation are explored. Are all types of work performance positively affected? This chapter attempts to answer this. Using psychological research from occupational psychology, three suggestions of things that have been shown to increase the happiness of employees are presented. Why might a trip to the garden centre help an office employee? Why have bags

■ **Figure 6.1** Having happy employees can reap benefits for an organization.

DOI: 10.4324/9781003329763-6

of candy been issued to NHS staff in some studies? And what role does the manager have to play in this story? This chapter aims to provide answers to all of these questions.

I'm sorry but I'm going to start on a rather depressing note. A recent survey conducted by Indeed in March 2021 found that 52% of workers were feeling burned out, a 9% increase from before the pandemic. Burnout can have the most devastating consequences, not just for physical health but for mental health also. It can leave employees feeling exhausted and drained but also it leads to negativity towards their workplace and a decline in productivity. Nobody wins in a burnout situation.

So, how do we avoid burnout in employees? Although it is not the full answer, one idea that has been suggested is to ensure employees are happy. Not rocket science I know but the evidence does suggest that happy people are significantly less likely to burn out (Iverson et al., 1998) and having happy employees brings with it a number of other benefits too. What are these benefits? And how do we keep employees happy? These are some of the questions we will explore in this chapter. Come with me on a journey through an organizational psychology theme.

HAPPY EMPLOYEES ARE MORE COMMITTED TO THE ORGANISATION

Having happy employees can reduce turnover in a company and lower the absenteeism rate (Pelled & Xin, 1999). Pelled and Xin collected questionnaire data, absenteeism data and turnover data for 148 employees at an electronics company. The employees spanned a number of roles from supervisors to technicians to administrative staff. The questionnaires measured affect (positive and negative feeling) and job satisfaction and were completed 5 months prior to the collection of turnover and absenteeism data. What did they find? As happiness increased, absenteeism decreased. Moreover, as happiness increased, turnover also decreased. Of course, the converse was also true. As negative affect increased, so did the turnover and absenteeism leading to the aptly named title of "Down and out" for their paper.

Not only do happy employees stick around longer, they are more committed to their organisation (Herrbach, 2006). Herrbach surveyed 365 engineers and reported an association between commitment to the organisation and the experience of positive affect (happiness!). Spector and Fox (2002) similarly suggest that becoming more involved in the organisation is something that is encouraged by situations that make us feel happy.

Singh et al. (2018) studied the effect of happiness on feelings towards an organisation in 136 workers from banks, software companies, academia, pharmaceutical companies and consultancies in India. All participants had worked at their organization for a minimum of one year. Those employees who saw their organization as being virtuous (having rules that promote harmony) felt proud to identify themselves with it, and rated themselves as happier. They were more engaged in their work as a result and showed a higher level of job satisfaction. They were also more likely to interact more with other employees and form strong social bonds. Which brings us to our next reason why we should promote happiness in our employees.

HAPPY EMPLOYEES WORK WELL WITH OTHERS

Let's take our story to a large retailer specialising in clothing and household goods in the South-Western United States. Jennifer George, did just that in 1991 when she distributed questionnaires to employees there. Supervisors were also asked to rate each of the people in their care. The findings were pretty clear. Experience a happy mood at work and you will not only engage more in your role but you are more likely to engage in "extrarole" behaviours too. In other words, you are more likely to be helpful in situations that are not part of your job responsibilities as well as those that are.

The idea that happy employees work well with others is now well established. Barsade et al. (2000) suggested that having a happy managerial team can mean less conflict and more co-operation for chief executives. And it is not just the day-to-day interactions that this applies to.

Imagine this scenario. You are asked to negotiate a deal on behalf of your company. You want to ensure you are successful and seal a good deal for your employer. Top tip? Be happy. Barsade et al. (2000) reported more co-operation and less conflict in a negotiating situation when negotiators were in a happy mood. Chances are the other person will like you more for being happy (Druckman & Broome, 1991), you will feel more confident (Kumar, 1997) and you are more likely to demonstrate innovative problem-solving (Carnevale & Isen, 1986). Who doesn't like a win-win negotiation!

Negotiations aside, being happy can lead to more positive evaluations and appraisals by supervisors. Staw et al. (1994) used a panel of employees from a hospital and two car manufacturers to demonstrate this relationship. Using face-to-face interviews, observations, structured field observations and ratings, they reported that employees who were happy in their workplace had more favourable evaluations from their supervisors and great support from co-workers. Incidentally, they also earnt more money 18 months later compared to those who had less positive emotions about their work. Wright and Staw (1999) have shown that these effects are long-lasting. Even 4 years after levels of happiness were measured, happy employees were still rated more favourably by their superiors.

It doesn't stop there either. Staw and Barsade (1993) discovered that positive individuals in the workplace were often considered to have made greater contributions to the effective working of a group than those with less positive emotions and their contributions were more valued and Singh et al. (2018) suggest this is largely a result of greater interactions with colleagues and the forming of strong social bonds as a result. Such bonds can make work feel more satisfying and meaningful for the employee as a result.

HAPPY EMPLOYEES ARE LIKELY TO PERFORM BETTER

Given the positive effects of happiness on team working, it may come as no surprise to know that happy employees are also more productive. George (1995) studied the behaviour of 64 sales managers from a leading US retailer. The quality of service or assistance provided to customers was significantly related to the levels of positive affect experienced at work. As one increased, so did the other.

It works in other industries also. Take insurance salesmen for example. Seligman and Schulman (1986) administered an Attributional Style Questionnaire, which measured, amongst other things, levels of optimism. Those who showed an optimistic outlook were more successful in selling policies in the second half of the year than those who didn't. Even in preschoolers, a happy mood leads to children setting higher goals for themselves and performing at a higher level on a digit substitution task.

Next time you visit a coffee shop, take note of whether the waiter or waitress seems happy. Barger and Grandey (2006) asked independent observers to rate the strength of smiles shown by employees and by customers in seven coffee shops offering counter food service. Customers were asked to complete surveys after their experience. Well, wouldn't you just know it. The strength of the smile shown by the employees predicted the strength of the smiles shown by the customers regardless of how much of a smile customers had when they entered. Customers reported a greater level of satisfaction with their experience too. Happiness, is clearly contagious.

Sometimes, in any job, we are likely to hit obstacles. But hey, happiness helps conquer all. Staw et al. (1994) point to more favourable outcomes for happy employees when facing such a circumstance, and consequently better evaluations from supervisors.

So, is it all good news? Happy employees equal productive employees? Well yes but I'm going to spoil the party here and raise a word of caution. When it comes to decision-making, not all decisions made by happy people may be good ones. Melton (1995) raised this possibility in a study which required participants

■ **Figure 6.2** Barger and Grandey's coffee shop study suggests that happiness can be contagious.

to engage in syllogistic reasoning. Syllogistic reasoning involves looking at some statements and seeing what conclusion follows from a selection of possibilities. The critical aspect of this task is it does not require the generation of a response. On this task, those reporting a happy mood did worse. They spent less time on the task, chose unqualified conclusions more often and were less likely to sketch out the relationship between the premises.

Similarly, Elsbach and Barr (1999) discovered that happy moods were detrimental to complex decision-making which required careful execution of a series of procedural steps and Bless et al. (1990) reported that happy participants were as likely to be swayed by weak counter-attitudinal arguments as they were to strong, unlike their sad counterparts who were only influenced by strong arguments. Happy people are less likely to engage in elaboration of a message the authors claim. Why do less happy people do so? One idea proposed by Martin et al. (1993) is that when we feel low, we engage in more effortful, active cognitive processing to try to solve the problem. Hence we become more analytical in our processing. Is there such a thing as a happy statistician? I'm going to leave that one there.

Well, all is not lost. At least if we believe Bodenhausen et al. (1994). We just need to make sure our happy employees are aware of the need for extra care on any task requiring such decisions. Take doctors for example. Here, accuracy in diagnosis is of utmost importance. It is reassuring to read then that being happy is not incompatible with making accurate diagnoses. Estrada et al. (1997) gave doctors a small bag of candy to facilitate a positive mood. Following this, they were asked to read a patient description and to verbalise their thinking about the diagnosis. There was no difference in the number of diagnoses considered by those in the happy group and those in the no-candy group but the correct diagnosis was identified earlier and was likely to be guided by the appropriate information in doctors who felt happy. Efficiency and flexibility rules when happiness abounds. Just for a minute stop to think about the implications of this finding in a world where doctors' shift patterns require them to work extortionate hours and often without a bag of candy to lighten the mood.

HAPPY EMPLOYEES ARE MORE CREATIVE

Our journey through the world of decision-making and happiness emphasised the importance of type of decision-making in the debate of whether happy people make better decisions. Where flexible thinking is concerned, happy employees have it in the bag. Let's take our journey to Bulgaria where Madjar et al. (2002) visited three organizations from the knitwear industry to conduct a questionnaire study. Using a measure called the Job Affect Scale, they were able to measure positive and negative mood of the employees and supervisors were asked to assess the creativity of each employee. As you might have guessed by now, positive mood was associated positively with creativity.

Amabile et al. (2005) studied employees in chemical industries, high tech companies and producers of consumer products. The daily diaries of over 200 employees were examined and just like the knitwear employees in Bulgaria, a linear relationship between positive affect and creativity was found. As one increased, so did the other.

Wherever we travel, we find a similar story. Bani-Melhem et al. (2018) surveyed 328 hotel employees in United Arab Emirates. What was the single most significant determinant of innovation? Yep. Happiness in the workplace. As Amabile et al. mention, there have been historical examples of creativity and happiness such as Henri Poincare, the mathematician. Henri was known as the last polymath and was responsible for discoveries that underlie modern chaos theory. As Amabile et al. mention, his most creative discoveries were made when he was at his most relaxed, on vacation. And how about Mozart? He himself is said to have declared that happiness was conducive to his ability to be creative (Vernon, 1970). Fredrickson (1998) believes happiness promotes the search for novel and often unscripted ways of thinking.

HAPPY EMPLOYEES ARE SAFER EMPLOYEES

If happy employees are more creative, does this mean they are more likely to be risk taking? Ragan and Carder (2019) argue exactly the opposite. One of the aspects of performance important to creativity, they argue, is intuition. This is also important to safety. Ever had that feeling that something might be wrong? Trusting our intuition and acting on that understanding can often pre-empt more serious incidents occurring. Let's try an exercise here. To start with, I want you think of a happy event in your life. Got it? Ok, now, I want you to think of a word that is associated with all three of the following:

SWISS   COTTAGE   CAKE

Did you get it? Hopefully if you thought long enough about the happy event in your life, you would have found the answer relatively quickly. The answer is cheese. How about this one:

DIVE   LIGHT   ROCKET

More difficult huh? These examples come from something called the Remote Association Test. The answer to the second example is of course sky if you were wondering. Let's try just one more:

DREAM   BALL   BOOK

Any thoughts? These are all examples mentioned by Ragan and Carder but their participants were given just 2 seconds to make a decision about whether there was a word that linked them or not. I confess, the last example has no associated linking word. Apologies if you spent a long time on that one. What Ragan and Carder were trying to measure was intuition. Two seconds is not long enough to solve the problem. The relevant part of Ragan and Carder's story, however, is the effect that happiness had on performance. Happy participants doing this task correctly identified whether there was an associated word or not much more accurately than those who were asked to think of a sad event in their life. Their intuition served them well.

If happiness has so many positive benefits to employees and employers alike, then how can we ensure we have happy employees? Here we are going to suggest just a few ideas stemming from the psychological literature.

Suggestion 1: Make sure there are a moderate number of plants in the office

In the early 1990s, Kaplan and Kaplan (1989) were already reporting a beneficial effect of having a view of nature on satisfaction and well-being. Having a view of trees and greenery from the office window for example is associated with greater enthusiasm for one's job and we are likely to find our job more challenging (in a good way of course). This is great if your office happens to overlook a beautiful green area outside and has lots of windows but what if it doesn't? Well don't despair. Bringing the outdoors in is the new trend in keeping your employees happy. Even photographs of restorative environments are sufficient to increase sustained attention (Berto, 2005) but an easy win here is to make sure there are some plants in the office.

■ **Figure 6.3** How many plants are there in your workplace?

Wolverton and Wolverton (1993) believe that having houseplants in the office can have numerous beneficial effects, particularly in removing air pollutants. For example, the Boston fern can remove formaldehyde from the air, a dwarf date palm can remove xylene and a lady palm can remove ammonia. Why are these chemicals relevant? Because, Wolverton and Wolverton argue, in modern offices these are often present in building products such as furnishings, paints, carpeting, panelling, and so on. Oyabu et al. (2003) similarly point to the value of houseplants in removing odours. They looked at the performance of a plant called Goldon pothos (Epipremnum aureum) as well as snake plants and rubber plants in removing this odour using laboratory techniques and suggested that in all cases, the plants were efficient diffusers of the bad odours. Wolverton and Wolverton were doing this research on behalf of NASA looking at air quality in space stations but the relevance for our day to day office space is clear.

Goodrich (1982) advocated the use of large plants to increase perceptions of privacy in the office. In a study of secretarial staff, Duvall-Early and Benedict (1992) identified that privacy enables employees to better use their abilities, empowers employees to have greater freedom of judgement and have a greater sense of accomplishment. The number of indoor plants proximal to a worker's desk has been associated with a significant reduction in sick leave (Bringslimark et al., 2007). It isn't just about the effect on the individual either. Sitting in a room with natural plants increases pro-social behaviour according to Weinstein et al. (2009) so you may have a happier office all round. (Incidentially, the presence of a dog in the workplace has also been shown to facilitate co-operation and interpersonal trust in those working together according to Christensen et al., 2012).

However, before you rush out to buy up the local garden centre supply of houseplants, there is a word of caution. If you over-do things and make the office appear like a local rainforest environment, you may end up with unproductive or uncomfortable employees. Smith and Pitt (2008), in a laboratory study, presented participants with photographs of an office space in which the number of plants varied from none at all, to 1 or 2 right up to 13. Participants were asked to rate how comfortable the office looked and whether they liked the look of it using a questionnaire. Participants certainly preferred offices with plants to those with none but the preference that was strongest was for the offices with low to moderate numbers of plants. It is interesting to note that the preference for low to moderate plants was highest in younger participants. Participants in older age groups preferred higher numbers of plants. Considering the age range of people in the office adds another consideration to the story.

It isn't just about employees feeling comfortable however. Having too many plants can have an adverse effect in productivity. Perhaps employees relax a little too much! Larsen et al. (1998) compared reactions to an office space that had either no plants, a moderate amount of plants or a high number of plants in it. Participants recruited from University of Illinois were asked to complete a sorting task and a productivity task in a pre-prepared office. In the sorting task, they were asked to sort a series of sheets of typeface fonts into groups and then rank their own preference for each type. In the productivity task, they were asked to identify as many occurrences of the letters t and f in passages of text written in different typeface fonts. Before leaving, participants were asked to complete a questionnaire exploring their perception of the tasks and the office. What did they find? Well, those participants who had completed the tasks in the office with the highest number of plants showed the lowest level of productivity on the productivity task. Those in the office with no plants showed the highest level of productivity. However, as Larsen et al. point out, the productivity task is repetitive and lacks any need for creativity. For tasks that require creative thinking, they argue, the value of plants may be heightened. Despite this, in terms of how attractive the office was seen to be, the one with many plants in won the day. For the participants themselves, their experience was rated the highest when a moderate level of plants were present and in this condition, that rating was associated with a more positive evaluation of their own performance.

And why stop at snake plants, spider plants or rubber plants? Evidence suggests that nice smells in the office are also conducive to happiness. Baron (1990) exposed participants to either pleasant or neutral air freshener scents. Those exposed to the pleasant smells not only set higher goals for themselves on a clerical task, but adopted more efficient strategies, set higher monetary goals in negotiations and showed reduced preferences for competitive conflict. Bring on the hyacinths.

There is just one additional reason why you may want to hold back from your garden centre mass purchase of plants (scented or otherwise). According to Knight and Haslam (2010), any increases in well-being and productivity are accentuated further still if workers themselves have input into the office decoration. Which brings us nicely to the second suggestion on our list of three: empower your staff!

Suggestion 2: Empower your staff

We have already established that giving staff a role to play in decorating the office can do wonders for their sense of well-being and can make them more productive also. How else can an employer empower their staff? Since the start of the global COVID-19 pandemic, there has been an increasing interest in exploring the effect of working from home and/or flexible working schedules as an avenue of empowerment. Breaugh and Farabee (2012) for example believe that working from home increases an employee's sense of control over their work and others have suggested that giving employees a chance to work in a comfortable, familiar environment can facilitate productivity and reduce clashes between home and work commitments (Hill et al., 2003). In a study of IBM employers in the United States, they also found that it has a positive effect on job retention.

However, home working is not as straightforward as it sounds as it is known to be linked with a greater tendency to work during unusual hours (Kristensen & Pedersen, 2017) and Palumbo (2020) reported a greater work-related fatigue in many. Perhaps the key to understanding the difference in findings is choice. Having the flexibility to decide what works best for you as an employee might explain this discrepancy.

That certainly does seem to be the case if we look at the results of a large-scale case study conducted by Atkinson and Hall (2011) within an NHS Acute Trust in the United Kingdom. Having flexibility in terms of working schedules might include part-time options and job sharing but it might also mean flexibility simply in terms of variation of working hours. Having such control over managing commitments at work and home as well as having control over the working environment was incredibly important to staff in Atkinson and Hall's study. Perhaps the biggest factor showing the beneficial effects for the organisation in turn was the fact that 18 employees reported how the offer of flexibility had made them respond by giving more or being more flexible themselves. Over a third of those involved recognised that they wanted to go over and above what was required in their role to help the Trust itself. It has been claimed that substantial flexibility in the workplace has an effect on happiness that is about as large as the effect of income and as the difference between good and excellent self-reported health! (Okulicz-Kozaryn and Golden (2018).

But empowering your employees is not just about allowing employees to decide what type of working arrangement suits them best. Empowerment is also about autonomy. Indeed, in their self-determination theory, Deci and Ryan (2008) argue that it is one of three needs that must be satisfied for employees to be intrinsically motivated, that is to engage in their work because they are genuinely interested in it or enjoy it. Similarly, Hackman and Oldman (1975) suggest that autonomy promotes increased responsibility in employees, leading to higher quality work, higher job satisfaction and lower absenteeism and Rothmann et al. (2013) demonstrated how being supportive of autonomy in your employees can lead to them reporting greater satisfaction with their employment and better well-being too. Indeed, in a meta-analysis, Humphrey et al. (2007) identified autonomy as one of nine work characteristics that underpin most work performance and satisfaction and in Seijts and Crim's (2006) 10 C's of engagement, allowing employees "control" or autonomy over the pace of their work is included amongst them.

Suggestion 3: Be a happy boss

To ensure our employees are empowered, it doesn't pay to be a miserable boss. In fact, quite the opposite. Jennifer George (1995) studied the experience of 53 sales managers leading groups ranging in size from 4–9 members. Questionnaires were sent to the managers and the salespeople in their teams. Even when the managers' own levels of job satisfaction were accounted for, their positive mood was significantly related to the performance of their group. Perhaps these managers had higher expectations for their groups as we know that this is predictive of performance at a higher level (Eden, 1990). Or perhaps it is reflective of the link between happiness and pro-social behaviour (George, 1991).

Whatever explanation we opt for, the effect is strong. Indeed, when compared to the content of a leader's message, their expression of emotion (happy or otherwise) is significantly more influential (Newcombe & Ashkanasy, 2002). Moreover, looking happy would appear to lead to employees rating the leader as more effective (Awamleh & Gardner, 1999) and incidentally, more attractive (Bono & Ilies, 2006). In fact, Mühlfeit and Costi felt so compelled by the power of the evidence that in 2016, they wrote a whole book on "The positive leader: How happiness and energy fuel top performing teams".

Visser et al. (2013) explains the effect of positive leaders as a form of emotional contagion. They presented students at a business school with a situation where they would be given instructions by a leader in another room that they would be able to see and hear. The leader was in fact a professional actor. The leader, they were told, would not be able to see or hear them back. Facial expressions and vocal intonations were used to portray the feeling of the leader, for example the happy leader smiled frequently and spoke with an enthusiastic intonation. The sad leader however looked glum and spoke in a quiet and pleading tone. After completing both a creative idea generation task and an analytical Sudoku puzzle, participants were asked to fill in a questionnaire asking for their impressions of the leader and their effectiveness.

As far as creativity was concerned, the happy leader ruled the roost! He enhanced the creative performance of the participants significantly and was rated as being a more effective leader. All was not lost for the sad leader though. He managed to enhance the performance of the participants on the analytical task. Happy leaders may still be seen as effective where analytical tasks are

■ **Figure 6.4** Screenshots from Visser et al.'s study showing a leader displaying happiness, sadness and an affective neutral state.

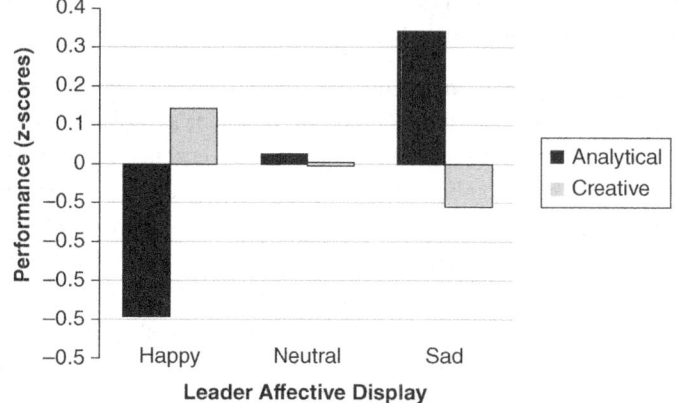

■ **Figure 6.5** The effect of a leader's happy, sad or neutral state on creative and analytical performance.

required but they won't enhance the analytical performance of their employees as much as their creative performance.

And for anyone planning to move into a managerial position, its worth remembering that those seen to be happy are more likely to be rated as higher in managerial potential. Staw and Barsade (1993) reported this in a study of 111 year 1 MBA students attending an assessment centre weekend. But even if a managerial position is not something you are keen to pursue, take pleasure (and happiness, why not) in the knowledge that people who consider themselves to be happy tend to earn more at later time points that those who don't (Diener et al., 2002). Whatever you are doing today, make sure you make time for some genuine smiles.

REFERENCES

Amabile, T. M., Barsade, S. G., Mueller, J. S., & Staw, B. M. (2005). Affect and creativity at work. *Administrative Science Quarterly*, *50*(3), 367–403.

Atkinson, C., & Hall, L. (2011). Flexible working and happiness in the NHS. *Employee Relations*, *33*(2), 88–105.

Awamleh, R., & Gardner, W. L. (1999). Perceptions of leader charisma and effectiveness-Charismatic political leadership. *Leadership Quarterly*, *10*, 345–373.

Bani-Melhem, S., Zeffane, R., & Albaity, M. (2018). Determinants of employees' innovative behavior. *International Journal of Contemporary Hospitality Management*, *30*(3), 1601–1620.

Barger, P. B., & Grandey, A. A. (2006). Service with a smile and encounter satisfaction: Emotional contagion and appraisal mechanisms. *Academy of Management Journal*, *49*(6), 1229–1238.

Baron, R. A. (1990). Environmentally induced positive affect: Its impact on self-efficacy, task performance, negotiation, and conflict 1. *Journal of Applied Social Psychology*, *20*(5), 368–384.

Barsade, S. G., Ward, A. J., Turner, J. D., & Sonnenfeld, J. A. (2000). To your heart's content: A model of affective diversity in top management teams. *Administrative Science Quarterly*, *45*(4), 802–836.

Berto, R. (2005). Exposure to restorative environments helps restore attentional capacity. *Journal of Environmental Psychology*, *25*(3), 249–259.

Bless, H., Bohner, G., Schwarz, N., & Strack, F. (1990). Mood and persuasion: A cognitive response analysis. *Personality and Social Psychology Bulletin*, *16*(2), 331–345.

Bodenhausen, G. V., Kramer, G. P., & Süsser, K. (1994). Happiness and stereotypic thinking in social judgment. *Journal of Personality and Social Psychology*, *66*(4), 621.

Bono, J. E., & Ilies, R. (2006). Charisma, positive emotions and mood contagion. *The Leadership Quarterly*, *17*(4), 317–334.

Breaugh, J. A., & Farabee, A. M. (2012). Telecommuting and flexible work hours: Alternative work arrangements that can improve the quality of work life. In *Work and quality of life* (pp. 251–274). Springer.

Bringslimark, T., Hartig, T., & Patil, G. G. (2007). Psychological benefits of indoor plants in workplaces: Putting experimental results into context. *HortScience*, *42*(3), 581–587.

Carnevale, P. J., & Isen, A. M. (1986). The influence of positive affect and visual access on the discovery of integrative solutions in bilateral negotiation. *Organizational Behavior and Human Decision Processes*, *37*(1), 1–13.

Christensen, M., Honts, C., & Colarelli, S. (2012). Effects of a companion dog on a group task. In *Poster presented at the 27th annual conference of the society for industrial and organizational psychology, San Diego, CA*.

Deci, E. L., & Ryan, R. M. (2008). Self-determination theory: A macrotheory of human motivation, development, and health. *Canadian Psychology/Psychologie canadienne*, *49*(3), 182.

Diener, E., & Biswas-Diener, R. (2002). Will money increase subjective well-being? *Social Indicators Research*, *57*(2), 119–169.

Druckman, D., & Broome, B. J. (1991). Value differences and conflict resolution: Familiarity or liking? *Journal of Conflict Resolution*, *35*(4), 571–593.

Duvall-Early, K., & Benedict, J. O. (1992). The relationships between privacy and different components of job satisfaction. *Environment and Behavior*, *24*(5), 670–679.

Eden, D. (1990). Pygmalion without interpersonal contrast effects: Whole groups gain from raising manager expectations. *Journal of Applied Psychology*, *75*(4), 394.

Elsbach, K. D., & Barr, P. S. (1999). The effects of mood on individuals' use of structured decision protocols. *Organization Science*, *10*(2), 181–198.

Estrada, C. A., Isen, A. M., & Young, M. J. (1997). Positive affect facilitates integration of information and decreases anchoring in reasoning among physicians. *Organizational Behavior and Human Decision Processes*, *72*(1), 117–135.

Fredrickson, B. L. (1998). What good are positive emotions? *Review of General Psychology*, *2*(3), 300–319.

George, J. M. (1991). State or trait: Effects of positive mood on prosocial behaviors at work. *Journal of Applied Psychology*, *76*(2), 299.

George, J. M. (1995). Leader positive mood and group performance: The case of customer service. *Journal of Applied Social Psychology*, *25*(9), 778–794.

Goodrich, R. (1982). Seven office evaluations: A review. *Environment and Behavior*, *14*(3), 353–378.

Hackman, R. J., & Oldman, G. R. (1975). General job satisfaction. In *Work redesign*. Addison-Wesley.

Herrbach, O. (2006). A matter of feeling? The affective tone of organizational commitment and identification. *Journal of Organizational Behavior: The International Journal of Industrial, Occupational and Organizational Psychology and Behavior*, *27*(5), 629–643.

Hill, E. J., Ferris, M., & Märtinson, V. (2003). Does it matter where you work? A comparison of how three work venues (traditional office, virtual office, and home office) influence aspects of work and personal/family life. *Journal of Vocational Behavior*, *63*(2), 220–241.

Humphrey, S. E., Nahrgang, J. D., & Morgeson, F. P. (2007). Integrating motivational, social, and contextual work design features: A meta-analytic summary and theoretical extension of the work design literature. *Journal of Applied Psychology*, *92*(5), 1332.

Iverson, R. D., Olekalns, M., & Erwin, P. J. (1998). Affectivity, organizational stressors, and absenteeism: A causal model of burnout and its consequences. *Journal of Vocational Behavior*, *52*(1), 1–23.

Kaplan, R., & Kaplan, S. (1989). *The experience of nature: A psychological perspective*. Cambridge University Press.

Knight, C., & Haslam, S. A. (2010). The relative merits of lean, enriched, and empowered offices: An experimental examination of the impact of workspace management strategies on well-being and productivity. *Journal of Experimental Psychology: Applied*, *16*(2), 158.

Kristensen, A. R., & Pedersen, M. (2017). 'I wish I could work in my spare time' Simondon and the individuation of work – life balance. *Culture and Organization*, *23*(1), 67–79.

Kumar, R. (1997). The role of affect in negotiations: An integrative overview. *The Journal of Applied Behavioral Science*, *33*(1), 84–100.

Larsen, L., Adams, J., Deal, B., Kweon, B. S., & Tyler, E. (1998). Plants in the workplace: The effects of plant density on productivity, attitudes, and perceptions. *Environment and Behavior*, *30*(3), 261–281.

Madjar, N., Oldham, G. R., & Pratt, M. G. (2002). There's no place like home? The contributions of work and nonwork creativity support to employees' creative performance. *Academy of Management Journal*, *45*(4), 757–767.

Martin, L. L., Ward, D. W., Achee, J. W., & Wyer, R. S. (1993). Mood as input: People have to interpret the motivational implications of their moods. *Journal of Personality and Social Psychology*, *64*(3), 317.

Melton, R. J. (1995). The role of positive affect in syllogism performance. *Personality and Social Psychology Bulletin*, *21*(8), 788–794.

Mühlfeit, J., & Costi, M. (2016). *The positive leader: How energy and happiness fuel top-performing teams*. Pearson UK.

Newcombe, M. J., & Ashkanasy, N. M. (2002). The role of affect and affective congruence in perceptions of leaders: An experimental study. *The Leadership Quarterly*, *13*(5), 601–614.

Okulicz-Kozaryn, A., & Golden, L. (2018). Happiness is flextime. *Applied Research in Quality of Life*, *13*(2), 355–369.

Oyabu, T., Sawada, A., Onodera, T., Takenaka, K., & Wolverton, B. (2003). Characteristics of potted plants for removing offensive odours. *Sensors and Actuators B*, *89*(1/2), 131–136.

Palumbo, R. (2020). Let me go to the office! An investigation into the side effects of working from home on work-life balance. *International Journal of Public Sector Management*, *33*(6/7), 771–790.

Pelled, L. H., & Xin, K. R. (1999). Down and out: An investigation of the relationship between mood and employee withdrawal behavior. *Journal of Management*, *25*(6), 875–895.

Ragan, P. T., & Carder, B. (2019). The happiness factor: Happy employees are safer employees. *Professional Safety*, *64*(09), 35–38.

Rothmann, S., Diedericks, E., & Swart, J. P. (2013). Manager relations, psychological need satisfaction and intention to leave in the agricultural sector. *SA Journal of Industrial Psychology*, *39*(2), 1–11.

Seijts, G. H., & Crim, D. (2006). What engages employees the most or, the ten C's of employee engagement. *Ivey Business Journal*, *70*(4), 1–5.

Seligman, M. E., & Schulman, P. (1986). Explanatory style as a predictor of productivity and quitting among life insurance sales agents. *Journal of Personality and Social Psychology*, *50*(4), 832.

Singh, S., David, R., & Mikkilineni, S. (2018). Organizational virtuousness and work engagement: Mediating role of happiness in India. *Advances in Developing Human Resources*, *20*(1), 88–102.

Smith, A., & Pitt, M. (2008, June 16–18). Preference for plants in an office environment. *Proceedings of the CIB W70 Conference in Facilities Management – Healthy and Creative Facilities*, Heriot-Watt University, Edinburgh, CIB No. 315, pp. 629–637.

Spector, P. E., & Fox, S. (2002). An emotion-centered model of voluntary work behavior: Some parallels between counterproductive work behavior and organizational citizenship behavior. *Human Resource Management Review*, *12*(2), 269–292.

Staw, B. M., & Barsade, S. G. (1993). Affect and managerial performance: A test of the sadder-but-wiser vs. happier-and-smarter hypotheses. *Administrative Science Quarterly*, 304–331.

Staw, B. M., Sutton, R. I., & Pelled, L. H. (1994). Employee positive emotion and favorable outcomes at the workplace. *Organization Science*, 5(1), 51–71.

Vernon, P. E. (Ed.). (1970). *Creativity: Selected readings*. Penguin.

Visser, V. A., van Knippenberg, D., Van Kleef, G. A., & Wisse, B. (2013). How leader displays of happiness and sadness influence follower performance: Emotional contagion and creative versus analytical performance. *The Leadership Quarterly*, 24(1), 172–188.

Weinstein, N., Przybylski, A. K., & Ryan, R. M. (2009). Can nature make us more caring? Effects of immersion in nature on intrinsic aspirations and generosity. *Personality and Social Psychology Bulletin*, 35(10), 1315–1329.

Wolverton, B. C., & Wolverton, J. D. (1993). Plants and soil microorganisms: Removal of formaldehyde, xylene, and ammonia from the indoor environment. *Journal of the Mississippi Academy of Sciences*, 38(2), 11–15.

Wright, T. A., & Staw, B. M. (1999). Affect and favorable work outcomes: Two longitudinal tests of the happy – productive worker thesis. *Journal of Organizational Behavior: The International Journal of Industrial, Occupational and Organizational Psychology and Behavior*, 20(1), 1–23.

Chapter 7

Is it possible to detect deception?

How good are you at detecting deceit in others? This question delves into the world of forensic psychology to address the question of whether it is possible to accurately detect deceit. What cues are reliable cues? Indeed, are there any? It is easy to imagine that there exists a specific list of cues that if used, lead us to successfully distinguish lie from truth. But psychological evidence suggests otherwise. In this chapter, factors that might affect the outcome such as experience, the method used to extract information and the idea of non-conscious detection are examined. The question of whether certain individuals are better lie detectors than others is raised and theories such as the Tipping Point Framework of lie detection, Social Defence Theory and Sentinel Behaviour are all discussed. In the second half of this chapter, three suggestions that may help to improve and develop our ability to detect deception are made, using psychological research as the basis. Find out why groups can be valuable, why drawing is an under-utilised but much valued tool and why unexpected questions may be the key to greater accuracy.

■ **Figure 7.1** We like to think we are good at detecting deception but are we deceiving ourselves?

Let me ask you a question? What connects the following: Arthur Smith Woodward, Suzanne Hardman, Hilary Clinton and yourself (I suspect)? Any ideas? Let me give you a clue. Arthur Smith Woodward was a renowned palaeontologist (someone who studies fossils), Suzanne Hardman was an avid internet user looking for love, Hilary Clinton is the wife of the former President of the United States and you? Got the link yet? Well, I'll not keep you guessing any longer. The one thing that connects all of these individuals is that they are all victims of lies. Yes, you included.

Arthur Smith Woodward had someone called Martin Hinton working for him but Arthur refused to pay Martin a weekly wage. It is thought that as revenge, Martin set up one of the biggest deceptions of all time, the Piltdown Man. In 1910, a skull and jawbone with molars attached, was discovered by Charles Dawson and taken along to Woodward for investigation. Woodward was convinced this was indeed a skull of an earlier form of human and it provided the "missing link" between ape and man. Unfortunately, it was later discovered to be a hoax. The jawbone was in fact that of an orangutan and the skull was thought to be only 600 years old. Whoever had created this deception had gone to the trouble to file down the molars and stain them. Word has it that a trunk belonging to Hinton contained bones which had been similarly stained, implicating him in the deceit.

How about Suzanne Hardman and Hilary Clinton? Well both were deceived in matters of the heart but in two quite different manners. Suzanne Hardman was reported to have lost £174,000 to an internet fraudster posing as a potential love match on an online dating site whilst Hilary was lied to in a public press conference when the then President of the United States, Bill Clinton, her husband, denied he had had an affair with Monica Lewinsky under oath. Through records of telephone calls, he was later shown to have lied and was impeached.

So how about you? Well, how tall would you say Napoleon was based on what you have learnt in your history lessons? Word has it that he was pretty short as men go, right? Well, no. We're going to expose that one as a lie because Napoleon was actually taller than most men of his era, at 5ft 7inches. The myth of him being short was simply due to a difference in measuring tools. Inches in France were longer than inches in England, hence the idea that he was short for his age.

These represent some quite diverse examples I agree but lies abound in day-to-day existence, not just in politics but in love relationships, friendships and in criminal environments too. Given the preponderance of lie-telling, the question is, how good are we are discriminating lie from truth? Good you might imagine, particularly given how frequently lies are told. One estimate from Meyer (2011) is that we are lied to between 10 and 200 times a day and over 90% of us tell them (Patterson & Kim, 1991). In fact Freud (1953/1905) believed betrayal oozes out of us in every pore.

Jensen et al. (2004), in a study of high school and college students, reported the majority of students had lied to their parents in the past year. Lying isn't always seen in a negative light however, for example you may have heard of white lies, lies told to avoid hurting someone's feelings and many of the students in Jensen's study described the lies they told as having pro-social and altruistic motives. Even if we look at cultural products such as books, films and music, the theme of deception abounds. In literature, for example, many of Shakespeare's works revolve around deceit. Take Othello for example. Desdemona reacts with a huge outburst of emotion at finding out that Cassio, her alleged lover, has been killed and therefore she has no alibi to protest her innocence. Othello takes this outburst as confirmation that she was unfaithful. This narrative has been used to term a concept in deception research. The Othello error refers to the error of interpreting certain behaviours as proof of deception too readily (Ekman, 2001; Vrij, Granhag, et al., 2010). And, as we shall see on our next journey into an area of applied psychology, this error makes us actually pretty poor at the business of detecting lies.

JUST HOW BAD ARE WE AT DETECTING DECEPTION?

Let's start by establishing just how bad we really are at detecting deception. Bond and DePaulo (2006) explored the results from over 24,000 judges of lie detection. They performed, on average, at a level of about 54% accuracy. If you consider that performing at chance would give you an accuracy of 50%, then you get an idea of just how poor we are. In fact in a review, Vrij (2000) reported an accuracy rate of just 44% for lie detection! And it doesn't matter if you are someone who has extensive experience in having to detect deception. Allwood and Granhag (2007) report that although professional "lie catchers" are more confident in their abilities, they actually are no more accurate than novices in detecting deception and Bond and

DePaulo (2006) suggest that the average person is no better at discriminating lie from truth than they could achieve by flipping a coin.

So, how come we are so bad? What explains our poor performance? One idea is that we just look for the wrong cues. For example, if someone was lying to you, how do you think their behaviour would change from if they were telling the truth? Well? Chances are you mentioned at least one of the following: they avoid eye contact, they fidget more, they look nervous. Am I right? Well, re-think those cues. None of these have been shown to be reliable predictors of lie-telling. However, don't despair because you are in the majority thinking that they would be. In a 2006 publication entitled "A world of lies", the Global Deception Research Team considered the cues used to detect deception by 2,320 residents from across 58 different countries. No, I am not lying. There actually is a Global Deception Research Team. Anyway, what do you think they found? The most commonly reported cue to deception, reported in this study, was gaze aversion, that is, avoiding eye contact with the interviewer. Of their subjects, 63% reported this as a reliable cue. Gaze aversion, however, has been shown to have little predictive validity in helping us distinguish lies from truth (Bogaard et al., 2016). Another common cue mentioned was signs of nervousness but as Bogaard et al (2016) reports, truth tellers can be just as nervous in an interview situation. How about fidgeting? Again, 25% of subjects reported this as a cue in the Global Deception Research Team study. And again, there is little evidence to support this. In fact, as Vrij, Granhag, et al. (2010) identified, liars will often try to suppress nervous behaviour and this often means they move *less* than honest individuals.

This idea that lots of movement is a cue to lying can cause problems for truth tellers in other ways. For example, when denying something, truth-tellers tend to use lots of hand and finger movements, which may cause observers to think they are lying (Vrij & Baxter, 1999). In a study of undergraduates, Vrij and Baxter demonstrated that when witnessing a video fragment of an individual denying something in an interview, they are much more likely to be considered deceitful when denying something than when they are elaborating with detail. Perhaps this offers instead a way to improve deception detection as liars are known to make fewer hand and finger movements (Caso et al., 2006). However, as Zloteanu et al. (2019) point out, in investigative and legal criminal contexts, suspects are often handcuffed, restricting the ability to produce movement and hence reducing the distinction between liars and truth-tellers.

This over-emphasis on non-verbal cues to deception, many of which are either not reliable or are actually contrary to what the evidence suggests, is not specific to individuals who have little experience in deception detection. Bogaard and Meijer (2018) compared the responses of police officers with those of undergraduate students. They were asked to identify what would be good cues for detecting deception and were then shown 8 statements taken from 13 interviews. In 7 of these interviews, the event being discussed was completely fake. Both police officers and students alike focused primarily on non-verbal cues such as gaze aversion and nervousness to make their judgements. Where verbal cues were used, accuracy was better but the years of experience of the police officers did not influence their success.

The emphasis placed on non-verbal cues is not entirely surprising given the way that lying is portrayed. Lying is seen often as morally wrong and therefore we expect liars to feel uncomfortable about telling lies and to be nervous about being caught (with all the consequences that might bring). Vrij, Granhag, et al. (2010) describe the process of deception detection in China in 1000 BC which involved suspected liars being forced to chew on rice powder and then spit it out. Dry powder was considered to demonstrate lying had occurred based on the idea that a dry mouth was indicative of a fear response (Kleinmuntz & Szucko, 1984).

ARE VERBAL CUES MORE RELIABLE?

So are verbal cues more reliable? It depends on what verbal cues are looked for. Strömwall and Granhag (2003) tested judges, prosecutors and police officers on their ability to detect deception. As well as the usual focus on non-verbal behaviours previously mentioned, there was also a marked tendency, in all three groups, to assume that liars were more inconsistent in their verbal reports. However, research suggests just the opposite (e.g. Strömwall et al., 2003). Liars often rehearse their stories thoroughly in preparation for interrogation.

One aspect of verbal behaviour that does seem to offer more hope for deception detectors is the amount of detail offered by an individual. Vrij, Mann, et al. (2010) report that truth-tellers are often concerned to tell everything they know pertaining to a situation whereas liars opt for a more cautious approach, giving only vague information. This does of course make logical sense since the more information we give, the greater the chance that any deception will be identified due to mismatches with other information or contradictions in story. Vrij and colleagues took participants, in pairs, to a restaurant to have lunch with the backstory that the experiment they were going to do was running late. On being collected, they were informed they were suspected of taking two £5 notes from a room during lunch and they would both be interviewed in 10 minutes time. Participants were informed that if the interviewer believed them, they would receive a £10 reward. However, that was only the case for the truth-tellers. For the liars, on arrival, they were told by an experimenter, that two £5 notes were hidden in a purse in an empty room. They were told to get it and share it. On returning, they were then told that they were suspected of taking two £5 notes from a room and they had 10 minutes to prepare an alibi. The alibi was that someone took them to the restaurant to have lunch because the experiment was running late. They had lunch together and then returned. Again, a £10 reward was offered if the experimenter believed them. In terms of non-verbal strategies discussed in the 10-minute window, truth-tellers and lie-tellers were indistinguishable. Both tried to suppress signs of nervousness. However, in terms of verbal strategies, they differed. The truth-tellers were concerned to tell as much as they could remember about what had happened. The lie-tellers on the other hand, were more concerned to prepare answers to possible questions, trying to give away as little detail as possible. Verbal cues, it was suggested, are much more diagnostic and useful when detecting deception.

This suggestion that verbal cues trump non-verbal cues has been borne out not just in criminal contexts but also in cases of infidelity. Hughes and Harrison (2017) presented voice samples to participants of people who had either been unfaithful in romantic relationships or who had always been faithful in romantic relationships. From the voice alone, participants were able to distinguish the two groups. Those individuals with lower pitched voices were considered to be more likely to be unfaithful. It is interesting to note, as the authors do, that low pitch in voices is linked to high levels of testosterone, which itself is linked to number of sex partners (Bogaert & Fisher, 1995). Probably a good one to bear in mind next time you go on a date. Those deep, dark tones may spell trouble further down the line.

WHY NOT ELIMINATE VISUAL INFORMATION ALTOGETHER?

Given the role that verbal behaviour plays in helping us detect deception, surely we would be more accurate deception detectors if we eliminated visual information altogether? Burgoon et al. (2008) suggest that we normally show a visual bias, ascribing greater weight and importance to visual information over other forms of socially available information. Perhaps when we have access to visual information, it distracts us from the verbal information. Mann et al. (2008) put this to the test. Are we more accurate lie detectors when we only have evidence to listen to as opposed to watch? The answer is yes. Accuracy leapt from 44% when visual information only was provided to 65% when auditory information only was provided. Similarly, Burgoon et al. (2008) reported 47% accuracy for video presentation compared to 60% for audio presentation. In an extension of this, Leach et al. (2016) demonstrated that covering part of the face when giving evidence leads to greater accuracy in lie detection. When witnesses wore niqabs or hijabs, participants were more accurate at detecting deception than when no face veil was worn. That is, covering part of the face improved accuracy without any negative biases. Obscuring part of the face, it is argued, forces people to use different strategies such as focusing on the voice and what is being said.

■ **Figure 7.2** Eliminating visual bias in deception detection can help.

Not everyone agrees with Leach et al.'s conclusions however. Denault et al. (2017) point to methodological limitations of the study such as an inaccurate experimental court situation used. This leads us to one of the main criticisms that has been levelled at research into deception detection, namely that the experiments we have encountered often use what are called "low stakes lies". It doesn't really matter how accurate we are on these tasks because after all, its only an experiment. There are no real world consequences for the individuals we are rating as lie or truth-tellers. To try and counter this, Shaw and Lyons (2017) used footage from 22 public appeals asking for help to find a missing relative. The stakes involved here were high. In 11 of the appeals, the person making the appeal was honest and uninvolved in the disappearance and/or death of the missing person. In the remaining 11, the person making the appeal was involved. Would participants be able to distinguish which was which?

Participants in this study were divided into two groups. The first group were given information about certain non-verbal cues that might be useful to focus on such as gaze aversion, fake emotions, shaking of the head, cues that individuals frequently associate with deception. The second group were not given any cue information at all. How did they do? Well, whether they were informed about cues or not made no difference to their ability to identify truth-tellers from the lie-tellers. But one thing did make a difference. And it isn't something you might consider at first glance. It was age. The older the participant, the better their accuracy. In particular, the judgements of accuracy were associated with a focus on emotion-based cues. Perhaps as people age, the authors suggest, they become more aware that the emotional expressions we portray do not always match how we feel internally. When the stakes are high, age matters and emotion rules.

This does point us in a different direction entirely, one which emphasises the need to focus on emotion rather than the actual words a person says. Indeed, Etcoff et al. (2000) demonstrated that aphasic individuals who are unable to understand spoken language are significantly more accurate at lie detection than those who are unimpaired in their language comprehension. Focusing on the aspects of interactions that are perhaps harder to control consciously is a key way forward.

THE UNCONSCIOUS LIE DETECTOR

Are we capable of detecting deception at an unconscious level? This is certainly the suggestion made by ten Brinke et al. (2014).

They created a set of videotapes in an experiment in which people pleaded innocent to their involvement in a crime, stealing $100 from an envelope. Only half were telling the truth. Participants were asked to make a judgement about whether the person in each video was telling the truth or not. On to the next part of the study. Participants were then asked to complete a task on a computer. On the screen, they saw "truth" and "lie" in the upper right and left corners. In the centre of the screen, photos from the videos and words associated with lies appeared. The participants' job? Decide whether to place that photo or that word in the left- or right-hand category. As in many previous studies, the ability of the participants to distinguish liars from truth-tellers was poor (46% accurate on average). However, in the computer task, viewing a liar did seem to make participants faster at categorising concepts associated with lying and viewing an honest person meant they categorised words associated with honesty quicker. In a second experiment, the photos from the videos were presented so quickly that participants were not consciously aware of their presence on the screen yet nonetheless, they influenced speed of categorisation of related words. What does all this mean? When we rely on unconscious cues, we do pretty well at outing the liars. But when we have to make a conscious and explicit decision, we're pretty bad.

This idea makes sense given the social rules of conversation (Vrij, 2000). There are serious consequences to accusing someone of lying and generally speaking, we like to think of people as being truthful and trustworthy. Vrij and Baxter (1999) refer to this as a truth bias, a bias because we often over-estimate the chances that someone is being honest. ten Brinke et al. (2016) point to the potential for misattributions of deception to reflect badly on the individual making these decisions, suggesting something pretty awful about their moral standing and demonstrating a lack of trust in the accused.

However, being able to detect when we are being lied to has an evolutionary advantage. It could threaten well-being and safety for example (ten Brinke et al., 2016). Take the capuchin monkey. It has been documented that often a capuchin will elicit a false alarm call in order to remove fellow monkeys from a food source, simply so they can benefit from it in their absence (Wheeler, 2010). If this happens often enough, not only will the safety of the group be threatened (alarm calls will eventually be ignored) but also it could threaten the well-being of other monkeys in terms of not having access to food. No surprise then that certain areas of the brain in these monkeys can automatically detect deception (e.g. Grézes et al., 2004).

ten Brinke et al. (2016) therefore proposed the tipping point framework of lie detection. It proposes that people are indeed able to accurately detect lie-telling but at non-conscious levels. Because social costs of accusing someone of lying are often high, this may explain why conscious ability to detect lies is weak. In support of this, Grézes et al. (2004) measured activity in a brain area called the amygdala, reporting an increase in activity when people see someone telling a lie. Such activation strengthens further if the person being lied to is ourselves as opposed to another (Grézes et al., 2004). And if that doesn't give the liar away, then measure skin temperature of the observer. Observing a lie causes a drop in skin temperature (van't Veer et al., 2015).

So, there is a lot going on in our brain and our body that gives us a feeling or impression of deception even if we can't demonstrate that in our explicit judgements. If you're still not convinced, take a look at the work of Anderson et al. (2002). They asked pairs of same-sex friends to take part in a study. One member of each pair told four life stories to their friend who had to make a decision about the truth or otherwise of the account they heard. As well as making this decision, participants were asked to rate their confidence, comfort and suspiciousness. This procedure was followed at two time points: 1 month after they had met and 5 months later. Not entirely surprisingly, more of the stories were judged to be true than to be false. Where change occurred over time, it was the less-close friends who showed a decline in the truth bias (that is, they were less likely to think their friend was telling the truth). Perhaps when we become very close, the truth bias dominates. Overall accuracy across time points was again near to chance (54%).

However (and this is the best bit), on the indirect measures, they successfully identified lies from truth consistently! For example, the mean suspiciousness rating for lies was 5.51 compared to 4.48 when their friend was telling the truth. Confidence was greater when the story told was true (6.38) than when it was false (5.75) and comfort was rated highest when the story was true (7.56) compared to when it was false (7.13). So, even though accuracy was at chance levels in terms of decision-making, the levels of discomfort, suspicion and confidence told a different story.

ARE CERTAIN INDIVIDUALS BETTER LIE DETECTORS THAN OTHERS?

Research by Ein-Dor and Perry-Paldi (2014) suggests that certain individuals, due to early attachment experiences, are more "in tune" with these instincts and hunches that we often overlook. In the Social Defence Theory or SDT (Ein-Dor et al., 2010) it is proposed that individuals who experience attachment anxiety are more accurate in identifying deception that those who are not. Let me explain. When we are young, we are driven to seek proximity (closeness) to those who look after us, our "significant others" (Ein-Dor & Perry-Paldi, 2014). Sometimes things don't work out as planned and those significant others don't protect us from threats in the way we hope. As a result, the individual starts to feel anxious about how they will cope in times of need. Will someone be available or be able to help? Such anxiety then leads to an increased search for signs of threat, something that Ein-Dor refers to as sentinel behaviour. These individuals are more likely to notice danger and to warn others about it.

To prove this point, Ein-Dor and Perry-Paldi asked participants to watch seven video clips of two women interacting. In four of these clips, the main character told a fake story to the other. In the rest, she told the truth. Alongside this task, participants were asked to complete a questionnaire about experiences in close relationships and an anxiety questionnaire. Who was able to perform best? Those scoring high in attachment anxiety, that is those who perhaps worried about being abandoned or worried about people not being there to protect them. General levels of anxiety did not predict accuracy. This was the case whether environmental and situational cues were present to help give an idea of truthfulness or not.

On the note of attachment anxiety, if you are playing poker, this could be important. Players high in attachment anxiety tend to be pretty successful. As Ein-Dor and Perry-Paldi found, they tend to win a lot of money. How do they do this? By considering the emotional condition of the other players amongst other cues (Wallace, 1976) and by being expert at deceiving others too. Ein-Dor et al. (2017) asked 68 card players to participate in a tournament. The card game used was called "Bullshit". Excuse the language but that's really what it was called. To be successful in this game, you need to try to deceive other players about what cards you are discarding and at the same time, make accurate judgements about who else is lying when they do the same. Lo and behold, those players who scored highly for attachment anxiety were more likely to cheat without being caught, were more likely to correctly detect cheating in other players and hence were more likely to win.

There is one downside to this tale of attachment anxiety however. It may indeed be the case that this makes you great at card games but unfortunately it does also mean that you are more likely to be unfaithful (Etcheverry et al., 2013). That behaviour also relies on your ability to cheat without being caught. Ein-Dor et al. (2017) presented participants with a computerised detection task. A matrix of 36 pictures were shown on a screen, most depicting neutral social interactions and one portraying signs of unfaithfulness. The task for participants was to click on the one picture that portrayed signs of unfaithfulness as quickly as possible. This was repeated ten times. Following this task, participants were asked to complete a questionnaire which asked, among other things, about their own experience of infidelity against them plus their own engagement in romantic affairs whilst in a committed relationship.

Those scoring high in attachment anxiety made fewest errors on this task suggesting that there were better able to detect infidelity in others. They were also more likely to cheat on their own romantic partners. The same skills required to keep their cheating behaviour secretive were deployed to detect unfaithfulness in others. A history of experiencing dishonesty leads to heightened vigilance and attention to deception in others (Ein-Dor et al., 2017). It is akin to a self-preservation strategy that has evolved.

Self-preservation is also relevant to another group of individuals who may or may not be high in attachment anxiety. Criminals! Criminals are more likely to live in a deceptive environment, raising their vigilance to deception around them. For example, Hartwig et al. (2004) believe that criminals are particularly good at using feedback from interrogations to help them develop good lie detection strategies. Jupe et al. (2016) compared secondary school students with young offenders. Having watched interview clips regarding the theft of an MP3 player, participants were not only asked to make a decision about whether the person in the clip was lying but also were asked to describe what cues they were using. Teenage offenders were significantly more accurate in this decision-making, detecting 73% of lies compared to only 50% for non-offenders but no clear picture emerged for the use of cues. The offender's superior performance, Jupe et al. suggest, may be due to the experience they have had themselves of seeing what strategies worked for them.

Similar results have also been obtained using prison inmates from a high security prison (Hartwig et al., 2004). A particularly gruelling tale was told. A man had been found stabbed and robbed. One woman and two men had been accused. Their story was that the stabbed man had inflicted the injury himself after accosting the woman and threatening them with the knife. The good news was that a witness had been identified and had been interviewed three times. The witness had previously met the accused people but no one really knew the nature of this meeting. Participants were asked to watch the recorded interviews and make a judgement as to whether the witness was telling the truth or a lie as well as to outline what factors influenced their judgement.

The accuracy of the prison inmates in detecting lies was astounding (88.5%), whereas the students were no better than chance (65.4%). However, there was no difference between them when it came to identifying truthful accounts correctly. This suggests that the prison inmates showed a lie bias, being more likely to see people as deceitful than as honest. Perhaps this is indicative of a more suspicious outlook, Hartwig and Bond (2014) suggest. In terms of the cues used, students relied on consistency most of all, a cue which, as we know from our aforementioned story, is unlikely to be helpful. However, prison inmates relied much more on plausibility which is a much more reliable and objective cue.

So, should we be using inmates to help detect deception in criminal cases? Despite Hartwig's encouraging results, and similar findings from other researchers (e.g. Granhag et al., 2004), there is reason to be cautious. Schindler and colleagues (2021) were unable to replicate previous findings and instead found that offenders were significantly *worse* at deception detection than non-offenders. They raise the possibility that the lower level of education of inmates may be an important factor to consider as well as the criminal background of those involved.

HOW CAN WE IMPROVE DECEPTION DETECTION?
Use a group
Given these findings, it sounds as though relying on individuals to make a decision about truth versus lie is often prone to error,

even if they do have a background of deceit or being deceived. With that in mind, Klein and Epley (2015) suggest that perhaps a more accurate way of detecting deception is to rely on group decisions instead. In the first two of their four experiments, they used video recordings of 18 different speakers providing answers to 10 questions. Some of the answers provided were truthful and some were not. Participants were shown these clips and asked to make a judgement about the answers provided either individually or through discussing as a group. In the group condition, only one survey form was given for participants to complete so it really did have to be a joint decision. As far as the individuals were concerned, performance was once again close to chance (53.6%). However, when making a decision as part of a group, accuracy leapt to 61.7%! This improvement was largely due to the fact that more lies were detected correctly. This was also the case when a larger sample was used and different statements.

The third experiment tested whether the group would be just as effective when the lies were high-stakes. This, remember, has been a criticism of some of the early laboratory studies, that they used only low-stakes lies where the consequences didn't really matter. In many real-life situations, criminal cases, insurance fraud and so on, the stakes are high. Klein and Epley chose to use the final segments from a British game show "Golden Balls". To be successful, one contestant must successfully deceive another with the consequence being that they get to win a significant amount of money (anything from 6k to 66k). How do contestants deceive each other? They have to decide whether to split the winnings, meaning that each contestant gets half, or to steal, meaning to take the whole lot for themselves. The critical thing is that both contestants have to make this decision. If both say "split", they each get half. If both say "steal", they each win nothing at all. If one says "split" and the other says "steal", the stealer keeps the whole lot. In the video clips, the contestants talk to each other about the decision, usually advocating a split decision. However, some contestants intentionally engage in deception and although they claim they will opt to split, actually choose to steal. Would participants be able to identify the deceivers before they knew the outcome?

That is what Klein and Epley wanted to find out. They showed six videos to each participant or to each group and asked them to make a decision about each of the participants in each. Yet again, groups were more accurate than individuals. Whilst individuals got it right 47% of the time, groups out-performed them with a

53% accuracy score. Again, the groups were able to identify the liars better than the individuals. This better performance appeared to be due to individuals being exposed to each others' point of view, what Klein and Epley termed the "synergy" account. ten Brinke et al. (2016) interpret such findings as supportive of their Tipping Point Framework, in that the costs to any one individual's reputation is lessened as a result of others coming to the same conclusion and making that decision. As social cost decreases, accuracy goes in the reverse direction.

So group decision-making rocks in the world of deception detection. It's still a long way from perfect but it does empower people to express their suspicions more easily. How about the liar themselves though? Are there things we can do to influence their behaviour that will make their deception more apparent? Well, yes there is. We have already seen that liars tend to be more consistent rather than less in their accounts. Possibly because they have already rehearsed their stories at length in preparation for questioning (Hines et al., 2010). How can we throw a curveball into proceedings? There are two suggestions in the literature that we will explore here. One is the idea of getting the suspect to draw an aspect of the situation or event they are describing. The other, that we will encounter shortly, is the idea of throwing in an unexpected twist to the interview.

Use drawing as a detection tool

Let's look at the effect of requesting a suspect to draw. Most suspects will be surprised at being asked to draw an aspect of the situation or event they are being interviewed about but drawings can be advantageous for other reasons also. Drawings require a certain level of specific detail to be included. Just cast your mind back to some of the previous studies. Imagine being asked to draw the restaurant where you had lunch if you hadn't actually been in the restaurant. Would you know where the counters and the till was? How would the seating be arranged?

Van Veldhuizen et al. (2018) utilised drawing as a focus for assessing asylum claims. Asylum seekers, by their nature, often have no access to necessary documents used to support their claims. How do we know that the stated country of origin is indeed truthful? Van Veldhuizen set about exploring the potential value of drawing as a means of assessing this. Residents from two Dutch cities (Tilberg and Maastricht) and a city in Sweden (Gothenburg), were asked to sketch the main square in Tilburg as part of a larger interview where they had to claim to be a resident of Tilburg, also answering general knowledge questions about the area. The number of details included in each drawing as well as the number of correct answers to the questions were monitored. In terms of the questions, these did not differentiate between the residents very well. Even those who were genuinely from Tilburg slipped up on some of the questions and those liars who were given time to prepare answers to the questions did just as well as some of the unprepared truth-tellers. As the authors point out, if we don't attend to certain details about the area, it is unlikely we can develop knowledge about them. In terms of the drawings they produced, however, the differences were striking. Those from Tilburg drew much more detailed sketches and included many more correct details. The experience of being in a place enables the observer to create a rich episodic memory complete with rich sensory information (Johnson et al., 1988), something which is not possible for liars.

Vrij et al. (2010) similarly tried using drawings to distinguish truth-tellers from liars. In this study, participants were asked to collect and deliver a package to another person. The participants were police and army officers. On completion, they were stopped and asked about their activity. In half of the cases, participants

■ **Figure 7.3** Drawing can be a useful way of improving detection deception.

had been asked to tell the truth. In the other half, they were told to lie. When asked to draw the place where the package had been given to them, important differences emerged. Not only did the truth-teller include the person who gave them the package in their drawings more often but they also were more likely to show the scene from a shoulder camera position rather than an overhead position. Bystanders were more likely to be included in their sketches. Based on simply whether the agent was shown though was sufficient for over 80% of truth-tellers and a similar proportion of liars to be correctly identified.

The potential of this as a tool extends beyond just theft cases. Take the example of identity theft. If you were asked to draw your workplace, would you be able to? Now imagine a person who is claiming to work for a certain company. Would they be able to draw their workplace? Vrij and colleagues (2012) were again on the case. They recruited participants from a range of professions including secretarial staff, pilots, social workers and an engineer amongst others. Half of the sample were asked to lie about their occupation in an interview and half were asked to tell the truth. In the interview, not only were participants asked questions about the workplace in terms of where desks were, any tea-making facilities and so on, but they were also asked to sketch a layout of the area. Not only were the drawings of truth-tellers more plausible, they included more people in them than those of lie-tellers. As Giolla et al. (2017) point out, type of detail may be more important than amount of detail.

One of the added advantages of using drawing as a tool to detect deception is the fact that it enables an investigator to look for consistencies between the pictorial and verbal accounts. Vrij et al. (2009) compared the verbal reports and drawings of truth-telling pairs that had had lunch together with those of lying pairs that had been asked simply to imagine this. Those telling the truth showed a greater consistency between their verbal reports and the details in their sketches. As Leins et al. (2011) have demonstrated it is the unexpected nature of the request to sketch that seems to disrupt the pre-prepared strategies of the liar.

Use unexpected questions

Are there other ways that we can throw some unexpected demands on the liar? Vrij et al. (2011) certainly think so. How about asking the suspect to tell their side of the story in reverse order? That surely will fox them – lying takes a lot of preparation. Not only does the liar need to ensure consistency in their reports but they need to make sure they don't give too much away that will oust them as a liar. They have to try to control any signs of nervousness and appear confident. Vrij et al. decided to try this out. They had participants play a game of Connect 4 during which they were interrupted first by someone coming in to wipe the board and then by someone who came in looking for their wallet. On finding the wallet, this person exclaimed that a £10 note had gone missing from it. That was the experience of the "truth tellers". The "liars" however were asked to take the £10 note from the wallet but to deny all knowledge of this when asked and pretend they too had been playing Connect 4.

When interviewed, half of the people in each condition were asked to report in as much detail as possible, what happened. The other half were asked to do so but in reverse order. Did it have any effect? Why yes. When asked to recall events in the reverse order, liars included fewer auditory details than truth-tellers, fewer spatial or temporal details and hesitated more in their speech. They also made more leg and foot movements. This was not the case when they were asked to recall in a natural order where liars showed less movement. In a follow up study, the effect of asking liars to recall in reverse order was shown to influence the judgements made by police officers as to their truth. They were able to spot the liars accurately 60% of the time compared to only 42% of the time when stories were recounted in a logical order.

If you don't fancy reverse order questioning, then how about the "Devil's advocate approach" (Leal et al., 2010)? This is particularly useful for situations where people are expressing opinions. Ask them to argue not just in favour of their view but also against it. As a rule, people usually generate more reasons in support of their point of view. In liars, this means they are more likely to generate reasons against their stated point of view. Leal et al. demonstrated this in a study where participants were asked to share their views about issues such as UK immigration laws, the rights of gay couples to adopt a child and abortion laws. Truth-tellers did indeed give longer answers in support of their point of view whereas for liars, they gave equally long answers for their stated point of view and the devil's advocate position. In a second study, they were able to demonstrate that truth-tellers were more emotionally involved and have more immediate responses too.

So, where does this leave our story of deception and intrigue? We know now that despite being prolific lie-tellers ourselves (for a multitude of reasons), we are desperately poor at detecting deceit in others, albeit explicitly. If we don't think about it too much, our instinct can serve us better but we're still not perfect. In the meantime, finding ways to reduce the social costs of outing deception, or increasing the demands on a liar cognitively seem to offer a good route forward to improving detection.

REFERENCES

Allwood, C. M., & Granhag, P. A. (2007). Feelings of confidence and the realism of confidence judgments in everyday life. In *Judgment and decision making* (pp. 131–154). Psychology Press.

Anderson, D. E., DePaulo, B. M., & Ansfield, M. E. (2002). The development of deception detection skill: A longitudinal study of same-sex friends. *Personality and Social Psychology Bulletin, 28*(4), 536–545.

Bogaard, G., & Meijer, E. H. (2018). Self-Reported beliefs about verbal cues correlate with deception-detection performance. *Applied Cognitive Psychology, 32*(1), 129–137.

Bogaard, G., Meijer, E. H., Vrij, A., & Merckelbach, H. (2016). Strong, but wrong: Lay people's and police officers' beliefs about verbal and nonverbal cues to deception. *PloS One, 11*(6), e0156615.

Bogaert, A. F., & Fisher, W. A. (1995). Predictors of university men's number of sexual partners. *Journal of Sex Research, 32*(2), 119–130.

Bond Jr, C. F., & DePaulo, B. M. (2006). Accuracy of deception judgments. *Personality and Social Psychology Review, 10*(3), 214–234.

Burgoon, J. K., Blair, J. P., & Strom, R. E. (2008). Cognitive biases and nonverbal cue availability in detecting deception. *Human Communication Research, 34*(4), 572–599.

Caso, L., Maricchiolo, F., Bonaiuto, M., Vrij, A., & Mann, S. (2006). The impact of deception and suspicion on different hand movements. *Journal of Nonverbal Behavior, 30*(1), 1–19.

Denault, V., & Dunbar, N. (2017). Nonverbal communication in courtrooms: Scientific assessments or modern trials by ordeal. *The Advocates' Quarterly, 47*, 280.

Ein-Dor, T., Mikulincer, M., Doron, G., & Shaver, P. R. (2010). The attachment paradox: How can so many of us (the insecure ones) have no adaptive advantages? *Perspectives on Psychological Science, 5*(2), 123–141.

Ein-Dor, T., & Perry-Paldi, A. (2014). Full house of fears: Evidence that people high in attachment anxiety are more accurate in detecting deceit. *Journal of Personality, 82*(2), 83–92.

Ein-Dor, T., Perry-Paldi, A., Zohar-Cohen, K., Efrati, Y., & Hirschberger, G. (2017). It takes an insecure liar to catch a liar: The link between attachment insecurity, deception, and detection of deception. *Personality and Individual Differences, 113*, 81–87.

Ekman, P. (2001). *Telling lies: Clues to deceit in the marketplace, politics and marriage*. Norton. (Original work published 1985).

Etcheverry, P. E., Le, B., Wu, T. F., & Wei, M. (2013). Attachment and the investment model: Predictors of relationship commitment, maintenance, and persistence. *Personal Relationships, 20*(3), 546–567.

Etcoff, N. L., Ekman, P., Magee, J. J., & Frank, M. G. (2000). Lie detection and language comprehension. *Nature*, *405*(6783), 139.

Freud, S. (1953 [1905]). Three essays on the theory of sexuality. In *The standard edition of the complete psychological works of Sigmund Freud, volume VII (1901–1905): A case of hysteria, three essays on sexuality and other works* (pp. 123–246). Psychoanalytic Electronic Publishing.

Giolla, E. M., Granhag, P. A., & Vernham, Z. (2017). Drawing-based deception detection techniques: A state-of-the-art review. *Crime Psychology Review*, *3*(1), 23–38.

Global Deception Research Team. (2006). A world of lies. *Journal of Cross-cultural Psychology*, *37*(1), 60–74.

Granhag, P. A., Andersson, L. O., Strömwall, L. A., & Hartwig, M. (2004). Imprisoned knowledge: Criminals' beliefs about deception. *Legal and Criminological Psychology*, *9*(1), 103–119.

Grézes, J., Frith, C., & Passingham, R. E. (2004). Brain mechanisms for inferring deceit in the actions of others. *Journal of Neuroscience*, *24*(24), 5500–5505.

Hartwig, M., & Bond Jr, C. F. (2014). Lie detection from multiple cues: A meta-analysis. *Applied Cognitive Psychology*, *28*(5), 661–676.

Hartwig, M., Granhag, P. A., Strömwall, L. A., & Andersson, L. O. (2004). Suspicious minds: Criminals' ability to detect deception. *Psychology, Crime and Law*, *10*(1), 83–95.

Hines, A., Colwell, K., Hiscock-Anisman, C., Garrett, E., Ansarra, R., & Montalvo, L. (2010). Impression management strategies of deceivers and honest reporters in an investigative interview. *European Journal of Psychology Applied to Legal Context*, *2*(1).

Hughes, S. M., & Harrison, M. A. (2017). Your cheatin' voice will tell on you: Detection of past infidelity from voice. *Evolutionary Psychology*, *15*(2), https://doi.org/10.1177/1474704917711513.

Jensen, E. N., Svebak, S., & Götestam, K. G. (2004). A descriptive study of personality, health and stress in high school students (16–19 years old). *The European Journal of Psychiatry*, *18*(3), 153–162.

Johnson, M. K., Foley, M. A., Suengas, A. G., & Raye, C. L. (1988). Phenomenal characteristics of memories for perceived and imagined autobiographical events. *Journal of Experimental Psychology: General*, *117*(4), 371.

Jupe, L., Akehurst, L., Vernham, Z., & Allen, J. (2016). Teenage offenders' ability to detect deception in their peers. *Applied Cognitive Psychology*, *30*(3), 401–408.

Klein, N., & Epley, N. (2015). Group discussion improves lie detection. *Proceedings of the National Academy of Sciences*, *112*(24), 7460–7465.

Kleinmuntz, B., & Szucko, J. J. (1984). Lie detection in ancient and modern times: A call for contemporary scientific study. *American Psychologist*, *39*(7), 766.

Leach, A. M., Ammar, N., England, D. N., Remigio, L. M., Kleinberg, B., & Verschuere, B. J. (2016). Less is more? Detecting lies in veiled witnesses. *Law and Human Behavior*, *40*(4), 401.

Leal, S., Vrij, A., Mann, S., & Fisher, R. P. (2010). Detecting true and false opinions: The Devil's Advocate approach as a lie detection aid. *Acta psychologica*, *134*(3), 323–329.

Leins, D., Fisher, R. P., Vrij, A., Leal, S., & Mann, S. (2011). Using sketch drawing to induce inconsistency in liars. *Legal and Criminological Psychology*, *16*(2), 253–265.

Mann, S. A., Vrij, A., Fisher, R. P., & Robinson, M. (2008). See no lies, hear no lies: Differences in discrimination accuracy and response bias when watching or listening to police suspect interviews. *Applied Cognitive Psychology: The Official Journal of the Society for Applied Research in Memory and Cognition*, *22*(8), 1062–1071.

Meyer, P. (2011). *How to spot a liar*. Retrieved February 7, 2022, from www.ted.com/talks/pamela_meyer_how_to_spot_a_liar?language=en

Patterson, J., & Kim, P. (1991). *The day America told the truth: What people really believe about everything that really matters*. Prentice Hall.

Schindler, S., Wagner, L. K., Reinhard, M. A., Ruhara, N., Pfattheicher, S., & Nitschke, J. (2021). Are criminals better lie detectors? Investigating offenders' abilities in the context of deception detection. *Applied Cognitive Psychology*, *35*(1), 203–214.

Shaw, H., & Lyons, M. (2017). Lie detection accuracy – The role of age and the use of emotions as a reliable cue. *Journal of Police and Criminal Psychology*, *32*(4), 300–304.

Strömwall, L. A., & Granhag, P. A. (2003). How to detect deception? Arresting the beliefs of police officers, prosecutors and judges. *Psychology, Crime and Law*, *9*(1), 19–36.

Strömwall, L. A., Granhag, P. A., & Jonsson, A. C. (2003). Deception among pairs: "Let's say we had lunch and hope they will swallow it!" Deception among pairs. *Psychology, Crime & Law*, *9*(2), 109–124.

ten Brinke, L., Stimson, D., & Carney, D. R. (2014). Some evidence for unconscious lie detection. *Psychological Science*, *25*(5), 1098–1105.

ten Brinke, L., Vohs, K. D., & Carney, D. R. (2016). Can ordinary people detect deception after all? *Trends in Cognitive Sciences*, *20*(8), 579–588.

van't Veer, A. E., Gallucci, M., Stel, M., & Beest, I. V. (2015). Unconscious deception detection measured by finger skin temperature and indirect veracity judgments – results of a registered report. *Frontiers in Psychology*, *6*, 672.

van Veldhuizen, T. S., Maas, R. P., Horselenberg, R., & van Koppen, P. J. (2018). Establishing origin: Analysing the questions asked in asylum interviews. *Psychiatry, Psychology and Law*, *25*(2), 283–302.

Vrij, A., & Baxter, M. (1999). Accuracy and confidence in detecting truths andlies in elaborations and denials: Truth bias, lie bias and individual differences. *Expert Evidence*, *7*(1), 25–36.

Vrij, A., Edward, K., Roberts, K. P., & Bull, R. (2000). Detecting deceit via analysis of verbal and nonverbal behavior. *Journal of Nonverbal Behavior*, *24*(4), 239–263.

Vrij, A., & Granhag, P. A. (2012). Eliciting cues to deception and truth: What matters are the questions asked. *Journal of Applied Research in Memory and Cognition*, *1*(2), 110–117.

Vrij, A., Granhag, P. A., Mann, S., & Leal, S. (2011). Outsmarting the liars: Toward a cognitive lie detection approach. *Current Directions in Psychological Science*, *20*(1), 28–32.

Vrij, A., Granhag, P. A., & Porter, S. (2010). Pitfalls and opportunities in nonverbal and verbal lie detection. *Psychological Science in the Public Interest*, *11*(3), 89–121.

Vrij, A., Leal, S., Granhag, P. A., Mann, S., Fisher, R. P., Hillman, J., & Sperry, K. (2009). Outsmarting the liars: The benefit of asking unanticipated questions. *Law and Human Behavior, 33*(2), 159–166.

Vrij, A., Leal, S., Mann, S., Warmelink, L., Granhag, P. A., & Fisher, R. P. (2010). Drawings as an innovative and successful lie detection tool. *Applied Cognitive Psychology, 24*(4), 587–594.

Vrij, A., Mann, S., Leal, S., & Granhag, P. A. (2010). Getting into the minds of pairs of liars and truth tellers: An examination of their strategies. *The Open Criminology Journal, 3*(1).

Wallace, F. R. (1976). *Poker: A guaranteed income for life by using the advanced concepts of poker*. I&O Publishing.

Wheeler, B. C. (2010). Production and perception of situationally variable alarm calls in wild tufted capuchin monkeys (Cebus apella nigritus). *Behavioral Ecology and Sociobiology, 64*(6), 989–1000.

Zloteanu, M., Salman, N., & Richardson, D. C. (2019). *Looking guilty: Handcuffing suspects influences judgments of deception*. Unpublished manuscript.

Chapter 8

Can you spot a criminal?

This chapter deals with a controversial issue from forensic and criminological psychology. Do criminals look different from non-criminals? Would you be able to identify a criminal from looks alone? The chapter takes us back initially to Victorian times when the idea first became apparent but brings us up to the present day in terms of our understanding of this topic. Evidence suggests that criminal stereotypes are frequently employed when asked to identify a suspect but what constitutes a criminal stereotype? Experimental evidence suggests that a number of features associated with unattractiveness may be to blame. Taking a critical view of the research, this chapter ends with consideration of the self-fulfilling prophecy and explores the implications of this area of research by asking why does it matter at all?

■ **Figure 8.1** Do criminals "look" different from law abiding individuals?

DOI: 10.4324/9781003329763-8

Time for a spot of time-travelling readers. Let's go back to 1859. We are in a place called Pavia, in Italy and we are in the army where we meet a person called Cesare Lombroso, whom we are told is the army surgeon. Lombroso trained in medicine at the local university where he obtained his degree in 1858. Take note of this man, because just a few years on from here, he will become established as the father of modern criminology and the most famous Italian thinker of his era. There will be a museum dedicated to his work and over 30 books and 1,000 articles published in his name (Gibson & Rafter, 2006). More importantly, he will play a vital part in our next story of applied psychology.

THE "CRIMINAL TYPE"

Lombroso's main claim to fame was back in Victorian times, when he proposed a theory of the born criminal "delinquent nato". Lombroso (1876/2006) believed that there were a number of physical abnormalities associated with criminality and his medical background prepared him well to explore this further. He worked not only with soldiers but also with asylum residents and prison inmates. Word has it that his interest was particularly sparked by a notorious thief called Giuseppe Villella. When he died, a post-mortem revealed an indentation at the back of his skull. This was not dissimilar from that seen in apes and Lombroso began to develop a theory of criminals as atavistic. That is, they are individuals who have regressed to an earlier evolutionary way of living and so represent a different type of human (Jones, 2008).

In his book *Criminal Man* first published in 1876, he listed a number of characteristics that set criminals apart from other people. These characteristics were identified as a result of extensive measurements of not only things such as arm spans, weight and height but also measurements of skulls as part of autopsies. Lombroso studied over 300 Italian criminals, claiming that 43% of them had 5 or more of the characteristics he had identified.

He characterised, amongst others, the appearance of a murderer: hawk-nose, strong jaw, thin lips, bloodshot eyes, scanty beard and dark, abundant hair. How about an arsonist? Well Lombroso observed a preponderance of thick, straight hair and a childlike appearance. As for thieves, they were more likely to have distorted or squashed noses, thick and close eyebrows, sloping foreheads and jug ears. This was very much focused on male criminals of course. But female criminals didn't escape Lombroso's gaze.

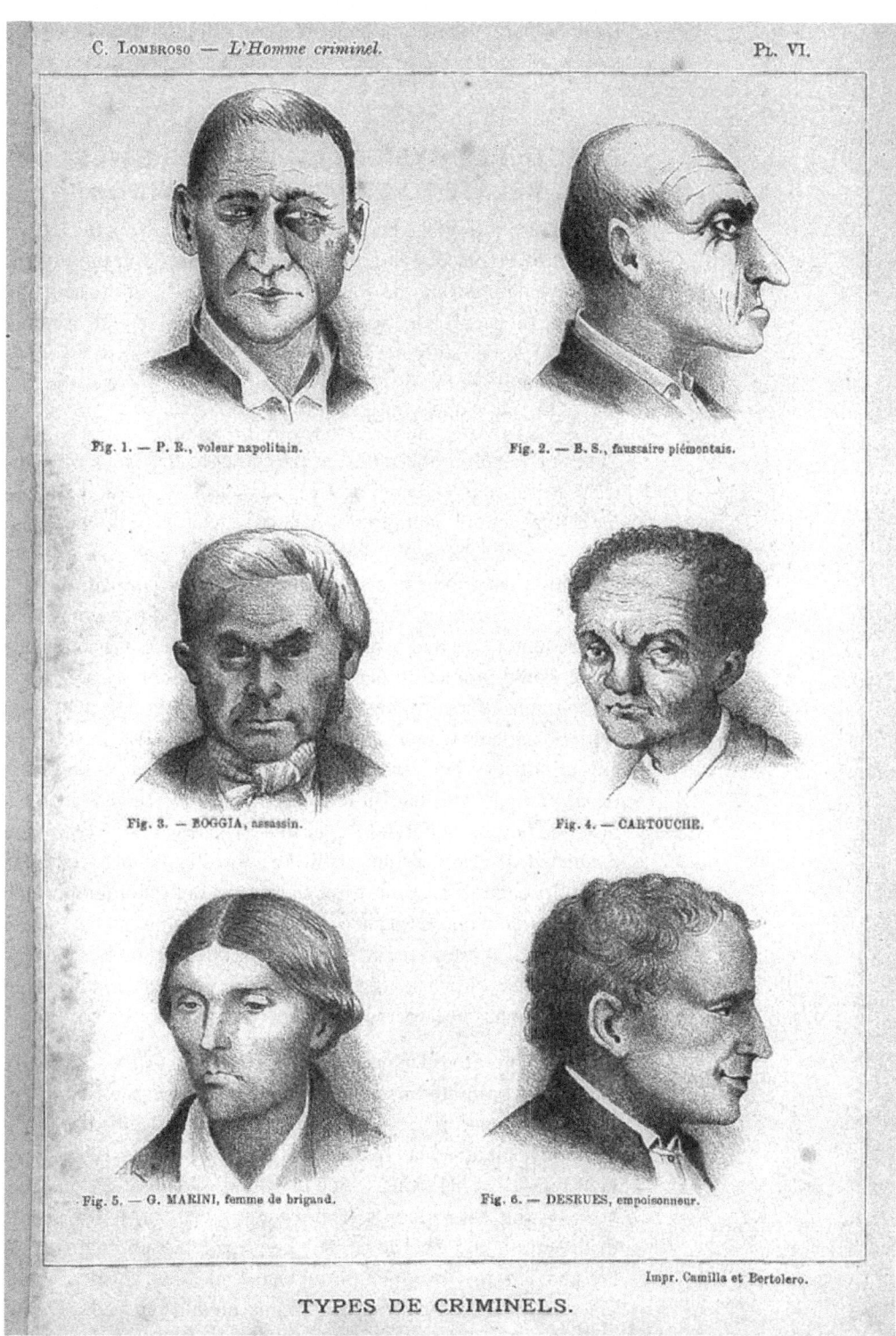

■ **Figure 8.2** Sketches by Lombroso depicting head shots of criminals.

He thought they were similar to men and were so unattractive that they were better able to adapt to an unappealing environment.

ARE THERE PHYSICAL CHARACTERISTICS THAT RELATE TO CRIMINAL BEHAVIOUR?

Ok so that was in Victorian times and Lombroso's work did indeed fall out of favour due largely to the role it played in the Eugenics movement during the Nazi era in particular. But the idea that there are physical characteristics that are associated with criminal behaviour is certainly not forgotten. In fact, in recent years it has seen something of a resurgence due to the concerns over the role it may play in courts of law.

First, let's explore the more recent evidence that links physical characteristics to criminality. I want you to imagine that you are looking at school photographs of people who were in your class in secondary school. Do you think you could make an accurate prediction from their photo of whether they had turned to criminality? Research reported by Royer (2018) suggests you might just be able to do this, and do this at a level greater than chance alone would predict. In her first study, Royer took the yearbook photographs of high school seniors. Half of the photographs used were of students who had since turned to criminality and not just any criminality but violent criminality! All of the photos were of white men who had little facial hair. None of the depicted men had tattoos. What did Royer find? Those who had been later convicted of criminal activity were more likely to be rated as likely to commit a crime from their yearbook photograph than those who had not. Of course, as Royer herself points out, we do not know if these individuals had committed crime before they left high school but the idea that we can detect criminality from appearance has been demonstrated in other contexts also.

In 1939, Thornton decided to ask participants to try to identify the crime committed by convicts from the Nebraska State Penitentiary. He was a wise man, Thornton, as he decided to try to avoid investigator bias by not looking at the photos of the convicts himself in selecting which ones to use in his study. Instead, he used the case records. Having narrowed down his search to 20 criminals, Thornton then presented the photographs of the convicts to 14 groups of students and asked them to make a note of which crime they had committed. They had a choice of four crimes to choose from for each individual, for example, for photograph 1, they could choose from arson, swindling, manslaughter, kidnapping. Swindling, in case you are wondering, is where people deceive others for the purpose of depriving someone of money or possessions. Again, the participants were able to make accurate judgements of what crime each person had committed using just the cues from their appearance in the photographs alone.

Even with more advanced technology than was probably available to Thornton in 1939, similar results have been reported. Johnson et al. (2018) used a series of photos taken from the NimStim photo catalogue (Tottenham, 2007) and photos from a Crime and Capital Punishment website to see if participants could reliably distinguish criminals from non-criminals. They used an application called Windows Paint to make sure only the head was shown and used Google Forms to create a survey to collect participants' views on whether the person shown was a criminal or not. Not only did participants discriminate between the two groups at a level greater than chance but this ability showed no relationship to demographic factors such as gender or career path.

Our view of what a criminal looks like is so pervasive that when asked to select faces which fit criminal or non-criminal occupations, we tend to show a high level of agreement (Yarmey, 1993). In a study that took as inspiration the work of Goldstein et al. (1984), participants were asked to rate each of 30 target individuals (white, male volunteers) in terms of nine personality traits and six voice characteristics. The personality traits included things like weak-strong, straightforward-deceitful and vulnerable-invulnerable. They were then given one additional trial in which they were asked to choose which person best represented each of the following: a mass murderer, a sexual assault criminal, an armed robber, a clergyman, a medical doctor and an engineer. Only one person could be chosen for each.

Far from being a random choice, the participants showed considerable agreement on who fitted the occupational descriptions best. That is, they were able to identify good exemplars for the "good guys" and the "bad guys" and did so with significant confidence, selecting similar personality traits for these individuals. Goldstein et al. (1984) suggest that we have a template for what a prototypical criminal looks like and this is what we compare with visual representations of individuals to make a judgement. This interpretation sits well with that of Shoemaker et al. (1973) who reported that participants showed a significant level of consistency in their choice of which individual was most or least likely to be associated with a particular crime. They compared four crimes: murder, robbery, treason and homosexuality. Bear in mind that this was a study done in the 1970s! Not only was there high consensus in the judgements made but these stereotypes were also associated with judgements of guilt or innocence. The only exception, importantly, was homosexuality. As the authors themselves claim, this was perceived as a different kind of deviance which suggests it shouldn't be classified as a crime at all. Thankfully, society agreed.

So in terms of Lombroso's ideas, the association of physical appearance and criminality is still pervasive. One word of caution is offered by Valla et al. (2011). They presented participants with a series of photographs, half of which were of criminals. Not only did they ask participants whether the person shown was likely to be a criminal, but if they did suspect criminality, they asked them to judge the likelihood that that person was a violent or non-violent criminal and the likelihood that they committed a specific crime from murder, rape, forgery or theft. Even with just the static photographs to go by, participants were significantly better than chance at distinguishing criminals from non-criminals. However, they were not able to identify the individual criminal sub-types and rapists were considered to be the least likely to have committed any crime.

These results suggest that the stereotype we use is more likely to represent what Gottfredson and Hirschi (1990) refer to as a "general theory of crime". That is, the stereotype helps us distinguish those who show a propensity for crime but not what type of crime they may produce. The fact that rapists escape this distinction is explained by Valla et al. in terms of deception. To be successful in committing their crime, rapists have to gain access to their victims. If they appear attractive, this can deceive their victims into finding them non-threatening. And the idea of attractiveness as a factor in our criminal stereotypes is exactly where we will journey to next.

SO WHAT DOES THIS CRIMINAL STEREOTYPE LOOK LIKE?

Imagine you have been asked to sketch what you think a criminal looks like. What would your sketch look like? Give it a try. MacLin and Herrera (2006) didn't ask their participants to sketch but they did ask them to list the top 10 things they thought of when they heard the word criminal along with details of clothing and hair that they associated with criminals. One of the words frequently mentioned was male. In terms of the clothing and hair descriptors, baggy, black clothing featured prominently and long or shaggy dark hair was frequently mentioned. Criminals were seen to have beady eyes, facial hair, scars and tattoos. It doesn't paint a very attractive picture, does it? Unfortunately, these results are consistent with others in this area. For example, Madriz (1997) reported dominant images of criminals amongst women which described the typical criminal as weird, dirty, tall and big. It would seem that being unattractive is very much a part of the criminal stereotype consistent with Cavior, Hayes and Cavior's claim, in 1975, that low levels of attractiveness contribute to criminal careers.

Shepherd et al. (1978) presented female participants with a target photograph. The person in the photograph was described as either being a brutal murderer or as being a lifeboat captain. The photo was then removed and the participants were asked to construct an accurate Photofit of the person they had seen in the photograph. Photofits are reconstruction devices which have lots of different photographic examples of five facial features. A witness is usually asked to try to construct a face that matches the suspect using a combination of these.

Independent raters were asked to rate the Photofit images that the participants had created using a series of dichotomous scales such as good-looking-unattractive. When the person was described as a murderer, the Photofit produced was rated as less good-looking than when the person was described as a lifeboat captain. Criminality, it seemed, was associated with being unattractive.

Royer (2018) reported that attractiveness correlated strongly with whether participants thought a person in a photograph was guilty of a criminal act. Ten mugshots of men who had been convicted of violent crime were interspersed with 10 mugshots of men who had been convicted but then later exonerated of violent crimes. Participants were asked to judge whether the person in each photograph was guilty or not of violent crime. Consistent with previous studies, convicted criminals were more likely than those who had been exonerated to be seen as guilty. Furthermore, this was more likely to be the case if the man was seen to be aggressive and less so if the man was seen to be physically attractive. Seeing a man as attractive leads us to believe that they are less likely to do unpleasant things (Eagly et al., 1991).

So, what constitutes attractiveness in this context? Zebrowitz and Montepare (1992) suggest babyfaceness helps. One of the key characteristics of a baby face is large eyes. Large eyes are seen to be synonymous with innocence and honesty. Berry and McArthur (1985) for example reported that eye size correlated with perceived honesty in a study where participants were asked to view male faces. Zebrowitz et al. also argue that baby faces have more symmetry than mature adult faces. The older we get, the more adverse environmental influences we come across and the less symmetry in our musculature. Zebrowitz reported a strong correlation between facial symmetry and attractiveness at almost every age and this itself was correlated with perceived honesty. Klatt et al. (2016) also add high cheekbones and thick lips to the list of babyface characteristics which is beginning to sound a little like the description offered in Victorian times by Lombroso.

Conversely, facial hair can lead to perceptions of greater maturity, dominance and potentially aggression which can strengthen criminal stereotypes. Neave and Shields (2008) constructed a series of faces of male individuals possessing five levels of facial hair from clean-shaven through to full bearded. As the amount of facial hair present increased, so did the perception of dominance and aggression. The optimum level for attractiveness however, was light stubble.

Aggression as a key part of the criminal stereotype is particularly relevant for violent crime. High levels of aggression are linked with the male hormone testosterone (Dabbs, 2000) and Stillman et al. (2010) suggest it can underlie assumptions about whether someone is a violent or non-violent criminal. They presented participants with photographs of 84 violent or non-violent sex offenders and asked them to distinguish which was which. They could indeed do this at a level significantly greater than chance. Quite impressive as the photos were shown for only 2 seconds! What were they using to make these judgements? According to Stillman and colleagues, signs of high testosterone, that is heavier

■ **Figure 8.3** Taken from Neave and Shields (2008). An example of one of the faces showing the difference degrees of facial hair used.

brows and signs of high physical strength. It is interesting to note that being happy was associated with less likelihood of violence. Being happy was also associated with low levels of criminality in Flowe's (2012) study and it is to that study that we shall travel next.

WHY ARE HONESTY AND DOMINANCE SO IMPORTANT?

Flowe used not only police mugshots of individuals but also photographs that had been manipulated to vary the expression the person was showing on their face. In some, the person was shown as being happy, in another as wearing a neutral expression and the third, shown looking angry. All photographs were presented on a computer screen. Participants not only rated criminal appearance but also other attributes such as trustworthiness and dominance.

As trustworthiness went up, criminality judgements decreased. In contrast, as dominance increased, criminality judgements went

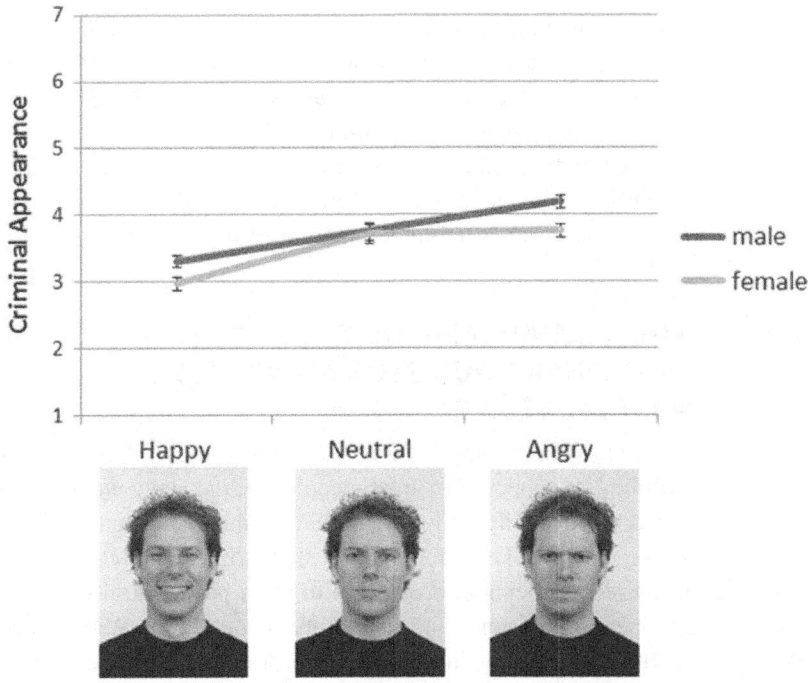

■ **Figure 8.4** Ratings of criminal appearance associated with each emotional expression condition and actor gender.

up. Criminality seemed to be seen as synonymous with threat. How about the emotional expressions? Angry faces were more likely to be judged as criminal and as less trustworthy. Happy expressions on the other hand, were associated with lower criminality ratings. According to Flowe (2012), understanding the criminal stereotype can be reduced to a 2D model. Being alert to honesty (or trustworthiness) and dominance seem to underpin this and may have evolutionary adaptive value. Knowing who to approach and who to avoid could be a life saving decision. It makes sense then that these decisions are made rapidly. Research conducted by Klatt et al. (2016) suggests that even the briefest of exposures to a face (less than 100ms!) is sufficient for these judgements to be made, suggesting a role to play for intuition.

Porter et al. (2008) demonstrated a similar finding but using the faces of Nobel Prize winners and America's Most Wanted Criminals. Would you be able to tell the difference? And how long would it take you? Porter's participants were as accurate if they saw the faces for 100 milliseconds as if they saw them for 30 seconds. In line with previous findings, aggressiveness was used as a dimension to make the decision along with perceived kindness, perhaps an indicator or trustworthiness? What Porter et al. did report however, was that the participants were more accurate at judging trustworthy faces than untrustworthy, suggesting we like to think the best of people and it is worth noting that in 40% of cases, inaccurate assessments were made – our criminal stereotype is not fool-proof. In fact, as Porter and ten Brinke (2009) point out, even the British Prime Minister, Neville Chamberlain made an error when he described Hitler as a man who could be relied upon after their meeting in 1938!

THE SELF-FULFILLING PROPHECY AND WHERE OUR STORY BECOMES A LITTLE LESS CLEAR

Perhaps what is happening here is something called the self-fulfilling prophecy. We treat people with certain unattractive facial features differently and this causes their behaviour to differ in response. We know for example that attractive individuals are often seen as being in possession of other positive traits such as kindness, intelligence and sociability (Dion, 1972). When asked to rate nursery children in terms of IQ, peer friendships and future educational potential, teachers have been shown to be influenced by the attractiveness of the child in a photograph. Even when the child's report card says exactly the same as everyone else's, they may get a more favourable rating if their photo is seen to be attractive (Clifford & Walster, 1973). (Incidentally, a similar phenomenon has been found with the marking of undergraduate students' essays by Bull & Stevens, 1979).

Perhaps, individuals who are seen to be less attractive are treated differently and criminality is one response to this. Zebrowtiz et al. (1996) reported that there was a marginal tendency for men who had been rated as honest looking early on in life to be become more honest in later years. Honest looks elicit trust in others which may in itself encourage honesty going forward. However, this only worked for men. For women, Zebrowitz claims, it might work slightly differently. Those who looked less honest early in life tended to become more honest looking in later years. Would this enable them to be more successful in their lying? Whether this in indeed the case remains to be seen but it does highlight the importance of assessing gender effects in research in this area.

Treating individuals in accordance with their looks can, however, backfire in certain groups according to Zebrowitz et al. (1998). Take the babyfaceness concept. This is often associated with child-like traits such as innocence but also with weakness. Zebrowitz studied adolescent boys from middle- and lower-class backgrounds. Those who were seen to have more babyfaceness were actually more likely than those with more mature faces to be delinquent but only if their background was one of a low socio-economic class. Zebrowitz et al. describe this as a compensation effect, compensating for the child-like traits that are attributed to them. Boys from more middle-class backgrounds also compensated but by showing heightened academic achievement due to higher motivation. Babyfacedness however had no similar effects in adolescent girls, again highlighting the importance of gender to these effects.

WHY DOES IT MATTER?

We started our story back in Victorian times with Lombroso and his study of skulls. Why are we still so interested in the idea that we can tell a criminal by looks alone? The answer is clear. It can have a significant impact on matters of justice. Let's take a deeper look.

Porter et al. (2008) reported that after the 9/11 attacks in America, the transportation agency in the United States developed training aimed at enabling airport staff to identify threats by reading faces. Not a new idea as in 1978, Robinson published a book in which he talked about the sixth sense policemen had when it came to identifying criminals. In the most skilled policemen, he claimed, they could not only recognise a criminal but also identify the type of conviction that criminal had.

It sounds as though our criminal stereotype is going to be useful in legal contexts. However, there are a number of reasons to be cautious. To understand why, I want you to imagine you are a juror, sitting in a court of law. In front of you, you see the defendant. What is going to influence your judgement of guilty versus innocent? Evidence you might think. Well yes, it does. But that's not all that is likely to influence your judgement. Imagine that that defendant matches your criminal stereotype. Chances are that you will not need to hear as much evidence before you reach a guilty verdict (Porter et al., 2010). Particularly if the defendant has a mature rather than a baby face, you are likely to not only find them guilty more often but also to consider them as having acted intentionally (Zebrowitz & McDonald, 1991).

Remember also that in some studies, it has been claimed that we can identify what crimes individuals have committed from their face alone (although Valla et al. beg to differ here). Does this have any bearing on judicial decisions? Dumas and Testé (2006) certainly think so. They wanted to try to replicate the legal decision-making process as closely as possible so gave their participants information about the principle of presumption of innocence and the concept of reasonable doubt. Participants were asked to read a written case summary and were able to see a picture of the defendant on the back. Unbeknownst to the participants, the photographs had already been categorised by a group of individuals, taken from a range of sectors in society, according to the type of crime they thought the person had committed. Each of the people photographed, they were told, had been convicted of one of the crimes listed. As in previous studies, there was a high level of agreement in terms of which faces were associated with which crimes.

The case summaries contained the legal definition of the offence that the defendant was accused of as well as both the defendant's and prosecutor's evidence. Was the suspect guilty? If so, what sort of sentence should they receive? How attractive would you say they were and how mature do they look? The decision of guilty versus innocent was heavily influenced by the picture accompanying the case summary. If the face was congruent with the offence mentioned, guilty verdicts were more likely to be given than innocent verdicts. If the suspect also had a mature face, they would be given longer sentences. This was the case regardless of how strong the prosecution evidence was against them. Dumas and Testé did note however, that attractiveness had little impact. This is in contrast to many studies that suggest physical attractiveness can reduce the chances of conviction (Efran, 1974; Kulka & Kessler, 1978) although others have suggested that it is the victim's level of attractiveness that can sway decisions (Villemur & Hyde, 1983).

In the de-briefing after their study, Dumas and Testé reported that participants frequently declared that they had not been influenced by the photograph, claiming that they had not paid much attention to it, if at all. Lown (1977) similarly has suggested that jurors may not be aware they even hold a criminal stereotype.

It isn't just significant criminal cases such as armed robbery or murder cases that are affected by our criminal stereotypes. Zebrowitz and McDonald (1991) demonstrated the influence of the criminal stereotype in small claims courts also. They observed 506 cases that had gone to the small claims courts in Massachusetts. Those having more of a baby face were more likely to win their cases if they involved intentional actions than those with more mature faces. If the defendant had a more mature face, they would be faced with having to pay larger payouts to plaintiffs if the plaintiff had a baby face.

Given the influence of the photograph on judgements, it is interesting to note that the Supreme Court of Canada, in 1993, ruled that jurors should be able to view a witness's face as it is an important cue to how trustworthy that person is. The automatic impressions we form of trustworthiness can influence how credible we see that evidence as outlined in Porter and ten Brinke's Dangerous Decisions Theory (DDT). In 2009, they outlined how assessments of whether a suspect is guilty or not can be influenced so heavily by facial appearance that they may in fact be irrational. Our initial "instinctive" assessments can colour our judgements made afterwards, leading to bias (Kahneman et al., 1982). Ask and Granhag (2007) refer to the tendency to be more sceptical of evidence that counteracts our initial beliefs as "asymmetrical scepticism".

It is possible, Porter et al. suggest, that judges are more likely to favour evidence that supports their initial instantaneous judgement. Porter and ten Brinke tested this using two severe crime vignettes and two minor crime vignettes. For each, participants were party to five sets of ambiguous evidence, five pieces of incriminating evidence and a piece of exonerating evidence. The photograph associated with each crime vignette was varied so that trustworthy and untrustworthy pictures were paired equally.

Less evidence was required for an untrustworthy looking individual to be found guilty of a severe crime. Given the same crime, those who were rated as looking untrustworthy were found guilty on the basis of fewer than five pieces of evidence on average. To convict someone who looked more trustworthy, more evidence was required. Not only did the photographs affect verdicts, they also affected confidence in the jurors. Confidence was much higher when declaring an untrustworthy suspect to be guilty than a trustworthy one. This was only the case however for severe crime.

THE CRIMINAL STEREOTYPE CAN INFLUENCE US EVEN BEFORE A CASE GETS TO COURT

So far we have explored the implications for jury decision-making in court cases. However, the criminal stereotype can also affect criminal cases even before the court process begins. Eyewitnesses may be required to identify a suspect from within a line of distractors in a police identity parade. Given the strength of our criminal stereotype, how might this affect judgements? MacLin and Malpass (2001) suggest that if there is an innocent person in the line-up who fits our criminal stereotype in terms of their appearance, we may be drawn to select them on this basis alone, with the result that the true criminal goes undetected. Flowe and Humphries (2011) used 11 police cases where a 6-person identity line-up had been employed to identify a suspect. In 6 of the 11 cases, the suspect had pleaded guilty.

Eyewitness descriptions were taken from the Crime Incident Reports and included information about physical appearance. Half of the participants were given a written physical description of the suspect along with the lineups showing the suspect and distractor individuals. The other half of participants were not given any accompanying description. Could their mock witnesses identify the suspect?

When no description was given, participants reported basing their judgement on criminal appearance. When a description was provided, this was used instead as the basis for the judgement given. Having the description did not increase the probability that the police suspect was identified however. Given the unreliability of eyewitness testimony or the fact that it is often weak in criminal cases, this does suggest that the criminal stereotype may introduce bias into the identification of a suspect. Indeed, in a second study, Flowe and Humphries reported that faces rated high in criminality were chosen more often when no description was provided. Even the eyewitnesses themselves may be influenced by the criminal stereotype as MacLin and MacLin (2004) reported. Faces that match our criminal stereotype are more likely to be remembered than those that don't.

PHYSICAL APPEARANCE IMPLICATIONS FOR CRIMINALS

The evidence pretty clearly points to a strong effect of appearance on criminal judgements, whether this is in a court of law or even in eyewitness identification. However, there is a more sinister side to our story and that is found when we explore the implications for convicted criminals themselves. Back in 1973, Longacre published a book called *Rehabilitation for the facially disfigured*. In this book, he raised the possibility of plastic surgery as a way of preventing further delinquent behaviour. It would be unfair to rest this one entirely on the shoulders of Longacre however as even back in 1966 Spira et al. were evaluating the effects of having plastic surgery on recidivism in Texas. Plastic surgery, Spira et al. claimed, was a way of helping an individual adjust satisfactorily to society once released. It wasn't just in Texas however that this was occurring. Spira reported that plastic surgery was being carried out on inmates in over 20 states in the United States and the results were striking. In one group of prisoners, re-offending occurred in only 17% of those who had received plastic surgery compared to 32% in those who had not.

Bull (1982) discusses the research of Lewison (1974) who published the results of a 20- year long study involving over 900 Canadian prisoners. Of 200 inmates who were seeking some form of facial surgery, 100 were selected randomly for treatment. Their recidivism rate was 48%, a lot steeper than that reported by Spira and colleagues. However, compared to those who were not selected, it was again striking. Of those who had not received surgery, 69% re-offended.

However, not all studies of plastic surgery and criminality have found equally impressive results. Meyer et al. (1973) for example offered plastic surgery to 14 of 21 individuals, some of whom have been identified as "delinquent" by the authorities and some of whom have come from areas seen to be high risk for criminality. One year later, improvement on a range of scores was measured. No difference was found between those who had had plastic surgery and those who had not.

In a review of studies in this area, Thompson (1990) points to a number of methodological failings of earlier studies such as the lack of random assignment to groups or the poor matching of those who did and didn't have surgery. Thompson also highlights that amongst nine studies that measured re-offending, two found no differences and one even found a higher level of recidivism following surgery. As Thompson concludes, perhaps we need to know more about the processes linking appearance and criminality before plastic surgery programmes are embraced more fully. For example, Kurtzberg et al. (1968) reported an almost equal recidivism rate for inmates who received surgery as well as social support as for those who simply received the social and vocational support alone. However, when drug addicts were removed from the analysis, those who received surgery had significantly lower recidivism rates. And that really highlights one of the additional reasons for caution in this area. Most of the studies discussed here treat criminality as a unitary concept with a fixed stereotype. As we have seen earlier in this chapter, specific faces are associated with specific crimes so we may be missing an important part of the story.

Reflecting back to where our story started, Lombroso's description of the criminal man has remained steadfast through more than a century of psychological investigation. In particular, our tendency to identify signs of trustworthiness or aggression in others may have an evolutionary origin in our drive to survive but it can also influence our judgements in less than useful ways in matters of the judiciary. It remains for future research to explore how the development of the criminal stereotype occurs, the role of the media in this and how this contributes to the nature/nurture debate around criminality itself.

REFERENCES

Ask, K., & Granhag, P. A. (2007). Motivational bias in criminal investigators' judgments of witness reliability 1. *Journal of Applied Social Psychology, 37*(3), 561–591.

Berry, D. S., & McArthur, L. Z. (1985). Some components and consequences of a babyface. *Journal of Personality and Social Psychology*, *48*(2), 312.

Bull, R. (1982). Physical appearance and criminality. *Current Psychological Reviews*, *2*(3), 269–281.

Bull, R., & Stevens, J. (1979). The effects of attractiveness of writer and penmanship on essay grades. *Journal of Occupational Psychology*, *52*(1), 53–59.

Cavior, H., Hayes, S., & Cavior, N. (1975). Physical attractiveness of female offenders. In A. Brodsky (Ed.), *The female offender*. Saga.

Clifford, M. M., & Walster, E. (1973). The effect of physical attractiveness on teacher expectations. *Sociology of Education*, 248–258.

Dabbs, J. M., & Dabbs, M. G. (2000). *Heroes, rogues, and lovers: Testosterone and behavior*. McGraw-Hill.

Dion, K., Berscheid, E., & Walster, E. (1972). What is beautiful is good. *Journal of Personality and Social Psychology*, *24*(3), 285.

Dumas, R., & Testé, B. (2006). The influence of criminal facial stereotypes on juridic judgments. *Swiss Journal of Psychology*, *65*(4), 237–244.

Eagly, A. H., Makhijani, G., Ashmore, D., & Longo, L. C. (1991). What is beautiful is good, but . . .: A meta-analytic review of the physical attractiveness stereotype. *Psychological Bulletin*, *110*, 109–128.

Efran, M. G. (1974). The effect of physical appearance on the judgment of guilt, interpersonal attraction, and severity of recommended punishment in a simulated jury task. *Journal of Research in Personality*, *8*(1), 45–54.

Flowe, H. D. (2012). Do characteristics of faces that convey trustworthiness and dominance underlie perceptions of criminality? *PLoS One*, *7*(6), e37253.

Flowe, H. D., & Humphries, J. E. (2011). An examination of criminal face bias in a random sample of police lineups. *Applied Cognitive Psychology*, *25*(2), 265–273.

Gibson, M., & Rafter, N. H. (2006). *Criminal man*. Duke University Press.

Goldstein, A. G., Chance, J. E., & Gilbert, B. (1984). Facial stereotypes of good guys and bad guys: A replication and extension. *Bulletin of the Psychonomic Society*, *22*(6), 549–552.

Gottfredson, M. R., & Hirschi, T. (1990). *A general theory of crime*. Stanford University Press.

Johnson, H., Anderson, M., Westra, H. R., & Suter, H. (2018). Inferences on criminality based on appearance. *Butler Journal of Undergraduate Research*, *4*(1), 6.

Jones, D. W. (2008). *Understanding criminal behaviour: Psychosocial approaches to criminality*. Willan Publishing.

Kahneman, D., Slovic, S. P., Slovic, P., & Tversky, A. (Eds.). (1982). *Judgment under uncertainty: Heuristics and biases*. Cambridge University Press.

Klatt, T., Maltby, J. J., Humphries, J., Smailes, H. L., Ryder, H., Phelps, M., & Flowe, H. D. (2016). Looking bad: Inferring criminality after 100 ms. *Applied Psychology in Criminal Justice*, *12*(2), 114–125.

Kulka, R. A., & Kessler, J. B. (1978). Is justice really blind?–The influence of litigant physical attractiveness on juridical judgment 1. *Journal of Applied Social Psychology*, *8*(4), 366–381.

Kurtzberg, R., Safar, H., & Cavior, N. (1968). *Surgical and social rehabilitation of adult offenders*. Proceedings of the 76th Annual Convention of The American Psychological Association.

Lewison, E. (1974). Twenty years of prison surgery: An evaluation. *Canadian Journal of Otolaryngology, 3*, 42–50.

Lombroso, C. (2006 [1876]). *Criminal man*. Duke University Press.

Longacre, J. J. (1973). *Rehabilitation of the facially disfigured*. Thomas.

Lown, C. (1977). Legal approaches to juror stereotyping by physical characteristics. *Law and Human Behavior, 1*(1), 87.

MacLin, M. K., & Herrera, V. (2006). The criminal stereotype. *North American Journal of Psychology, 8*(2), 197–208.

MacLin, O. H., & MacLin, M. K. (2004). The effect of criminality on face attractiveness, typicality, memorability and recognition. *North American Journal of Psychology, 6*(1), 145–154.

MacLin, O. H., & Malpass, R. S. (2001). Racial categorization of faces: The ambiguous race face effect. *Psychology, Public Policy, and Law, 7*(1), 98.

Madriz, E. I. (1997). Images of criminals and victims: A study on women's fear and social control. *Gender & Society, 11*(3), 342–356.

Meyer, J. K., Hoopes, J. E., Jabaley, M. E., & Allen, R. (1973). Is plastic surgery effective in the rehabilitation of deformed delinquent adolescents? *Plastic and Reconstructive Surgery, 51*(1), 53–58.

Neave, N., & Shields, K. (2008). The effects of facial hair manipulation on female perceptions of attractiveness, masculinity, and dominance in male faces. *Personality and Individual Differences, 45*(5), 373–377.

Porter, S., England, L., Juodis, M., ten Brinke, L., & Wilson, K. (2008). Is the face a window to the soul? Investigation of the accuracy of intuitive judgments of the trustworthiness of human faces. *Canadian Journal of Behavioural Science/Revue canadienne des sciences du comportement, 40*(3), 171.

Porter, S., & ten Brinke, L. (2009). Dangerous decisions: A theoretical framework for understanding how judges assess credibility in the courtroom. *Legal and Criminological Psychology, 14*(1), 119–134.

Porter, S., ten Brinke, L., & Gustaw, C. (2010). Dangerous decisions: The impact of first impressions of trustworthiness on the evaluation of legal evidence and defendant culpability. *Psychology, Crime & Law, 16*(6), 477–491.

Royer, C. E. (2018). *Convictable faces: Attributions of future criminality from facial appearance*. Cornell University.

Shepherd, J. W., Ellis, H. D., McMurran, M., & Davies, G. M. (1978). Effect of character attribution on Photofit construction of a face. *European Journal of Social Psychology, 8*(2), 263–268.

Shoemaker, D. J., South, D. R., & Lowe, J. (1973). Facial stereotypes of deviants and judgments of guilt or innocence. *Social Forces, 51*(4), 427–433.

Spira, M., Chizen, J. H., Gerow, F. J., & Hardy, S. B. (1966). Plastic surgery in the Texas prison system. *British Journal of Plastic Surgery, 19*, 364–371.

Stillman, T. F., Maner, J. K., & Baumeister, R. F. (2010). A thin slice of violence: Distinguishing violent from nonviolent sex offenders at a glance. *Evolution and Human Behavior, 31*(4), 298–303.

Thompson, K. M. (1990). Refacing inmates: A critical appraisal of plastic surgery programs in prison. *Criminal Justice and Behavior, 17*(4), 448–466.

Thornton, G. R. (1939). The ability to judge crimes from photographs of criminals: A contribution to technique. *The Journal of Abnormal and Social Psychology, 34*(3), 378.

Tottenham, N. (2007). *NimStim face stimulus* set. John D. and Catherine T. MacArthur Foundation Research Network on Early Experience and Brain Development.

Valla, J. M., Ceci, S. J., & Williams, W. M. (2011). The accuracy of inferences about criminality based on facial appearance. *Journal of Social, Evolutionary, and Cultural Psychology, 5*(1), 66.

Villemur, N. K., & Hyde, J. S. (1983). Effects of sex of defense attorney, sex of juror, and age and attractiveness of the victim on mock juror decision making in a rape case. *Sex Roles, 9*(8), 879–889.

Yarmey, A. D. (1993). Stereotypes and recognition memory for faces and voices of good guys and bad guys. *Applied Cognitive Psychology, 7*(5), 419–431.

Zebrowitz, L. A., Collins, M. A., & Dutta, R. (1998). The relationship between appearance and personality across the life span. *Personality and Social Psychology Bulletin, 24*(7), 736–749.

Zebrowitz, L. A., & McDonald, S. M. (1991). The impact of litigants' baby-facedness and attractiveness on adjudications in small claims courts. *Law and Human Behavior, 15*(6), 603–623.

Zebrowitz, L. A., & Montepare, J. M. (1992). Impressions of babyfaced individuals across the life span. *Developmental Psychology, 28*(6), 1143.

Zebrowitz, L. A., Voinescu, L., & Collins, M. A. (1996). "Wide-eyed" and" crooked-faced": Determinants of perceived and real honesty across the life span. *Personality and Social Psychology Bulletin, 22*(12), 1258–1269.

Chapter **9**

Where is a good place to live?

The theme of this chapter is to explore environmental psychology, specifically focusing on the role of green space on well-being. The chapter begins with a look at the historical origins of the idea that green space is good for us and leads us on to a critical exploration of the psychological research in this area. The effect of green space on emotions, cognition and longevity are discussed. But is it just being near green space that is important? A critical analysis of the issue follows with questions raised over whether all green space has the same effect, whether it is the green space itself that is important or how we use it, and whether pictures of green space might have the same effect. Studies from across the world are explored in an attempt to answer these questions and in the process, theories such as Attention Restoration Theory, the Biophilia Hypothesis and Perceptual Fluency Theory are examined.

■ **Figure 9.1** To what extent is green space good for our mental and physical well-being?

Take a look outside at the area where you live. Would you say that the area where you live is "good for you"? A concern with the environment in which we live dates back as far as Hippocrates. Hippocrates was a Greek doctor who has since become known as the father of medicine. Back in the time of the Ancient Greeks, he was already espousing the benefits of a scenic environment, a good climate and water quality for health. More recently, the COVID-19 epidemic has once more highlighted the importance of green space for health and well-being. So, our next adventure in applied psychology will take us on a journey through environmental psychology, to find out more.

THE LUNGS OF LONDON

In 1783, William Pitt became the youngest Prime Minister of Great Britain. His relevance for our story however is because of his turn of phrase "Lungs of London" which he used to refer to the health benefits offered by the capital's parks and squares (Jones, 2018). The phrase was later taken up by Charles Dickens who used it in a sketch he wrote for a newspaper *The Evening Chronicle* in 1835 (Mangham, 2016).

The Lungs of London phrase was used to emphasise the way that members of the public could escape the miasmas that evolved from the squalor and filth of city living (Crompton, 2017). Indeed, in 1833, a Select Commission on Public Walks was set up to survey what open space existed in London, reporting back that parks were beneficial for health, not only because they offered an escape from the miasmas but also because they offered an opportunity for exercise and would keep the working classes out of the pubs. Because of the social opportunities offered by greenspaces, it would also reduce class tension as individuals from all social classes could mix (Hoskins, 2004).

It is no accident that London was chosen as the focus for health and well-being. As Crompton (2017) explains, city living at the time of Pitt and Dickens was not pleasant. Horse dung on roads, cesspools rather than sewers and overcrowding plagued city-dwellers. Overcrowding in particular has been shown to have significant negative effects on health. Armario et al. (1984) reported that if 10 rats were put together in a cage, they showed lower body weight gain, ate less and drank more water than if they were in a less crowded cage of 3. Calhoun (1971) even reported heightened death rates, exaggerated aggression (they actually ate each others' tails!) and social withdrawal.

I know what you are thinking – yes, but these were rats. Humans are not susceptible to the same effects of crowding. But in fact, the evidence suggests we are. Living in a crowded place is not very good for us if the evidence is to be believed. In fact, it suggests you are more likely to feel ill and less likely to interact with those around you. McCain et al. (1976) for example reported higher numbers of illness complaints for prisoners who had been required to share a cell with others compared to those who had their own cell. And Valins and Baum (1973) studied the effect of crowding on university students living in student residences. Those living in a suite housing 4 or 6 students were less likely to feel crowded, and less likely to meet people when interaction was not wanted than students living in long corridors housing 34 students. When these students arrived in the laboratory, to take part in an experiment, those from the long corridor residences sat further away from a confederate who already sat waiting, spent less time looking towards them and were less likely to talk to them than those from a suite residence. The good news is that all it takes is a wall to divide the residences into smaller areas. When a wall was inserted in the middle of a long corridor in student residences, the amount of stress due to crowding decreased and friendship groups formed more readily (Baum & Davis, 1980).

GENDER EFFECTS EXIST

Not everyone reacts in the same way to crowding, however, whether mice or men. Brown and Grunberg (1995) compared the effects of crowding on male and female rats' behaviour. They either housed the rats individually or in groups of four in a small cage. In the crowded conditions, male rats showed a striking stress reaction with higher levels of corticosterone, a stress marker, in their blood. The female rats, however, showed a higher level of stress when housed individually. This gender difference has also been reported in human populations. Booth and Cowell (1976) for example suggested that males are more negatively affected by the experience of crowding compared to females and both Regoeczi (2008) and Epstein (1982) suggest that men are more likely to withdraw from social interaction in crowded situations. This effect is exacerbated if men are crowded with others who have incompatible personalities (Smith & Haythorn, 1972).

THE PHYTOPHILIC EFFECT

So, we've established that crowded living is not beneficial, particularly so for men. Women like to be with others but small groups rule. No wonder then that William Pitt was moved to emphasise the value of parks which offer plenty of open space. Parks do offer something other than just space though. Plants of all kinds are known to have a beneficial effect on emotions, something that Tifferet and Vilnai-Yavetz (2017) refer to as the Phytophilic Effect. After walking or running in a natural environment such as a park, people have been shown to experience fewer negative emotions such as anger or sadness in comparison to a synthetic environment. Bowler et al. (2010) reviewed no less than 25 studies to reach this conclusion.

There doesn't seem to be an age limit on this effect either. Talbot and Kaplan (1991) studied the effect of having an apartment that overlooked a natural setting on the satisfaction of elderly adults. Those living in a low-rise complex were more likely than those in a high-rise complex to mention specific natural elements in describing views they enjoyed such as trees and gardens. However, in both residences, 44% said that their favourite place to sit was at or near a window and those who could see natural environments through it were more likely to rate their residential satisfaction as high. This is not an isolated finding. Kaplan and Austin (2004) presented participants with black and white photographs of views showing differing levels of vegetation. When asked to indicate their preferences, the photos that were more popular were those which showed a view of nature with trees being seen as particularly relaxing.

So, satisfaction and relaxation seem to be associated with access to views of nature. A good place to live will probably have this. Time to turn our attention to some more specific benefits that might accrue with access to green space.

SPECIFIC BENEFITS ASSOCIATED WITH GREEN SPACE
You might just live longer

It's true. Takano et al. (2002) suggested this was indeed the case based on a large-scale study of over 3,000 residents of Tokyo born between 1903 and 1918. Takano studied these elderly residents for a 5-year period. Consistent with the phytophilic effect, those individuals who were able to walk down a street lined with trees, or in a local park were more likely to outlive those who couldn't.

You might perform better at work or school

Have you ever performed a digit span task? If not, try one now. Read the numbers in the table below, one row at a time. Then, without looking back at the table, try to recall them, in order. Go on, give it a go.

2, 5, 8
2, 5, 8, 2
2, 5, 8, 2, 6
2, 5, 8, 2, 6, 1
2, 5, 8, 2, 6, 1, 4
2, 5, 8, 2, 6, 1, 4, 3
2, 5, 8, 2, 6, 1, 4, 3, 9

How did you get on? Chances are, the more numbers there were to recall, the more difficult it became. Try the task again but this time, once you have read the numbers in each row, try to recall them in backwards order. This is what is known as a backwards digit-span task. So why am I suggesting you give these tasks a go? Because they are the exact tasks used by Berman, Jonides and Kaplan in 2008 to demonstrate the effects of nature on cognitive ability. Do these sort of tasks often enough and for long enough and you will probably find that your ability to attend to the digits fades as you become tired. Trying to maintain focus on the digits and block out any distractions causes fatigue. Attention Restoration Theory, proposed by Kaplan and Kaplan (1989), suggests that views of nature help to restore and replenish this sort of directed attention, which is why green space has such a positive effect on us. Berman et al. (2008) certainly agree. They gave participants the opportunity to take a 50–55-minute walk either in a tree-lined park near the university campus, away from traffic or downtown in Ann Arbor, a traffic-heavy, office-building lined street. When participants walked in nature, their performance on the backwards digit span task improved. That was not the case for those who walked the downtown route.

Given the boost to our cognitive performance, it is not surprising to learn that the benefits of views of nature are particularly noticeable in educational settings. Benfield et al. (2015) compared the feelings of undergraduate students about a college writing course they had enrolled on when they either had a view of a natural setting or a view of a concrete retaining wall through the windows. By the end of the semester, those students seeing a natural setting through the windows gave more positive ratings of the course, classroom resources and curriculum than those who saw only a brick wall. Strikingly, their grades were also higher. Benfield and colleagues suggest that perhaps the natural view restored attention more effectively and in so doing, lowered stress levels, raised mood and led to better performance on the course. I expect the tutors were pleased too with their higher ratings!

These findings hold out in university settings also. Tennessen and Cimprich (1995) studied university dormitory residents comparing the effect of having windows with more or less natural views on measures of attention. They used a range of tasks designed to measure attentional capacity. One was the Digit Span task that we mentioned earlier. One was the Necker Cube Pattern Control Test and another was the Symbol Digit Modalities Test. The Necker Cube is a 3D object that can be viewed in two different ways, dependent on what side of the cube you see as the foreground and which the background. The ability to inhibit switching attention from one to the other is seen as a test of directed or focused attention. The Symbol Digit Modalities Test requires individuals to substitute numbers for geometric symbols. In line with the findings already mentioned, those who had natural views from their windows, scored higher on all attention measures.

Regardless of your status as a student or otherwise, if you ever happen be asked to do any proof-reading, do make sure you take a nice walk in a natural environment first. Hartig et al. (1991) reported better proof-reading performance in college students who had taken a walk through a park than those who had walked through a more urban setting or those who had stayed indoors, in a comfortable setting. You might think that sitting on a comfortable sofa helps you to focus but walking through a park is far more advantageous it seems. Hartig et al. also compared proof-reading performance in three groups of individuals: those who had had no vacation, those who had a vacation in an urban environment and those who had been on a wilderness vacation. Guess who performed best? Yes, those who had been on a wilderness vacation. Hartig and colleagues interpret this as demonstrating the role of nature in ensuring recovery from attentional fatigue.

Kaplan (1978) wouldn't disagree. Restorative environments, according to Kaplan are characterised by fascination. This is where certain objects in the environment such as animals can capture our involuntary attention. Whilst our involuntary attention is captured, directed attention (the one that requires lots of effort) is restored. These sorts of environments allow us to escape from our everyday lives (what Kaplan calls "Being away") and leave behind the often overwhelming level of stimulation and demands we often face. Restorative environments also enable us to feel immersed and engaged. There is nothing unexpected in the features we see and so we can relax (what Kaplan called "Extent"). And of course, no environment is restorative unless you choose to be in it and feel enjoyment at being there (what Kaplan called "Compatibility").

SO, WHAT HAPPENS IF THERE ARE NOT MANY NATURE WALKS OR PARKS LOCALLY?

So what happens if there are few nature walks locally? A picture can do just as well, or a video and failing that, use your imagination. Following on from their first study, Berman et al. demonstrated that the restorative effect of nature works even when it is a photograph that we are looking at. Backward digit span was enhanced after looking at a series of 50 nature pictures. A similar suggestion was made by Felsten (2009). Felsten studied psychology students studying at a small, surburban campus. Having been asked to imagine themselves in a state of cognitive "fatigue", they were asked to assess the perceived restorativeness of campus settings. In some cases, no view of nature was present, in others, a view of nature could be seen through the window but with buildings present. In other cases, nature murals were shown. No surprises that views with no nature present were seen to be the least restorative. Views of nature through a window, albeit with buildings present were seen to be more restorative but guess which view won the day? Yes, the nature murals. Particularly if water was shown in the mural, these were seen to be particularly restorative.

Whilst I hope you never find yourself living there, prisons have been able to benefit from knowing this. In a study of prisoners at a medium-security prison in the United Kingdom, Moran (2019) suggested that outdoor green spaces *and* photographic displays of green, natural environments can have a restorative effect on prisoners. Self-reports from 86 prisoners indicated that green spaces helped prisoners to feel calm, find a sense of peace and gave them a sense of normality. Having access to these views enabled prisoners to think about things that they normally wouldn't and helped to remind them of their connection with the outside world. This was the case whether natural green spaces were explored or the photographic images were explored.

How about videos? Hartig et al. (1997) found no difference between restorative properties when walking through a forest or when viewing a video of a walk through a forest. Whilst our ability to interact with a natural setting may be limited in a video, it may also remove some of the less pleasant qualities associated with natural environments, cancelling out any differential effects. Laumann et al. (2001) similarly reported that watching a nature video could be as restorative as walking through a natural location. They used an attention orienting task. Imagine you are sitting in front of a computer screen in the middle of which you see a central fixation point. Your job? To look at that central point and when you see a target (an asterisk) appear in a rectangle on the left or right of the screen, press the corresponding button on the response box. Sometimes one of the rectangles will light up to cue you to the right location. Sometimes, the central fixation point will turn into an arrow which will point either left or right to help you. Just to make things a little more complicated though, sometimes the cues will be helpful and other times they will mislead you. Can you respond just as fast?

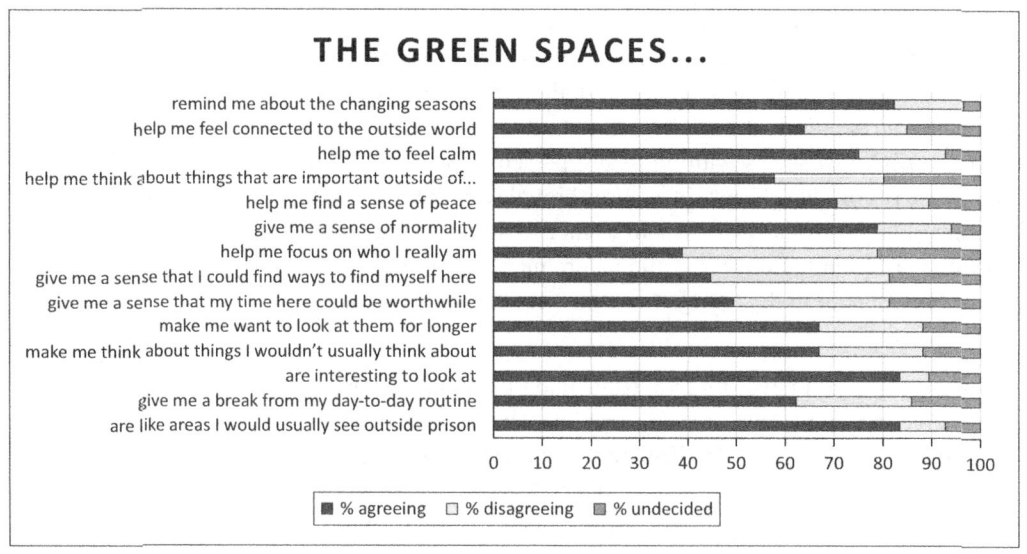

■ **Figure 9.2** Taken from Moran (2019). The responses of prisoners to questions about the effects of green space.

Once you have had a go at this task, you then sit back and watch a video. If you are lucky enough to be in condition A, you will be watching a nature video showing an island off of the coast of Norway. If you are in condition B, you will be watching a video of the urban environment, specifically a pedestrian street and bus station. You will hear cars and people talking for example. So what did Laumann et al. find? Well before watching the video, there was no difference between the people in the two conditions. However, having watched the video, those who watched the nature version had lower heart rates and performed just as fast on the attention task when invalid cues were used as when valid cues were used compared to those who watched the urban version of the video. In other words, they appeared to be less distracted by the invalid cues. As for the group who watched the urban video, well, they were still slower when invalid cues were given.

Perhaps even more striking is the claim of Laumann et al. (2001) that even imagining a natural environment can have restorative properties. Norwegian students were asked to imagine themselves in either a nature environment (a mountain area with snow) or in a city environment (in Spring). Using a questionnaire measure, they demonstrated that imagining the nature environment had a significantly greater restorative effect than imagining a city environment.

You might feel better mentally

Can greenspace improve mental health? Depression, anxiety and the effects of stress are all significant difficulties that many of us face in our daily lives. Can greenspace offer some reprieve? Nutsford et al. (2013) certainly think so. They conducted their study in New Zealand and looked at anxiety and mood disorder data in three different age groups ranging from 15 years to 65+ years. They measured access to total green space, reporting a strong relationship between this and anxiety and mood disorder prevalence. Specifically, having access to green space within 3km served as a protective factor. For Nutsford et al., being able to observe green space is a valuable tool in promoting good mental health.

Similar suggestions have been identified in other areas of the world. Honold et al. (2016) for example, conducted their study in Berlin, Germany. Participants who could view high amounts of diverse vegetation from their homes were significantly more likely to show low cortisol levels. Cortisol is used as an indicator

■ **Figure 9.3** Taken from Laumann et al. (2003). Examples of scenes from the environmental videos. The four photos at the top are from the natural environment and the four photos at the bottom are from the urban environment.

of stress. Participants who regularly visited a canal walk which had lots of greenery along it, similarly showed low levels of cortisol. And in Barcelona, Gascon et al. (2018) identified a link between access to green spaces and reduced need to take benzodiazepines (an anti-anxiety medication). Even in Taiwan, it has been demonstrated that having a view of nature can lead to less anxiety than when either a window view or indoor plants were not visible (Chang & Chen, 2005).

The idea that greenspaces can reduce stress was developed into a theory by Ulrich (1983) called the Stress Recovery Theory. According to Ulrich, seeing natural views triggers an automatic positive feeling in the perceiver. Natural views are more likely to have structural features such as complexity, a focal point that attracts our attention, depth, a ground surface texture that allows movement (e.g. evenly cut grass), a deflected vista (an element of mystery in the environment that captures attention) and no threat. This in turn causes neurophysiological responses in the body which ease stress and are restorative. In our evolutionary past, Ulrich suggests, survival would have depended on access to natural resources such as trees and bushes. Ulrich et al. (1991) demonstrated this in a study where they asked participants to watch a stressful movie about work accidents. They then exposed them to videos showing one of six natural or urban settings. Recovery was faster (as measured by heart rate, muscle tension and skin conductance for example) when participants viewed natural landscapes in the video.

The good news is it doesn't have to be about the total amount of greenspace that you have access to. It's all about our perception of green space. Hipp et al. (2016) studied students at three universities and asked them to complete a survey asking them about their perceived level of green space on campus and how they perceived the restorative potential of the campus. They measured the students' feelings of Quality of Life also. Hipp and colleagues found that those students who perceived a higher level of green space on campus were more likely to report a higher quality of life and this relationship was partly explained by how restorative they perceived the campus to be.

You might feel better physically

It isn't just mental health that seems to benefit from green space around where we live. Physical health does too. De Vries et al. (2003) studied the general health of over 10,000 Dutch residents. The one key finding that emerged from this study was the positive benefit that living in greener neighbourhoods had on health. It didn't matter what type of green space was available, but the quantity of it did make a difference. Those who lived in a greener environment tended to report fewer symptoms. In fact, the effect was so significant that the authors claimed that 10% more green space in the environment where people lived was sufficient to lead to a decrease in reported symptoms equivalent to a decrease in age by 5 years. Living near greenspace can make you feel young again!

Not only are you likely to experience fewer symptoms, but even if you do experience symptoms, chances are you are less likely to feel the need to visit a doctor if you are a local park user compared to if you are not a local park user (Godbey et al., 1998). Even in populations that can't access local parks, having a view of nature can be sufficient to prevent physical illness. Moore (1981) studied prisoners incarcerated in Michigan, USA. Similar, to Moran's studies, he reported that having a view of nature (in this case farmland and forests) resulted in 24% fewer sick cell visits compared to those whose cell looked out onto the prison yard. There could be added benefits for a prison population too. Using a combination of focus groups and interviews with prisoners and prison staff, Moran and Turner (2019) reported that views of nature had a de-stressing effect on prisoners and more recently Moran et al. (2020, 2021) also reported that access to greenspace can reduce self-harm in a prison population as well as reducing prisoner-on-prisoner assaults.

If you are unlucky enough to need surgery, well, access to views of nature can help there too. Ulrich (1984) monitored the post-operative recovery of patients who had undergone cholecystectomy (gall bladder removal). He matched patients so that one member of each pair had a view of nature from their room (a view of trees) and the other had a view of a brick wall. Not only did those seeing nature recover faster as measured by the length of their hospital stay but they also required fewer painkillers between days 2 and 5. Nurses noted the patients' condition as they recovered. Notes made about those who had access to a view of nature were significantly more positive than those who saw the brick wall. A similar pattern was identified by Lechtzin et al. (2010) who studied a different patient group. All of Lechtzin's patients were adults undergoing bone marrow aspiration and biopsy as part of their cancer treatment. This is a painful process completed with only local anaesthetic. Patients were asked to rate their pain level during the procedure. In the standard condition, 78.4% of patients reported moderate to severe pain. However, make sure there is a mural of a mountain stream in a spring meadow on a stand and play nature sounds through headphones and that percentage reduces to 60.5%, a significant reduction in pain.

Some researchers are so convinced of the role of greenspace in well-being that they advocate it as being the equivalent of a vitamin. In their "vitamin G" research programme Groenewegen et al. (2006) distinguish between Vitamin G1 (natural environments – healthy environments), Vitamin G2 (effects of greenery in the neighbourhood on health and well-being) and Vitamin G3 (health benefits from allotments) suggesting that green space can affect well-being in a number of ways rather than just one.

You might benefit economically too

The story we have told so far has advocated the role of nature in promoting good attention and good mental and physical health but there are reasons to think that nature leads to economic benefits too. Let's take worker productivity for example. Raanaas et al. (2011) demonstrated the impact of having four indoor plants in an office on a reading span performance task. The task involved participants reading aloud sentences as they appeared on a computer screen and remembering the last word in each sentence. After 8 or 12 trials, they were then asked to recall the last words they had heard in each of the sentences, in the same order as they were presented. This was repeated at three time points in an office which either had four plants in it or an office which had no plants in it. To begin with, no differences emerged. But on the second time of testing, the participants completing the task in the foliage filled office outperformed those in the bare office, showing improved performance.

And it's not only productivity that might be enhanced. Your workers may be happier too and report greater satisfaction with their work. Finnegan and Solomon (1981) delivered a 33-item questionnaire to American employees working in either a windowless or a windowed office. Those in the windowless offices were significantly less positive in terms of job satisfaction, rating their employment as less pleasurable and stimulating than those in the windowed environments. As well as replicating these findings, Kaplan (1993) also reported that having a view of nature from a window impacted positively factors such as feeling of privacy from co-workers and led to workers feeling more patient and less frustrated with their employment. If a nature view is not available, bring the outside in – indeed, in windowless environments, workers were much more likely to compensate by bringing indoor plants into the office or by posting up pictures of outdoor scenes (Heerwagen & Orians, 1986).

Not only might your employees be more productive and happier, but they might also be less likely to take time off for sick leave. Kaplan (1993) reported that workers were less likely to report common health ailments over a 1-month period if they had access to a view of a natural environment from their office. It is also worth noting that faculty of higher academic rank have significantly more windows in their office than those holding junior ranks (Farrenkopf & Roth, 1980) suggesting that status is linked to better access to views of nature.

There may be other economic benefits also. Lange and Schaeffer (2001) travelled to Zürich in Switzerland to explore the effect of a view of nature on hotel room prices. The Hotel Zürichberg offers visitors panoramic views. On one side, the rooms look out over the city and Lake Zürich whilst on the other side they look out to the forest. Hotel Storchen on the other hand is situated in the middle of the old town. Some rooms face the Limmat river, some provide views of the old town and some look out towards the Lake Zürich and the Alps. What effect did a green view have on room pricing? It increased the price and meant that the room occupancy rate was almost 100%. For Hotel Zürichberg for example, the authors estimated that the total profit impact of having a green view was approximately 456,980 US dollars!

A similar effect is seen in house prices. Barton and Pretty (2010) for example outline the results of studies such as Luttik (2000) that demonstrate the benefit of having a home with a garden that overlooks a lake on its monetary value and that of Luther and Gruehn (2001) showing how having a street that is lined with trees can inflate the value of real-estate. White and Gatersleben (2011) asked participants about their attitudes to photos of houses which either had vegetation growing on them or had no vegetation on them. The vegetation was either a turf roof, a flowering Sedum roof, a tall flowering meadow roof, an ivy façade or a brown roof. Houses with vegetation on them, regardless of type, were considered more aesthetically pleasing and beautiful than those without. Ivy facades were particularly pleasing.

Buber et al. (2007) pointed to the advantages of having nature displays in shopping malls. They created areas that had plants, water and animals in them and compared shoppers' behaviour in these

■ **Figure 9.4** Flowering plants have a particularly restorative effect.

environments with that in environments where simple wooden pillars were used or where single features (i.e. just plants, just a water fountain, just animals) were used. Over 100,000 consumers were observed over a 56-day period and 2,047 minutes of video recording was analysed. The presence of natural displays, particularly those incorporating multiple natural features, resulted in consumers not only spending longer in the mall, but also resulted in them exploring the products and interacting with salespeople significantly more. This is a particularly striking finding given that the plants and animals used were all artificial.

Aside from shopping malls, consumer satisfaction and willingness to pay is positively associated with the presence of plants in service areas such as dental surgeries, hair salons and libraries (Tifferet & Vilnai-Yavetz, 2017). In an innovative study, they recruited participants through Amazon Mechanical Turk, a crowdsourcing platform where individuals seeking work assignments for payment can be identified. Over 500 participants were recruited using this platform and were each asked to view one photo of a service delivery setting, after which they were asked to complete a questionnaire. The photo showed one of nine possible scenes created from a 3 x 3 design. 1 of 3 service settings was shown (dentist clinic, hair salon or library) and 1 of 3 conditions was shown (with a plant, with a vase or with no stimulus). Settings where a plant was present were rated as higher in perceived service quality and service satisfaction. This in turn was linked to a greater willingness to pay a higher amount for the service provided. However, the associations the authors identified were significant only for those who reported low exposure to greenery in their everyday lives.

THE BIOPHILIA HYPOTHESIS

Together, these studies suggest that nature is restorative and stress reducing. We have a preference for natural environments and seek these out where possible. Wilson (1984) developed the Biophilia Hypothesis to explain this effect, pointing to the way in which humans have an innate tendency to "focus on life and lifelike processes" (p. 1). The natural environment, he argues, is a key part of human history and evolution. Looking back at our ancestral past, Gullone (2000) argues that 99% of our history is characterised by hunter-gatherer living. Areas of water would have promoted the growth of plants and would have attracted animals that our ancestors would have harvested for survival. Trees would have offered safety in times of danger as well as offering look-out posts for enemies. These features are those that characterise the African savannahs, where our ancestors would have lived for over two million years. Balling and Falk (1982) reported a preference for savannahs over other environmental biomes in children aged 12, which, they suggest, is evidence that such preferences may be innate. Similarly, Lohr and Pearson-Mims (2006) report that certain types of trees, which are representative of those found in savannah environments are preferred over others. They compared preferences for trees that had "spreading crowns" with trees that were rounded in shape. The former were much preferred.

This also may explain why we like parks so much (Kaplan & Kaplan, 1989). Parks offer trees, and open spaces of grassland, much more similar to the savannah environment of our ancestors than dense forests or deserts that are less preferred.

And as far as animals are concerned, Wilson (1992, 1993) points out that visits to zoos in the United States and Canada outstrip attendance at major sporting events in number and Gullone (2000) points to the work of Newby (1999) showing the level of pet ownership in America to be colossal. The estimate provided is that there are 40 million pet cats and 55 million pet dogs! For anyone having to undergo oral surgery, it is also worth checking out the clinic beforehand to see if they have an aquarium in there. If DeSchriver and Riddick (1990) are to be believed, watching fish in an aquarium is as relaxing as having hypnosis!

BUT NOT ALL GREEN SPACE HAS THE SAME EFFECT

Our story so far makes a pretty convincing case for green space being good for us. In terms of where it is good to live, green space and a view of nature tops the shopping list. But as you now know, nothing is ever that straightforward in psychology. Not all green space has been shown to have similar effects on our feelings of relaxation and restoration. Park et al. (2002) reported that introducing flowering plants into a room increased pain tolerance compared to just having foliage plants present. Pain tolerance, at least for the female participants, was increased during a Cold Pressor Test where the hand is placed into icy cold water for 5 minutes. Adachi et al. (2000) also advocate the use of flowering plants to improve confidence. They asked participants to watch a video about the University of Reading, following which they were asked to complete a questionnaire asking about their feelings about the treatment room they were in. In one condition, there was a vase containing flowering plants such as sweet peas and delphiniums. In another condition, five popular foliage potted plants were present and in another condition, no display of plants were used at all. After being in the room with the cut flowers, participants reported feeling more confident as well as feeling more relaxed after being in the treatment room. In the foliage condition, however, no effect in relaxation was shown and in fact, bad temper increased. Be careful of the type of greenery you choose! Tifferet and Vilnai-Yavetz (2017) suggest that cacti may not have the same restorative effect as flowering plants as the thorns on them highlight an unpleasant aspect of them.

It's not just the type of greenery in a room that is important either. The type of greenery outside makes a difference too. Reid et al. (2017) distinguished between the amount of trees and grass in a residential area and their connection with self-reported health. Better ratings of health were connected with the presence of trees but not grass density.

But are lots of trees always a good thing? Ask Milligan and Bingley (2007). They invited young participants aged 16–21 to take part in interviews, group discussions and craft sessions held either in a rural village hall or in an area of woodland. For many of the young people, woodland offered an opportunity to find a space where they could collect their thoughts and relax. However, for some, dense woodlands with overhanging trees and narrow paths created a feeling of anxiety and being trapped. Some participants mentioned the lack of security in case of attack, having watched media coverage of attacks in wooded areas. Maas, van Dillen, et al. (2009) similarly pointed to the way in which enclosed green spaces in urban areas can increase feelings of threat and reduce social safety, particularly in women. They interviewed just short of 84,000 Dutch residents. It could be, the authors suggest, due to poorer maintenance of green spaces in these areas or it could be due to the size of buildings in urban areas. Whichever explanation we go along with, the important point is that not all green space is equally restorative.

In fact, in some cases, greenery has been seen to be a barrier to community relationships. Speller et al. (2002) studied a traditional mining village which was being relocated. Originally, rows of terraced houses had had no front gardens or dividing barriers such as hedges and residents would frequently meet each other as they went to and from their homes. In the new village, residents had gardens but these were separated by high fences. Did they like it? No they didn't. The sense of community that once existed had been eroded and isolation was increased.

EXPERIENCE MATTERS

Our experience as children makes a big difference to our response to and liking for green space as an adult. The attitudes towards green spaces shared by children in Milligan and Bingley's study for example were largely derived from childhood experiences and parental attitudes. Those who had been permitted to play unsupervised as children were more likely to feel positively about woodland. Growing up in areas near to green space is likely to increase engagement in pro-environmental behaviour when those same individuals reach adulthood (Cheng & Monroe, 2012).

The idea of individual differences like these affecting preference for particular types of greenspace was also demonstrated by Hartmann and Apaolaza-Ibanez (2010) in a study involving 750 participants. Emotional responses to 13 different green energy advertisements were assessed. Those showing nature scenes were preferred, consistent with earlier studies. However, lush green landscapes with water were preferred over typical Savannah environments. Familiarity with a landscape had a big impact on emotional response, suggesting perhaps that experience modifies our liking for particular settings.

Familiarity with a landscape has been used in a positive way to help refugees make links between new homes and former homes. Rishbeth and Finney (2006) enrolled 12 asylum seekers and refugees onto a 12-week photography programme focusing on urban open space. Ten sites in Sheffield were visited and participants kept photographic journals. Not only did the visits provide an enjoyable contrast to the everyday routines of the individuals involved but they also helped them to integrate into their communities. The more familiar the plants and landscapes, the more easily participants were able to make a link between former and current homes. Not only did it help them remember but it also empowered them by putting them in a knowledgeable position which in turn helped them to build confidence in their new communities.

PERHAPS IT IS NOT THE GREEN SPACE ITSELF THAT IS IMPORTANT AT ALL BUT WHAT WE DO IN THE GREEN SPACE

The studies we have encountered so far suggest a strong role for green spaces in well-being. But is it the presence of the green space itself or the opportunities it affords for us to engage in physical activity and to meet people? Holt et al. (2019) explored this question in a study that used over 200 undergraduate students studying at a liberal arts university in the United States as participants. They were asked to complete a survey which explored their use of green spaces in and around the campus. As mentioned earlier, having the opportunity to visit green spaces as a child was associated with use of green space as a student. But those who rated their quality of life and mood to be highest were those who used the green space in active ways. Just having green space available was not sufficient to improve health and well-being. It is possible then, that the restorative benefits of green spaces are an indirect result of the physical activity that takes place within them rather than being directly attributable to the green space itself.

This was also suggested by the findings obtained by Nutsford et al. (2013). Their study took place in New Zealand. They identified an association between anxiety or mood disorder and green space but it was the distance to useable green space that was associated with decreased treatment counts in an area not to un-useable green space.

And it may not just be physical activity that is important. Maas, van Dillen, et al. (2009) suggested that social support may explain the connection between green space and subjective mental health. In a study conducted in the Netherlands, they calculated the percentage of green space located within a 3km radius of each participant's home. As in previous studies, those who had more green space around their home did indeed report better health and the nearer the green space was to their home, the more significant the association. However, this association was mediated by the amount of social contact the participants had. Those who had more green space nearby felt less lonely and had more supportive interactions from their social network. Zhou and Rana (2012) explicitly mention the enhancement of social ties as one of the social benefits of green space and point to the findings of Kweon et al. (1998) demonstrating the benefit of accessible green space to the accumulation of social ties for older people in inner cities.

In an interesting attempt to try to make sense of the effect of these mediating variables, Sugiyama et al. (2008) distinguished between the effects of physical activity and social interaction on physical and mental health. In Adelaide, Australia, they collected data on not only perceived green space availability but walking for recreation, social coherence and physical and mental health. The association between physical health and green spaces was completely explained by walking for recreation. In other words, the link between green space and physical health was an indirect link, explained by what we use the green space for. However, for mental health, whilst walking and social coherence explained some of the association, it didn't explain it all. Green space does indeed have a restorative effect they argue in terms of its effects on our mental well-being independent of what we do in that space.

IS IT JUST OUR EVOLUTIONARY PAST HAVING AN EFFECT?

So, are we just succumbing to our evolutionary past? Is our preference for green space down to our need to survive and the affordances of the environment to sustain us? Joye and van den Berg (2011) raise a number of difficulties for earlier theories that argue this. In modern times, the environment provides us with rich opportunities to find food and shelter so why would nature still be restorative? Why would we need to have an immediate positive feeling towards nature? Plants (and hence food) do not move quickly if at all, so why the need for speed? And why should restoration itself be so rapid?

Joye and van den Berg postulate that the benefits of green space are the result of perceptual fluency. Green environments are beneficial because they are easier to process perceptually. If things are easier to process without difficulty, they tend to make us feel more positive. In environments such as natural scenes, we are able to process the visual scene more fluently.

Why are we able to process natural scenes more fluently? Joye and van den Berg argue that natural scenes have higher visual coherence due to fractal characteristics. What does that mean? Imagine seeing a branch on a tree. The structure of that branch is like a miniature of the tree itself. It is like a smaller copy. This means that a tree has a certain predictability about it. Because it has a predictability about it, there are less distracting elements to compete for visual attention so we have a chance to restore and relax. We process the scene easily. This approach, Joye and van den Berg claim provides a more coherent explanation of the benefits of nature than stress reduction theory or attention restoration theory alone.

LOOKING FORWARD

One thing is for sure. Green space does have benefits for us and if there is one take home message from our journey through this chapter, it is the importance of maintaining green space for well-being. This has never been more important than in recent times with the COVID-19 pandemic sweeping the world. Soga et al. (2021) asked residents of Tokyo, Japan to complete an online questionnaire asking about five health measures including depression, life satisfaction, happiness, self-esteem and loneliness as well as two measures of green space access during the

COVID-19 pandemic: how often they used green spaces and whether they had views of green spaces from their windows. The more frequently people used green spaces around their homes or accessed views of green spaces through their residence windows, the happier they felt, the more satisfied with their lives they reported feeling and the higher their reported self-esteem. In terms of loneliness and depression, these both decreased. Soga et al. suggest that green spaces can be used as one possible solution for public health.

Corley et al. (2021) studied the effect of having a garden during the Scottish lockdowns due to COVID-19. Older adults who completed an online survey reported spending more time in the garden during the lockdown and a corresponding improvement in physical health, mental health and sleep quality. In terms of what they did in the garden, this had little effect on their self-reports. It was the time spent in the garden that seemed to be key. The authors suggest a number of reasons why this is the case, from engaging in physical activity to greater access to sunshine and fresh air to providing opportunities to interact with neighbours.

The need to physically distance alongside the benefits green spaces offer make the role of urban planning a central concern for planners (McCunn, 2020). Soga and Gaston (2016) highlight the danger in seeing such natural components as being luxuries rather than necessities in planning and policy making. Making the importance of green space a central issue, they argue, is essential to reduce what Pyle (1993) refers to as the extinction of experience.

REFERENCES

Adachi, M., Rohde, C. L. E., & Kendle, A. D. (2000). Effects of floral and foliage displays on human emotions. *HortTechnology*, *10*(1), 59–63.

Armario, A., Ortiz, R., & Balasch, J. (1984). Effect of crowding on some physiological and behavioral variables in adult male rats. *Physiology & Behavior*, *32*(1), 35–37.

Balling, J. D., & Falk, J. H. (1982). Development of visual preference for natural environments. *Environment and Behavior*, *14*(1), 5–28.

Barton, J., & Pretty, J. U. L. E. S. (2010). Urban ecology and human health and wellbeing. *Urban Ecology*, *12*(1), 202–229.

Baum, A., & Davis, G. E. (1980). Reducing the stress of high-density living: An architectural intervention. *Journal of Personality and Social Psychology*, *38*(3), 471.

Benfield, J. A., Rainbolt, G. N., Bell, P. A., & Donovan, G. H. (2015). Classrooms with nature views: Evidence of differing student perceptions and behaviors. *Environment and Behavior*, *47*(2), 140–157.

Berman, M. G., Jonides, J., & Kaplan, S. (2008). The cognitive benefits of interacting with nature. *Psychological Science*, *19*(12), 1207–1212.

Booth, A., & Cowell, J. (1976). Crowding and health. *Journal of Health and Social Behavior*, 204–220.

Bowler, D. E., Buyung-Ali, L. M., Knight, T. M., & Pullin, A. S. (2010). A systematic review of evidence for the added benefits to health of exposure to natural environments. *BMC Public Health*, *10*(1), 1–10.

Brown, K. J., & Grunberg, N. E. (1995). Effects of housing on male and female rats: Crowding stresses males but calms females. *Physiology & Behavior*, *58*(6), 1085–1089.

Buber, R., Ruso, B., Gadner, J., Atzwanger, K., & Gruber, S. (2007, December). Evolutionary store design. How water, plants, animals and sight protection affect consumer behaviour. In *Proceedings of the Australian and New Zealand marketing academy (ANZMAC) conference* (pp. 325–331).

Calhoun, J. B. (1971). Space and the strategy of life. In *Behavior and environment* (pp. 329–387). Springer.

Chang, C. Y., & Chen, P. K. (2005). Human response to window views and indoor plants in the workplace. *HortScience*, *40*(5), 1354–1359.

Cheng, J. C. H., & Monroe, M. C. (2012). Connection to nature: Children's affective attitude toward nature. *Environment and Behavior*, *44*(1), 31–49.

Corley, J., Okely, J. A., Taylor, A. M., Page, D., Welstead, M., Skarabela, B., . . . Russ, T. C. (2021). Home garden use during COVID-19: Associations with physical and mental wellbeing in older adults. *Journal of Environmental Psychology*, *73*, 101545.

Crompton, J. L. (2017). Evolution of the "parks as lungs" metaphor: Is it still relevant? *World Leisure Journal*, *59*(2), 105–123.

DeSchriver, M. M., & Riddick, C. C. (1990). Effects of watching aquariums on elders' stress. *Anthrozoös*, *4*(1), 44–48.

De Vries, S., Verheij, R. A., Groenewegen, P. P., & Spreeuwenberg, P. (2003). Natural environments – healthy environments? An exploratory analysis of the relationship between greenspace and health. *Environment and Planning A*, *35*(10), 1717–1731.

Epstein, Y. (1982). Crowding stress and human behavior. *Environmental Stress*, 133–148.

Farrenkopf, T., & Roth, V. (1980). The university faculty office as an environment. *Environment and Behavior*, *12*(4), 467–477.

Felsten, G. (2009). Where to take a study break on the college campus: An attention restoration theory perspective. *Journal of Environmental Psychology*, *29*(1), 160–167.

Finnegan, M. C., & Solomon, L. Z. (1981). Work attitudes in windowed vs. windowless environments. *The Journal of Social Psychology*, *115*(2), 291–292.

Gascon, M., Sánchez-Benavides, G., Dadvand, P., Martínez, D., Gramunt, N., Gotsens, X., . . . Nieuwenhuijsen, M. (2018). Long-term exposure to residential green and blue spaces and anxiety and depression in adults: A cross-sectional study. *Environmental Research*, *162*, 231–239.

Godbey, G., Roy, M., Payne, L., & Orsega-Smith, E. (1998). *The relation between health and use of local parks*. National Recreation Foundation.

Groenewegen, P. P., Van den Berg, A. E., De Vries, S., & Verheij, R. A. (2006). Vitamin G: Effects of green space on health, well-being, and social safety. *BMC Public Health*, *6*(1), 1–9.

Gullone, E. (2000). The biophilia hypothesis and life in the 21st century: Increasing mental health or increasing pathology? *Journal of Happiness Studies*, *1*(3), 293–322.

Hartig, T., Korpela, K., Evans, G. W., & Gärling, T. (1997). A measure of restorative quality in environments. *Scandinavian Housing and Planning Research*, *14*(4), 175–194.

Hartig, T., Mang, M., & Evans, G. W. (1991). Restorative effects of natural environment experiences. *Environment and Behavior*, *23*(1), 3–26.

Hartmann, P., & Apaolaza-Ibanez, V. (2010). Beyond savanna: An evolutionary and environmental psychology approach to behavioral effects of nature scenery in green advertising. *Journal of Environmental Psychology*, *30*(1), 119–128.

Heerwagen, J. H., & Orians, G. H. (1986). Adaptations to windowlessness: A study of the use of visual decor in windowed and windowless offices. *Environment and Behavior*, *18*(5), 623–639.

Hipp, J. A., Gulwadi, G. B., Alves, S., & Sequeira, S. (2016). The relationship between perceived greenness and perceived restorativeness of university campuses and student-reported quality of life. *Environment and Behavior*, *48*(10), 1292–1308.

Holt, E. W., Lombard, Q. K., Best, N., Smiley-Smith, S., & Quinn, J. E. (2019). Active and passive use of green space, health, and well-being amongst university students. *International Journal of Environmental Research and Public Health*, *16*(3), 424.

Honold, J., Lakes, T., Beyer, R., & van der Meer, E. (2016). Restoration in urban spaces: Nature views from home, greenways, and public parks. *Environment and Behavior*, *48*(6), 796–825.

Hoskins, J. A. (2004). The green lungs of London. *Indoor and Built Environment*, *13*, 247–248.

Jones, K. R. (2018). 'The lungs of the city': Green space, public health and bodily metaphor in the landscape of urban park history. *Environment and History*, *24*(1), 39–58.

Joye, Y., & Van den Berg, A. (2011). Is love for green in our genes? A critical analysis of evolutionary assumptions in restorative environments research. *Urban Forestry & Urban Greening*, *10*(4), 261–268.

Kaplan, R. (1993). The role of nature in the context of the workplace. *Landscape and Urban Planning*, *26*(1–4), 193–201.

Kaplan, R., & Austin, M. E. (2004). Out in the country: Sprawl and the quest for nature nearby. *Landscape and Urban Planning*, *69*(2–3), 235–243. Duxbury.

Kaplan, R., & Kaplan, S. (1989). *The experience of nature: A psychological perspective*. Cambridge University Press.

Kaplan, S. (1978). Attention and fascination: The search for cognitive clarity. In S. Kaplan & R. Kaplan (Eds.), *Humanscape: Environments for people* (pp. 84–93). Duxbury.

Kweon, B. S., Sullivan, W. C., & Wiley, A. R. (1998). Green common spaces and the social integration of inner-city older adults. *Environment and Behavior*, *30*(6), 832–858.

Lange, E., & Schaeffer, P. V. (2001). A comment on the market value of a room with a view. *Landscape and Urban Planning, 55*(2), 113–120.

Laumann, K., Gärling, T., & Stormark, K. M. (2001). Rating scale measures of restorative components of environments. *Journal of Environmental Psychology, 21*(1), 31–44.

Laumann, K., Gärling, T., & Stormark, K. M. (2003). Selective attention and heart rate responses to natural and urban environments. *Journal of Environmental Psychology, 23*(2), 125–134.

Lechtzin, N., Busse, A. M., Smith, M. T., Grossman, S., Nesbit, S., & Diette, G. B. (2010). A randomized trial of nature scenery and sounds versus urban scenery and sounds to reduce pain in adults undergoing bone marrow aspirate and biopsy. *The Journal of Alternative and Complementary Medicine, 16*(9), 965–972.

Lohr, V. I., & Pearson-Mims, C. H. (2006). Responses to scenes with spreading, rounded, and conical tree forms. *Environment and Behavior, 38*(5), 667–688.

Luther, M., & Gruehn, D. (2001). Putting a price on urban green spaces. *Landscape Design*, 23–26.

Luttik, J. (2000). The value of trees, water and open space as reflected by house prices in the Netherlands. *Landscape and Urban Planning, 48*(3–4), 161–167.

Maas, J., Spreeuwenberg, P., Van Winsum-Westra, M., Verheij, R. A., Vries, S., & Groenewegen, P. P. (2009). Is green space in the living environment associated with people's feelings of social safety? *Environment and Planning A, 41*(7), 1763–1777.

Maas, J., Van Dillen, S. M., Verheij, R. A., & Groenewegen, P. P. (2009). Social contacts as a possible mechanism behind the relation between green space and health. *Health & Place, 15*(2), 586–595.

Mangham, A. (2016). *Dickens's forensic realism: Truth, bodies, evidence.* Ohio State University Press.

McCain, G., Cox, V. C., & Paulus, P. B. (1976). The relationship between illness complaints and degree of crowding in a prison environment. *Environment and Behavior, 8*(2), 283–290.

McCunn, L. J. (2020). The importance of nature to city living during the COVID-19 pandemic: Considerations and goals from environmental psychology. *Cities & Health*, 1–4.

Milligan, C., & Bingley, A. (2007). Restorative places or scary spaces? The impact of woodland on the mental well-being of young adults. *Health & Place, 13*(4), 799–811.

Moore, E. O. (1981). A prison environment's effect on health care service demands. *Journal of Environmental Systems, 11*(1), 17–34.

Moran, D. (2019). Back to nature? Attention restoration theory and the restorative effects of nature contact in prison. *Health & Place, 57*, 35–43.

Moran, D., Jones, P. I., Jordaan, J. A., & Porter, A. E. (2020). Does nature contact in prison improve well-being? Mapping land cover to identify the effect of greenspace on self-harm and violence in prisons in England and Wales. *Annals of the American Association of Geographers*, 1–17.

Moran, D., Jones, P. I., Jordaan, J. A., & Porter, A. E. (2021). Nature contact in the carceral workplace: Greenspace and staff sickness absence in prisons in England and Wales. *Environment and Behavior*. https://doi.org/10.1177/00139165211014618.

Moran, D., & Turner, J. (2019). Turning over a new leaf: The health-enabling capacities of nature contact in prison. *Social Science & Medicine*, *231*, 62–69.

Newby, J. (1999). *The animal attraction: Humans and their animal companions*. ABC Books.

Nutsford, D., Pearson, A. L., & Kingham, S. (2013). An ecological study investigating the association between access to urban green space and mental health. *Public Health*, *127*(11), 1005–1011.

Park, S. H., Mattson, R. H., & Kim, E. (2002, August). Pain tolerance effects of ornamental plants in a simulated hospital patient room. In *XXVI international horticultural congress: Expanding roles for horticulture in improving human well-being and life quality 639* (pp. 241–247). ISHS.

Pyle, R. M. (1993). *The thunder tree: Lessons from an urban wildland* (Vol. 337). Houghton Mifflin.

Raanaas, R. K., Evensen, K. H., Rich, D., Sjøstrøm, G., & Patil, G. (2011). Benefits of indoor plants on attention capacity in an office setting. *Journal of Environmental Psychology*, *31*(1), 99–105.

Regoeczi, W. C. (2008). Crowding in context: An examination of the differential responses of men and women to high-density living environments. *Journal of Health and Social Behavior*, *49*(3), 254–268.

Reid, C. E., Clougherty, J. E., Shmool, J. L., & Kubzansky, L. D. (2017). Is all urban green space the same? A comparison of the health benefits of trees and grass in New York City. *International Journal of Environmental Research and Public Health*, *14*(11), 1411.

Rishbeth, C., & Finney, N. (2006). Novelty and nostalgia in urban greenspace: Refugee perspectives. *Tijdschrift voor economische en sociale geografie*, *97*(3), 281–295.

Smith, S., & Haythorn, W. W. (1972). Effects of compatibility, crowding, group size, and leadership seniority on stress, anxiety, hostility, and annoyance in isolated groups. *Journal of Personality and Social Psychology*, *22*(1), 67.

Soga, M., Evans, M. J., Tsuchiya, K., & Fukano, Y. (2021). A room with a green view: The importance of nearby nature for mental health during the COVID-19 pandemic. *Ecological Applications*, *31*(2), e2248.

Soga, M., & Gaston, K. J. (2016). Extinction of experience: The loss of human – nature interactions. *Frontiers in Ecology and the Environment*, *14*(2), 94–101.

Speller, G. M., Lyons, E., & Twigger-Ross, C. (2002). A community in transition: The relationship between spatial change and identity processes. *Social Psychological Review*, *4*(2), 39–58.

Sugiyama, T., Leslie, E., Giles-Corti, B., & Owen, N. (2008). Associations of neighbourhood greenness with physical and mental health: Do walking, social coherence and local social interaction explain the relationships? *Journal of Epidemiology & Community Health*, *62*(5), e9–e9.

Takano, T., Nakamura, K., & Watanabe, M. (2002). Urban residential environments and senior citizens' longevity in megacity areas: The importance of walkable green spaces. *Journal of Epidemiology & Community Health*, *56*(12), 913–918.

Talbot, J. F., & Kaplan, R. (1991). The benefits of nearby nature for elderly apartment residents. *The International Journal of Aging and Human Development, 33*(2), 119–130.

Tennessen, C. M., & Cimprich, B. (1995). Views to nature: Effects on attention. *Journal of Environmental Psychology, 15*(1), 77–85.

Tifferet, S., & Vilnai-Yavetz, I. (2017). Phytophilia and service atmospherics: The effect of indoor plants on consumers. *Environment and Behavior, 49*(7), 814–844.

Ulrich, R. S. (1983). Aesthetic and affective response to natural environment. In *Behavior and the natural environment* (pp. 85–125). Springer.

Ulrich, R. S. (1984). View through a window may influence recovery from surgery. *Science, 224*(4647), 420–421.

Ulrich, R. S., Simons, R. F., Losito, B. D., Fiorito, E., Miles, M. A., & Zelson, M. (1991). Stress recovery during exposure to natural and urban environments. *Journal of Environmental Psychology, 11*(3), 201–230.

Valins, S., & Baum, A. (1973). Residential group size, social interaction, and crowding. *Environment and Behavior, 5*(4), 421–439.

White, E. V., & Gatersleben, B. (2011). Greenery on residential buildings: Does it affect preferences and perceptions of beauty? *Journal of Environmental Psychology, 31*(1), 89–98.

Wilson, E. O. (1984). *Biophilia: The human bond with other species*. Harvard University Press.

Wilson, E. O. (1992). The diversity of life. Allen Lane. *The Penguin Press, 178*, 6–7.

Wilson, E. O. (1993). Biophilia and the conservation ethic. In S. R. Kellert & E. O. Wilson (Eds.), *The biophilia hypothesis*. Island Press.

Zhou, X., & Rana, M. P. (2012). Social benefits of urban green space: A conceptual framework of valuation and accessibility measurements. *Management of Environmental Quality: An International Journal, 23*(2), 173–189.

Chapter 10

Is it good to spend time by the sea?

On a hot bank holiday, many people flock to the beach. This chapter questions whether spending time by the sea is beneficial to physical and/or to mental health. Certainly in Victorian times, a dip in the sea was seen to have medicinal qualities and the study of the effect of blue space (the sea, ocean, lakes, rivers and canals) on well-being has established itself as a key area within the study of environmental psychology. Does blue space have restorative effects in the same way as green space? What factors might mediate this relationship? And are there limits to the effect of blue space on our health and well-being? This chapter challenges readers to think about the limitations of blue space effects but also to consider how culture may play an important role in our interpretation of what it means to spend time by the sea.

■ **Figure 10.1** Crashing waves and a sea mist: is it good to spend time by the sea?

DOI: 10.4324/9781003329763-10

For my summer holidays, on many occasions, I have visited the Yorkshire Dales, one of my favourite spots. As part of my vacation travels, I usually stop off in Harrogate and it just so happens that Harrogate has a lot to offer in terms of our next psychology adventure because Harrogate is famous for its sulphur wells. From the 17th century, visitors flocked to Harrogate to sample the chalybeate water, that is natural mineral spring water containing a high percentage of iron. It was said to have medicinal properties and once the sulphurous water was discovered, its popularity rocketed. In fact, writing in 1845 George Kennion reported that partaking of the Harrogate waters was sufficient to cause an improvement in glandular swellings, health and strength and even to produce a new and vigorous state of the digestive system. Harrogate, he claimed, had a quality of air that was more similar to that of sea air, with its freshness and elasticity, than any other inland area. Kennion was a physician at the Harrogate Bath Hospital.

BLUE SPACE AS HEALTH-ENABLING

By the mid 18th century, doctors were recommending a stay of not less than 3 weeks to ensure permanent benefit and were prescribing bathing treatments for their patients, in some cases followed by a trip to the seaside (Holman, 2018). This early focus on the positive benefits of natural water, and its link to the sea was also advocated by Dr Richard Russell who pointed to the benefits of bathing in sea water. In 1750, he published a book documenting over 25 years of experience with sea-water use. Not only did he write about the benefits, he practised what he preached and in 1753 brought a residence near the seafront. Known as Russell House, it was on the site of what is now the Royal Albion Hotel (Lauste, 1972). Thanks to the work of Dr Russell, the rich and wealthy were attracted to Brighton in the second half of the 18th century to make the most of the remedies suggested by him in relation to the sea water and air.

Now, I know what you may be thinking. This is all very well but this was in the 18th century! However, the idea of blue space as being health-enabling is still very much a topical theme (Foley & Kistemann, 2015). We know for example that people who live near the coast have higher levels of self-reported physical activity (Bauman et al., 1999), which is mainly due to more time spent walking. For children this can be particularly important as childhood obesity has been found to be lower in children who live near the coast compared to those who live inland (Wood et al., 2016).

■ **Figure 10.2** Dr Richard Russell who advocated the benefits of sea water.

We know from the work of Elliott et al. (2015) that walking tends to last longer in coastal settings compared with urban green spaces.

However, not everyone has reported a significant effect of blue space on physical health. Vert et al. (2020) studied office workers at the Barcelona Biomedical Research Park, based at the Barcelona seafront. Participants were asked to walk on their own for 20 minutes along either a blue or urban route or to rest for 20 minutes at a control site. The blue route was along the seafront to a breakwater on the beach. The urban route took individuals down the side streets around the Research Park and the control site was a room at the Research Park. Participants were allocated to either one of the routes or the control site for a week each, during which time they were asked to complete a set of questionnaires about their well-being and mood. Not only did participants rate the blue route more positively than the urban route in terms of quality, safety and cleanliness but they also reported feeling more satisfied when walking along it. Moreover, they reported better mood and well-being after walking along the blue route. Whilst mental health certainly seemed to benefit, there was less evidence for a positive benefit on physical health. Both blood pressure and pulse rate showed little difference after participants had walked any of the routes or used the control condition room.

This is not an isolated finding. Gascon et al. (2017) in a comprehensive review, reported a less consistent association between outdoor blue space exposure and measures of obesity, cardiovascular health and general health than for mental well-being.

BLUE SPACE AND MENTAL HEALTH

Whilst the evidence for blue space being healthy for our hearts is mixed at best, the evidence for its impact on mental well-being is more consistent. Nutsford and colleagues, in 2016, reported a lower rate of poor mental health in those individuals who had a sea view and Dempsey et al. (2018) also reported a lower risk of depression amongst those who had the highest level of sea views. Völker et al. (2018) recruited over 1,000 participants for their study of blue space use. Völker chose to question participants from two German towns, one that had a poor supply of blue space and one that had a better supply of blue space. Demographic variables and socio-economic variables were all controlled yet the researchers still identified a strong association between use of blue space and mental health. Critically, it was the use of blue space that was significant rather than the perceived walking distance to the blue space.

A similar conclusion was obtained in a study conducted in Hong Kong by Garrett et al. (2019). Hong Kong, as Garrett reminds us, is one of the most densely populated countries in the world, yet at the time of publication of Garrett's work, about 40% of land was designated as a conservation or park area. Using survey methods, Garrett obtained higher well-being scores from participants who visited blue spaces more often and engaged in higher intensity activities in the blue space such as swimming. Even having a view of blue space led to better self-reported general health but it was the "intentional exposure" to the blue spaces that promoted a sense of well-being.

It is important to note that it isn't just the fact that in blue spaces, people might engage in physical exercise, that leads to our conclusion that such spaces are good for mental health. Blue spaces also offer an opportunity for people to connect with others, much like green spaces. De Bell and colleagues (2017) for example drew on data collected as part of an Opinions and Lifestyle survey of British adults run by the Office for National Statistics and identified social interaction as one of two key benefits of visiting blue spaces (the other being psychological benefits). Increased social and family interaction was identified by Ashbullby and colleagues (2013) also as a significant benefit of visits to the beach.

In fact, nature has been proposed as a "buffer" to feelings of loneliness (Cartwright et al., 2018). They collected data from 359 individuals who responded to an online survey via a survey distribution platform. One of the measures included was a 5-item well-being index measure developed by the World Health Organisation, used to give an indication of subjective well-being. Having a view of nature nearby was associated with high levels of well-being even in individuals with poor social connectedness. Such positive effects seem to be particularly noticeable when people are able to see blue space. How do we know? One source of evidence comes from the innovative work of MacKerron and Mourato (2013). Using smart phone technology, they were able to identify the geolocation of participants at various points during the day when they were asked to rate their emotional state. No surprises that the most positive responses were obtained at locations where there was blue space present, but particularly so at coastal locations.

EXPLAINING THE RESTORATIVE EFFECTS OF BLUE SPACE

So why is blue space, particularly coastal blue space, so restorative and health-promoting? There are a number of ideas that have been proposed, one of which we have already encountered which is the association between visiting blue space and engaging in physical exercise. Before we explore an alternative idea, try a quick imagination experiment. Close your eyes and imagine you are walking alongside a small mountain stream. Think about what you hear around you. Chances are it's not silent. Many poets in fact have written about the sound of water such as William Bryant's "warbling waters" in "The Rivulet" or the sound of waves breaking on the shore as in Matthew Arnold's "Dover Beach". There is good reason for this focus. Thoma (2018) allocated 60 healthy women to one of three conditions: listening to water sounds, a relaxing piece of music or silence for 10 minutes. Once the 10 minutes was up, they were asked to complete a stress- inducing test called the Trier Social Stress test: Participants are asked to prepare a 5-minute presentation as part of a job interview. During the 5-minute presentation, judges observe without passing any comments. After the presentation, participants are asked to complete a mental arithmetic task involving counting backwards in 13s. To assess stress levels, salivary cortisol was measured before, during and after the social stress test. The group that had listened to water sounds for 10 minutes showed an interesting pattern of responses. This experience moderated the effect of somatic complaints on cortisol secretion. In other words, it lessened the impact of existing bodily complaints on stress levels. This is consistent with previous research that has suggested that water sounds can have a direct effect on the nervous system. Arai et al. (2008) for example, reported that salivary alpha-amylase, used as a marker for the sympathetic nervous system, was reduced as a result of listening to natural sounds during an operation under epidural anaesthesia.

An alternative, or should I say potentially complementary idea, is that blue space is restorative due to the higher levels of biodiversity that such places possess. White et al. (2017) report that it is the perception of biodiversity that is important in terms of well-being. Indeed, this is the case even when the actual measure of biodiversity is lower (Dallimer et al., 2012)!

MEDIATING FACTORS

Whatever the reason, one thing that is consistent in the research in this area is that the potential benefits of blue space for psychological well-being seem to be particularly pronounced for elderly individuals. Chen and Yuan (2020) studied elderly residents of Guangzhou, a city in China. Exposure to blue space was found to be significantly associated with mental health in these participants even after the role of pollution, stress and opportunities for socialising were accounted for. A similar conclusion was reached by Hunter and colleagues in 2019 who described the effect of being in blue space as a "nature pill". The hormone cortisol, used to measure stress levels, showed a significant reduction in elderly individuals who spent time in blue space. This was true whether they sat at or walked along a riverbank. Dempsey et al. (2018) studied older adults in Ireland and suggested that simply having a house or flat that has a view of coastal blue space can be sufficient to lower the risk of depression.

Age is not the only factor that mediates the relationship between blue space and psychological health however. Gender makes a difference too. Both the type of blue space visited and the activity undertaken in those blue spaces tend to differ for men and women. Who is more likely to visit a beach for example? According to research by Elliott et al. (2018) it is women whilst men are more likely to visit inland waterways. This is linked to the type of activity they undertake there as men are more likely to engage in activities such as fishing whilst women are more likely to sunbathe or paddle in the sea. This was supported by Vert et al.'s study of a riverside regeneration project in Barcelona in 2020 which demonstrated that predominant users of the riverside area were male.

THE TYPE OF BLUE SPACE MATTERS

Now, as you may have gathered by now, nothing is ever straightforward in psychology and just as in other areas we have explored, there are some limitations to our claim that blue space is good for our mental well-being. In a seminal paper looking at preference for waterscapes, Herzog (1985) asked undergraduate students to rate 70 slides of natural environments containing water. Some included beautiful mountain streams, some contained rivers and others swampy creeks and stagnant ponds. You won't be surprised to know that swampy lakes were very rarely rated highly but mountain lakes were. Large bodies of water were also preferred over smaller bodies of water, a point which Herzog suggests might be due to the spaciousness of these areas. As he reminds us, "content matters" (p. 240).

The clarity and freshness of the blue space is important in assessing its effects on us. More recently, Julian et al. (2018) reported that 66% of undergraduate students studying at Texas State University said they would not be able to enjoy the San Marcos River that runs through campus if the water clarity was reduced.

Wyles et al. (2016) asked undergraduates to rate 24 photographs. Some of the photographs showed the beach at high tide and some at low tide. Some showed the beach littered and some not. Not only did the presence of litter reduce ratings of restorativeness but this was particularly the case for the photographs of the beach at high tide. This raises a related issue which is that of safety. Pitt

(2018) reminds us that for some adults and young individuals, they may be afraid to visit blue spaces due to the fear of falling in, particularly if they are unable to swim. Similarly Olive and Wheaton (2021) point to the potential health risk for people who use blue space for recreation, even when beaches are perceived to be clean.

Such concerns do not apply to prisoners of course but early research in this area suggested that the sight of the sea could help to relieve psychological distress experienced by these individuals (Sykes, 1958). Jewkes et al. (2020) however acknowledged that for many prisoners the sound of other people enjoying the blue space only served to exacerbate their own sense of "enforced isolation" (p. 393).

IS THIS A EUROCENTRIC VIEW?

The idea of blue space as being therapeutic and restorative is not culturally universal. Wheaton et al. (2020) challenge what they see as Eurocentric assumptions about blue spaces as sites of well-being and Collins and Kearns (2007) point to the view of some New Zealanders that sees beaches as sites where cancer risk is increased due to sun exposure. Ways of relating to and understanding the power of blue space do show cultural differences. In Maori aboriginal communities, there is no dichotomy between humans and the natural world (Patterson, 1992). Rivers are granted the same legal rights as a person and water safety is considered not just in terms of preventing drowning but also in terms of re-awakening connections with ancestors (Jackson et al., 2016, p. 28).

SOME BLUE SPACE IS GOOD BUT NOT TOO MUCH

Perhaps a more graduated approach to the topic is required. Certainly, if we believe the findings of research conducted by White et al. (2010). In this study, 120 photographs were shown to participants showing built and natural scenes. In half of the scenes, blue space was present. The proportion of blue space in these photographs was manipulated to fill either one-third or two-thirds of the photograph. Most of their participants showed a preference for views that were made up of two-thirds blue space. Anything less than one-third of blue space or scenes containing only water were rated less positively. White and colleagues argue for the importance of diversity in

■ **Figure 10.3** Examples of the scenes used in White et al.'s study of blue space. (A) Aquatic only (B) Aquatic-Green (C) Aquatic-Only + Object (D) Green-Only (E) Green-Aquatic (F) Green-Only + People (G) Built-Only (H) Built-Aquatc (I) Built + Green + Animals

terms of the effect of blue space. The interface between blue space and green space may be the optimal environment.

LOOKING TO THE FUTURE

An important issue to take forward from this is the way in which childhood experiences with blue space can feed into our experiences with nature as an adult. Calogiuri (2016), in a Norwegian study, suggests that blue space exposure in childhood may indeed have lasting positive effects. In an age where climate concerns predominate, this is an important consideration but one which we need to ensure is available to all. Even though they lived further from urban waterways, Haeffner et al. (2017) found that it was high socioeconomic status respondents who used these blue spaces more. Combined with the fact that house prices tend to be up to 10% higher for houses with the presence of water features nearby (Luttik, 2000), this points to the essential need to ensure that blue spaces cater to and are accessible for all.

REFERENCES

Arai, Y. C., Sakakibara, S., Ito, A., Ohshima, K., Sakakibara, T., Nishi, T., . . . Kuniyoshi, K. (2008). Intra-operative natural sound decreases salivary amylase activity of patients undergoing inguinal hernia repair under epidural anesthesia. *Acta Anaesthesiologica Scandinavica, 52*(7), 987–990.

Ashbullby, K. J., Pahl, S., Webley, P., & White, M. P. (2013). The beach as a setting for families' health promotion: A qualitative study with parents and children living in coastal regions in Southwest England. *Health & Place, 23*, 138–147.

Bauman, A., Smith, B., Stoker, L., Bellew, B., & Booth, M. (1999). Geographical influences upon physical activity participation: Evidence of a 'coastal effect'. *Australian and New Zealand Journal of Public Health, 23*(3), 322–324.

Calogiuri, G. (2016). Natural environments and childhood experiences promoting physical activity, examining the mediational effects of feelings about nature and social networks. *International Journal of Environmental Research and Public Health, 13*(4), 439.

Cartwright, B. D., White, M. P., & Clitherow, T. J. (2018). Nearby nature 'buffers' the effect of low social connectedness on adult subjective wellbeing over the last 7 days. *International Journal of Environmental Research and Public Health, 15*(6), 1238.

Chen, Y., & Yuan, Y. (2020). The neighborhood effect of exposure to blue space on elderly individuals' mental health: A case study in Guangzhou, China. *Health & Place, 63*, 102348.

Collins, D., & Kearns, R. A. (2007). Ambiguous landscapes: Sun, risk and recreation on New Zealand beaches. In A. Williams (Ed.), *Therapeutic landscapes* (pp. 15–32). Farnham.

Dallimer, M., Irvine, K. N., Skinner, A. M., Davies, Z. G., Rouquette, J. R., Maltby, L. L., . . . Gaston, K. J. (2012). Biodiversity and the feel-good factor: Understanding associations between self-reported human well-being and species richness. *BioScience, 62*(1), 47–55.

De Bell, S., Graham, H., Jarvis, S., & White, P. (2017). The importance of nature in mediating social and psychological benefits associated with visits to freshwater blue space. *Landscape and Urban Planning, 167*, 118–127.

Dempsey, S., Devine, M. T., Gillespie, T., Lyons, S., & Nolan, A. (2018). Coastal blue space and depression in older adults. *Health & Place, 54*, 110–117.

Elliott, L. R., White, M. P., Grellier, J., Rees, S. E., Waters, R. D., & Fleming, L. E. (2018). Recreational visits to marine and coastal environments in England: Where, what, who, why, and when? *Marine Policy, 97*, 305–314.

Elliott, L. R., White, M. P., Taylor, A. H., & Herbert, S. (2015). Energy expenditure on recreational visits to different natural environments. *Social Science & Medicine, 139*, 53–60.

Foley, R., & Kistemann, T. (2015). Blue space geographies: Enabling health in place. *Health & Place, 35*, 157–165.

Garrett, J. K., White, M. P., Huang, J., Ng, S., Hui, Z., Leung, C., . . . Wong, M. C. (2019). Urban blue space and health and wellbeing in Hong Kong: Results from a survey of older adults. *Health & Place, 55*, 100–110.

Gascon, M., Zijlema, W., Vert, C., White, M. P., & Nieuwenhuijsen, M. J. (2017). Outdoor blue spaces, human health and well-being: A systematic review of quantitative studies. *International Journal of Hygiene and Environmental Health*, *220*(8), 1207–1221.

Haeffner, M., Jackson-Smith, D., Buchert, M., & Risley, J. (2017). Accessing blue spaces: Social and geographic factors structuring familiarity with, use of, and appreciation of urban waterways. *Landscape and Urban Planning*, *167*, 136–146.

Herzog, T. R. (1985). A cognitive analysis of preference for waterscapes. *Journal of Environmental Psychology*, *5*(3), 225–241.

Holman, G. (2018). *Taking the waters-The lighter side of the Harrogate Cure, through the humorous postcards of the 1900s*. Retrieved from https://core.ac.uk/download/pdf/228319372.pdf on 30/04/22

Hunter, M. R., Gillespie, B. W., & Chen, S. Y. P. (2019). Urban nature experiences reduce stress in the context of daily life based on salivary biomarkers. *Frontiers in Psychology*, *10*, 722.

Jackson, A. M., ki Puketeraki, H., Mita, N., Kerr, H., Jackson, S., & Phillips, C. (2016). One day a waka for every marae: A southern approach to Maori water safety. *New Zealand Physical Educator*, *49*(1), 26–28.

Jewkes, Y., Moran, D., & Turner, J. (2020). Just add water: Prisons, therapeutic landscapes and healthy blue space. *Criminology & Criminal Justice*, *20*(4), 381–398.

Julian, J. P., Daly, G. S., & Weaver, R. C. (2018). University students' social demand of a blue space and the influence of life experiences. *Sustainability*, *10*(9), 3178.

Kennion, G. (1845). On the medicinal springs of Harrogate. *Provincial Medical and Surgical Journal*, *9*(35), 540.

Lauste, L. W. (1972). The development of the hospitals in Brighton and Hove. *Royal Society of Medicine*, 65, 221–226.

Luttik, J. (2000). The value of trees, water and open space as reflected by house prices in the Netherlands. *Landscape and Urban Planning*, *48*(3–4), 161–167.

MacKerron, G., & Mourato, S. (2013). Happiness is greater in natural environments. *Global Environmental Change*, *23*(5), 992–1000.

Nutsford, D., Pearson, A. L., Kingham, S., & Reitsma, F. (2016). Residential exposure to visible blue space (but not green space) associated with lower psychological distress in a capital city. *Health & Place*, *39*, 70–78.

Olive, R., & Wheaton, B. (2021). Understanding blue spaces: Sport, bodies, wellbeing, and the sea. *Journal of Sport and Social Issues*, *45*(1), 3–19.

Patterson, J. (1992). *Exploring maori values*. Dunmore Press.

Pitt, H. (2018). Muddying the waters: What urban waterways reveal about bluespaces and wellbeing. *Geoforum*, *92*, 161–170.

Sykes, G. (1958 [1974]) *The society of captives: A study in a maximum security prison*. Princeton University Press.

Thoma, M. V., Mewes, R., & Nater, U. M. (2018). Preliminary evidence: The stress-reducing effect of listening to water sounds depends on somatic complaints: A randomized trial. *Medicine*, *97*(8).

Vert, C., Gascon, M., Ranzani, O., Márquez, S., Triguero-Mas, M., Carrasco-Turigas, G., Arjona, L., Koch, S., Llopis, M., Donaire-Gonzalez, D., Elliott, L. R., & Nieuwenhuijsen, M. (2020). Physical and mental health effects of repeated short walks in a blue space environment: A randomised crossover study. *Environmental Research, 188*, 109812.

Völker, S., Heiler, A., Pollmann, T., Claßen, T., Hornberg, C., & Kistemann, T. (2018). Do perceived walking distance to and use of urban blue spaces affect self-reported physical and mental health? *Urban Forestry & Urban Greening, 29*, 1–9.

Wheaton, B., Waiti, J., Cosgriff, M., & Burrows, L. (2020). Coastal blue space and wellbeing research: Looking beyond western tides. *Leisure Studies, 39*(1), 83–95.

White, M., Smith, A., Humphryes, K., Pahl, S., Snelling, D., & Depledge, M. (2010). Blue space: The importance of water for preference, affect, and restorativeness ratings of natural and built scenes. *Journal of Environmental Psychology, 30*(4), 482–493.

White, M. P., Weeks, A., Hooper, T., Bleakley, L., Cracknell, D., Lovell, R., & Jefferson, R. L. (2017). Marine wildlife as an important component of coastal visits: the role of perceived biodiversity and species behaviour. *Marine Policy, 78*, 80–89.

Wood, S. L., Demougin, P. R., Higgins, S., Husk, K., Wheeler, B. W., & White, M. (2016). Exploring the relationship between childhood obesity and proximity to the coast: A rural/urban perspective. *Health & Place, 40*, 129–136.

Wyles, K. J., Pahl, S., Thomas, K., & Thompson, R. C. (2016). Factors that can undermine the psychological benefits of coastal environments: Exploring the effect of tidal state, presence, and type of litter. *Environment and Behavior, 48*(9), 1095–1126.

Chapter 11

The psychology of Christmas

How do you get the most out of the festive season? Should we give gifts and if so, what type? How can we maximise our guests' enjoyment of the Christmas dinner? And why is it good to sing Christmas carols? The psychological evidence explored here can apply to most festive occasions that involve gatherings to enjoy meals, to sing or to celebrate and draws on experimental studies to establish a plan for a happy time. Find out how to choose the most appropriate gift, why you should be aware of the Millman effect when you go Christmas shopping and what your Christmas decorations could be saying about you. Explore the holiday happiness curve but avoid the "Bah Humbug" syndrome that might establish itself over time!

■ **Figure 11.1** Is buying or receiving gifts the secret to a happy festive season?

DOI: 10.4324/9781003329763-11

What do you think of when you think of Christmas? Lights? Turkey? The Christmas tree? Or the presents? Perhaps you relish the thought of catching up with friends and family or maybe it is just a chance to relax and unwind for a while that appeals. Whatever your thoughts are about the festive period, and for that matter any celebratory holiday, psychology may have something to say about how you can make the festive period go with a bang.

HOW TO PROMOTE HAPPINESS IN THE FESTIVE SEASON

What is the best way to promote happiness at Christmas? Is it gift-giving? Is it being with family and friends? Or is it chilling out in front of the TV for an evening of Christmas specials? Kasser and Sheldon (2002) asked 117 individuals to rate their emotional states, satisfaction and stress levels during the Christmas period. They were asked to discuss their experiences and to share how they used money. Kasser and Sheldon originally sent out surveys to 400 randomly selected individuals living in Knox County but with only an 18% response rate, they followed up by administering 70 surveys to undergraduates at Knox College the following month.

What was it that predicted happiness? Well, it wasn't the materialistic aspects at all. In fact, these served only to undermine well-being. Focusing on spending money was a definite fun stopper. And even receiving gifts was a happiness suppressant. Think of all the time spent choosing, buying and wrapping presents. Think also of the economic debt that rises around the Christmas tradition of gift buying. None of this related to a sense of well-being. What really boosted happiness and well-being was being with family and engaging in religious experiences. This effect was particularly noticeable for individuals who were male and who were older and also for those who engaged in environmentally-conscious consumption practices. For Kasser and Sheldon, the key to understanding this effect is the way that Christmas festivities enable us to satisfy our need to relate to others. We like to feel a sense of connectedness and in the holiday season, the opportunities to do so are heightened. It could also be, as Kasser and Sheldon point out, that we feel happy because we are meeting the expectation that we should be social at this time of the year and we like to be consistent with society's expectations. I, for one, prefer their first interpretation.

Kasser and Sheldon are not alone in advocating the role of spiritual and family activities over the Christmas period. Páez et al. (2011) similarly point to the positive influence of participation in rituals of the holiday season on stress and subjective well-being. Paez and colleagues reject the common assumption that Christmas is a time of stress and argue that evidence for conflict caused by Christmas is weak and instead it is the positive emotions that dominate. Participation in family celebrations plays a positive role in cementing social support and reducing loneliness. They do, however, acknowledge that this is not always possible and where negative interactions occur, it can undermine positive affect and social well-being. But generally speaking, participation in the rituals of Christmas elevates well-being and life satisfaction, reduces loneliness and helps remove negative affect.

SHOULD WE GIVE GIFTS AT ALL?

So, should we ditch gift-giving then? Sounds like a lot of hard work for little reward. Not so fast! Dunn et al. (2008) gave participants an envelope containing either 5 or 20 dollars. They were given the instruction to spend it by 5pm that afternoon either by paying a bill, buying something for themselves or buying a gift for someone else. Participants were asked to rate their happiness in the morning and again in the afternoon. In the morning there was no difference between the groups. But by the end of the day, the participants who had been asked to spend their money on others or to make a charitable donation were significantly happier than those who spent it on themselves. Moreover, it didn't matter how much money they were given in the envelope. This had no effect at all on their ratings of happiness. It was simply the way it was spent that made the difference.

Perhaps what is important here is the choice associated with gift-giving. If we feel compelled to buy someone a gift, we may not feel happy at all about this, and it is unlikely to lead to a greater sense of well-being. But if we do so out of choice, well, that is a different matter. Weinstein and Ryan (2010) asked students to keep a diary recording their mood each day and whether they had engaged in any pro-social behaviour. Helping another person led to more positive ratings of how they felt but only in situations where they had a choice in whether to act pro-socially. If they felt they didn't have a choice, they actually felt worse!

Not only does choice matter, but who we are buying for makes a difference too. Aknin et al. (2011) recruited 80 people from the campus of the University of British Columbia for their study exploring how people spend money. Participants were asked to recall the last time they spent approximately 20 dollars on someone they considered to be a strong social tie or someone they considered to be a weak social tie. After describing this, they were asked to rate their affect using a questionnaire called the Positive and Negative Affect Schedule. This requires participants to use a 1–5 scale to assess how strongly (or otherwise) they feel in terms of hostility, happiness, alertness, and so on. What did the researchers find? Spending money on strong ties, those we know well, leads to greater happiness than spending on people we consider to be just acquaintances. For maximum happiness, when it comes to gift-buying, we should focus our efforts on those we feel closest to.

I am sure Caplow (1984) would not disagree. Caplow believes that the tradition of giving presents is an important way of maintaining social networks. Without this tradition, we may increase stress because we feel less able to express affection to our relatives.

HOW TO CHOOSE THE MOST APPROPRIATE GIFT

So, if we are not rejecting the idea of gift-giving, then how do we go about choosing the most appropriate gift? Indeed, why ask such a question? The reason lies in the work of Dunn et al. (2008) who argue that good and bad gifts can influence relationships. In the first of their studies, they led participants to believe that a new opposite sex acquaintance had selected either a desirable or undesirable gift for them. Participants were paired with a previously unknown acquaintance to complete a 4-minute experiment. Then, each participant was asked to order 12 gift certificates in terms of how much they would like to receive them before choosing one for their new acquaintance that they had only recently met. In reality, the experimenter manipulated the outcome so that for those in the good gift condition, they saw that their acquaintance had selected their first-choice gift certificate for them. In the bad gift condition, they saw that their 11th choice had been selected. Before participants left the study, they were asked to complete a survey rating their similarity to their new acquaintance and how much they liked the gift chosen for them. So, what did they find? Well there was a striking gender difference. Men receiving a "bad gift" saw themselves as being less similar to their new acquaintance than those receiving a "good gift". For women however, no differences in similarity were identified.

I know what you are thinking – this is all about new acquaintances. We are probably not even considering buying gifts for them at Christmas if we only met them for 4 minutes just before. But let's see what happened when Dunn et al. took their study to the next level. Rather than new acquaintances, what happens when the participants are heterosexual couples in dating relationships? Well, the same thing! Men perceived themselves as more dissimilar from their girlfriends when receiving a bad gift than when they received a good gift and moreover this led to a more negative evaluation of the future of the relationship. For women, they tended to behave rather differently, inflating their perception of similarity to their boyfriend after receipt of a bad gift. Dunn et al. suggest this may be a psychological defence to the threat posed by receipt of a bad gift.

So what constitutes a "good gift"? In Dunn's study, it appears to be one that the receiver would choose for themselves. Receiving a gift that matches what we would choose for ourselves acts as a form of self-verification of our values. However, we also know, from the work of Davis et al. (1986) that people's predictions about which products their spouse would like are driven by their own preferences for certain products. It should come as no surprise then to hear that they argue that similarity to a spouse can lead to greater accuracy in predicting preferences. The more similar we are to our partner, the more likely it is we will choose something that both they (and we) will like.

More recently however, Aknin and Human (2015) have argued that as a relationship develops, we would be well advised to choose a gift that reflects something about ourselves. Giver-centric gifts may act as a form of self-disclosure. The gift may heighten a sense of intimacy as it reveals or verifies something about the giver themselves. Such self-disclosure can act to increase feelings of closeness between the giver and the recipient for relationships that have already been established. It may also have additional benefits for the giver in that they are likely to feel closer to the receipient of that gift if it required a lot of thought. Recipients on the other hand are less likely to appreciate the effort invested in the process of gift purchasing unless prompted by contextual cues (Zhang & Epley, 2012).

There is one golden rule that is worth remembering though when it comes to gift-giving. Paul Webley and Richenda Wilson (1989) advise strongly against giving money as a gift. This may come as a surprise to many of us as we know that gifts of money give us the option of selecting something of our own choosing. Webley et al. (1983) quizzed students on their views about receiving money as a gift. All of them ranked money as less acceptable than a selected gift and pointed to the lack of time and effort involved. Webley and Wilson (1989) asked students to think of someone they knew either friendly or informally, as an equal or a superior and were asked to consider whether giving either money (one condition) or a present (the other condition) would be acceptable. The students were asked to estimate how much they would spend/give in each case. All students were then asked to rank order five gifts in terms of their own preference in receiving them. These were: a surprise present of their own choice, a surprise present of the giver's choice, a general token, a specific token or money. Webley and Wilson reported looks of horror on students' faces at even being asked to imagine giving money to others as a gift. Presents were considered to be a preferable option to money both to give and to receive. Of the students questioned, 75% rated this as the least preferable gift to receive out of the five options considered. Status played a role too. When the person receiving the gift was of higher status than the giver, more was spent on a monetary gift than on a present. Perhaps, the authors claim, this served as compensation for the unacceptability of this as a gift choice? When the person receiving the gift was of lower status, less was spent on monetary gifts than on a present, making for a very poor gift indeed.

So why is money considered to be undesirable? Lea et al. (1987) argue that it puts a precise monetary value on the relationship and Gregory (1982) points to the commercial connotations of money blurring the boundaries between commodity and gift exchange. Webley et al. (1983) suggest instead that it is the lack of effort and care taken by the giver that is crucial whereas Gouldner (1973) points to the difficulty of reciprocal giving. There is an unwritten rule that there needs to be a balance in exchange with gift-giving. Pryor and Graburn (1980) highlight how monetary gifts may make any imbalance more visible, damaging the relationship. Burgoyne and Routh (1991), like Webley and Wilson, quizzed undergraduate students about their views on monetary gifts. Only in certain situations such as an older person giving money to a younger person was this seen as acceptable. In fact, in 91% of cases where money was given, it was given by an older relative to a younger one. When status is equal, there is the possibility of insulting insinuations about the receiver's financial status.

■ **Figure 11.2** Giving money as a gift can be detrimental.

It is important to bear in mind that our exploration of gift-giving has so far focused primarily on Western cultures and on Christmas per se. There is reason to believe that for other festivities such as Chinese New Year, where money is exchanged in red envelopes, Hudik and Fang (2020), such social conventions differ and attitudes towards monetary gifts may differ.

CHRISTMAS SHOPPING

Given the role of gift giving in strengthening social connections, how do retail stores entice us to buy gifts within their stores? In short, by appealing to our senses. What smells do you associate with Christmas? Pine? Cinnamon? Mulled wine? And what music springs to mind? Slade's "Merry Christmas Everybody"? Brenda Lee's "Rockin' around the Christmas Tree"? Or, as in my case, Rod Stewart's Christmas Album? Well, believe it or not, the smells and sounds of Christmas might have a significant impact on your willingness to spend money in a retail store. Spangenberg et al. (2005) tells us more in his Christmas study. Participants were initially asked to evaluate a series of nine scents in terms of pleasantness, intensity and familiarity as well as the degree to which they evoked thoughts of Christmas. In the main study, participants were given an elaborate cover story, saying that they were being asked to provide feedback to a retail chain that was considering opening a new department store. Eighty slides were displayed to participants showing some of the merchandise that would be sold and evaluations of the store and merchandise were collected. Intentions to visit the store were assessed.

In one condition, Christmas scents were sprayed into the room. In another condition, no scent was sprayed. Within each condition, for half of the participants, Christmas music was played (Amy Grant's "Home for Christmas") and for the other half, music not associated with Christmas was played (Amy Grant's "Heart in Motion").

What led to the most favorable attitudes towards the store? Having an ambient Christmas scent in the air whilst listening to Christmas music. The combination of Christmas scent and Christmas music worked wonders. Not only did the participants show a more positive evaluation of the retail environment but they also expressed stronger intentions to visit the store. In contrast, smelling Christmassy smells in the presence of non-Christmas music actually led to less favorable attitudes and less intention to visit!

The picture may be more complicated than that however. In what has now been termed the "Milliman Effect" (Knoferle et al., 2012) the tempo of the music has been shown to be an important consideration. Slow tempo tends to lead to a more leisurely stroll around the store (Milliman, 1982) or a slower pace of eating which ultimately leads to more money being spent (Milliman, 1986).

A further factor that may help to slow the pace of eating is the type of scent used. Guéguen and Petr (2006) conducted their study in a pizzeria restaurant in Brittany, France. They compared the length of stay of customers and the amount purchased when either a lemon scent was sprayed, a lavender scent was sprayed or when no scent was sprayed through fragrance diffusers placed in wall sockets. Lemon is considered to have stimulating effects whilst lavender is considered to be relaxing (Diego et al., 1998). Whilst the lemon scent had little effect on behaviour, the lavender scent certainly did. According to Gueguen et al., the scent of lavender had a relaxation effect which led to customers ordering more items such as alcohol and/or coffee.

Notice that simple scents are used here. This is significant given the research reported by Herrmann et al. (2013). Herrmann et al. compared the effect of a simple orange scent with that of a basil-orange with green tea scent versus no scent at all. The study was an innovative field study conducted in an actual retail store. No prizes for guessing which scent led to the most spending. Yes, the plain orange scent. The simple scent, the authors argue, was more easily processed and led to the purchase of more items more quickly than in either of the other conditions.

THE CHRISTMAS DINNER

Which brings us nicely to the subject of the Christmas dinner. How do you ensure that your guests will leave feeling both full and happy? We can learn a lot from the work of Brian Wansink and colleagues here. According to Wansink et al. (2005), how we present food to our guests will make a lot of difference. They undertook a 6-week study, conducted in the cafeteria at the University of Illinois to demonstrate this point. Six products that were regularly offered in the café were chosen as the focus for the study. In each test week, two of the items were presented with their basic name, e.g. Grilled chicken, two items were presented with a descriptive name, e.g. Succulent Italian Seafood Fillet and two items were not presented at all. This procedure was rotated through each week. Individuals who purchased any one of the target items were asked to complete a simple one-page questionnaire at the till, to assess their sensory perceptions of the food and dietary habits as well as their rating of the food itself.

Did the descriptive label make a difference? Why yes it did. Those seeing the descriptive names made significantly more positive comments about the food compared to those who saw the basic names. Not only was it rated as being more tasty, it was also seen as being more appealing. The sensory label of the food, had, it seems, influenced evaluation of it.

Even the label on your wine bottle can make a difference. Wansink et al. (2007) gave participants a complimentary glass of wine with their restaurant meal. In one condition, the bottle had a label suggesting it was a favourable Calfornian wine. In another condition, it had a label suggesting it was from North Dakota, a less favourable wine. Did the positive expectation of tasting good wine have any impact on consumption of food? It did! Those who believed they were drinking Californian wine ate 12% more of their meal compared to those who believed they were drinking

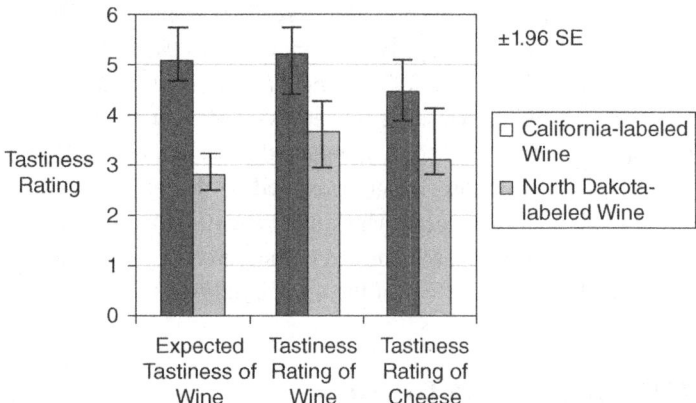

■ **Figure 11.3** Taken from Wansink et al. (2007). Even the label on your bottle of wine can bias diner's expectations and tastiness ratings.

North Dakotan wine and spent 17% longer at the table. So, at the Christmas table, make sure you draw attention to the nostalgic labels, and draw on sensory words to describe what you are serving. Chances are, your guests will approve!

THE CHRISTMAS SPIRIT

Even if cooking isn't your forte, the festive period is a good opportunity to put up decorations. If Werner et al. (1989) are to be believed, it won't just boost your spirits but it will give an important message to your neighbours. How can this be? Werner et al. (1989) explored the effect of outdoor exterior decorations on perceptions of sociability. Naïve raters were asked to look at pictures of homes and to make two judgements: how "accessible" and how "communal" to neighbours the resident was. Accessibility is about the degree of openness displayed to others. Communal identity is about the extent to which an individual shares common bonds with a larger social group. The photos showed either a close-up of the entrance or a full view showing both the home and the yard. In addition, the female heads of the households were interviewed about their attitudes to cohesiveness with, and their ratings of social contact with those in the neighbourhood.

What effect did Christmas decorations have? They gave the impression that the resident of that property was particularly sociable. Homes that were decorated were considered to be more neat, open and attractive and this was particularly the case for residents "in transition", that is residents who did not yet know many of their neighbours but liked them. For these individuals, putting up Christmas decorations on the exterior of the house served as a signal that they wished to interact with their neighbours.

Such findings confirm Werner, Brown and Peterson-Lewis's earlier work published in 1984, that reported more friends and more positive attitudes for people who put Christmas decorations on the entrance to their home than those who put their decorations away from the entrance. Perhaps, the authors argue, placing decorations at the entrance to the home serves as a welcome sign.

Of course, here we are assuming that those in the neighbourhood are also celebrators of the festive period. This may well not be the case everywhere so caution must be urged. Schmitt et al. (2010) argue that the effect of seeing Christmas decorations may be different for those who do not celebrate it. In a laboratory study, celebrators and non-celebrators were asked to complete a questionnaire in a cubicle which either had a small Christmas tree on the desk next to the computer or didn't. The questionnaire asked participants about their preferred work space before quizzing them on their mood state. The presence of the Christmas tree had a positive effect for celebrators but for non-celebrators, resulted in a less positive mood. Perhaps, the authors argue, this reflects a sense of not being included which in turn may be harmful to our sense of self-esteem.

Perhaps a better way to increase social bonding would be to engage in a spot of karaoke? Keeler et al. (2015) suggest that singing decreases stress and increases our sense of social attachment. Keeler and colleagues compared both pre-composed and improvised singing and measured the effects on ACTH and oxytocin levels in the blood. Oxytocin is known to regulate stress and anxiety and is involved in the attachment process between a child and parent. ACTH is used as a measure of stress and arousal. In both the pre-composed and improvised singing conditions, ACTH levels fell after singing, suggesting a reduction in stress. Oxytocin levels increased in the improvised singing condition, perhaps reflecting the social element of improvisation.

Keeler is not alone in advocating the value of singing to reductions in stress and increases in social bonding. Kreutz et al. (2004) similarly reported an increase in positive emotion and a reduction in negative emotion after singing in a choir and even listening to choral music was sufficient to reduce cortisol levels, a stress hormone.

DOES THE CHRISTMAS SPIRIT EXIST?

We've explored the role of decorations, singing, the Christmas dinner and gift buying but so far, we haven't really mentioned the Christmas spirit. We talk about it often enough but is there such a thing? Well, no surprises here. Psychologists have already been on the case. Hougaard et al (2015) decided to exploit the technology of MRI scans to answer our question. Hougaard, working in Copenhagen, recruited 20 volunteers, 10 of whom were celebrators of Christmas and 10 of whom were not. Whilst in the MRI scanner, participants were shown a series of pictures. Some of the pictures were Christmas themed but others were neutral containing nothing that symbolized Christmas at all. Was there any difference in the brain scans of those who celebrated Christmas and those who did not? Yes! In the sensory motor cortex, premotor and primary motor cortex and the parietal lobe, significantly more clusters of activation were found in the celebrators. Why are these areas significant? Because, Hougaard claims, these are areas associated with spirituality. It is as though celebrators have a Christmas spirit network in the brain! The brain, it would appear, does indeed play a central role in the festive cultural traditions of Christmas. Beware though, Hogaard et al. do highlight the existence of "Bah Humbug" syndrome, a deficiency in Christmas spirit that occurs after many years of celebrating the same tradition.

CHRISTMAS AS A TIME OF RELAXATION

Before we leave our psychological exploration of Christmas, there is just time to mention one last point and that is to make sure that you use the festive period to unwind and relax. To maximise the effectiveness of this, ensure that any unfinished tasks are completed before the holidays begin. Syrek et al. (2018) asked 145 employees working in industry to complete a survey regarding their work. This was repeated twice each week for 15 weeks. The study spanned the Christmas period, 4 weeks before and the remaining weeks after. Participants were asked to rate their positive and negative affect, anticipation, the number of unfinished work-related tasks and detachment and relaxation activities. Syrek identified a curvilinear relationship, that Nawijn (2010) termed the "holiday happiness curve". Positive feelings increased in the lead-up to Christmas, showed a peak at Christmas and then slowly decreased through January and February. Anticipation of the Christmas season seemed to make the biggest impact on positive affect but as far as the reduction in negative affect was concerned, it was the number of unfinished tasks that had the biggest impact. As the number of unfinished tasks increased, so the reduction of negative affect in the run-up to Christmas slowed down. On return to the workplace after Christmas, the number of unfinished tasks also impaired positive affect during the next few weeks. Individuals with fewer unfinished tasks to return to showed a slower increase in negative affect after Christmas. Detachment and relaxation were seen to be powerful influences in terms of slowing the reduction of positive affect after the Christmas period. So, what is the key message? Enjoy the anticipation, get those work tasks finished where you can and make sure you relax and detach from the workplace where possible.

REFERENCES

Aknin, L. B., & Human, L. J. (2015). Give a piece of you: Gifts that reflect givers promote closeness. *Journal of Experimental Social Psychology*, *60*, 8–16.

Aknin, L. B., Sandstrom, G. M., Dunn, E. W., & Norton, M. I. (2011). It's the recipient that counts: Spending money on strong social ties leads to greater happiness than spending on weak social ties. *PLoS One*, *6*(2), e17018.

Burgoyne, C. B., & Routh, D. A. (1991). Constraints on the use of money as a gift at Christmas: The role of status and intimacy*. *Journal of Economic Psychology*, *12*(1), 47–69.

Caplow, T. (1984). Rule enforcement without visible means: Christmas gift giving in Middletown. *American Journal of Sociology*, *89*(6), 1306–1323.

Davis, H. L., Hoch, S. J., & Ragsdale, E. E. (1986). An anchoring and adjustment model of spousal predictions. *Journal of Consumer Research*, *13*(1), 25–37.

Diego, M. A., Jones, N. A., Field, T., Hernandez-Reif, M., Schanberg, S., Kuhn, C., . . . Galamaga, R. (1998). Aromatherapy positively affects mood, EEG patterns of alertness and math computations. *International Journal of Neuroscience*, *96*(3–4), 217–224.

Dunn, E. W., Aknin, L. B., & Norton, M. I. (2008). Spending money on others promotes happiness. *Science*, *319*(5870), 1687–1688.

Dunn, E. W., Huntsinger, J., Lun, J., & Sinclair, S. (2008). The gift of similarity: How good and bad gifts influence relationships. *Social Cognition*, *26*(4), 469–481.

Gouldner, A. W. (1973). The norm of reciprocity: A preliminary statement. In A. W. Gouldner (Ed.), *For sociology: Renewal and critique in sociology today* (pp. 226–260). Allen Lane. (Orig. pub. 1960).

Gregory, C. A. (1982). *Gifts and commodities*. Academic Press.

Guéguen, N., & Petr, C. (2006). Odors and consumer behavior in a restaurant. *International Journal of Hospitality Management*, *25*(2), 335–339.

Herrmann, A., Zidansek, M., Sprott, D. E., & Spangenberg, E. R. (2013). The power of simplicity: Processing fluency and the effects of olfactory cues on retail sales. *Journal of Retailing, 89*(1), 30–43.

Hougaard, A., Lindberg, U., Arngrim, N., Larsson, H. B., Olesen, J., Amin, F. M., . . . Haddock, B. T. (2015). Evidence of a Christmas spirit network in the brain: Functional MRI study. *BMJ, 351*.

Hudik, M., & Fang, E. S. (2020). Money or in-kind gift? Evidence from red packets in China. *Journal of Institutional Economics, 16*(5), 731–746.

Kasser, T., & Sheldon, K. M. (2002). What makes for a merry Christmas? *Journal of Happiness Studies, 3*(4), 313–329.

Keeler, J. R., Roth, E. A., Neuser, B. L., Spitsbergen, J. M., Waters, D. J. M., & Vianney, J. M. (2015). The neurochemistry and social flow of singing: Bonding and oxytocin. *Frontiers in Human Neuroscience*, 518.

Knoferle, K. M., Spangenberg, E. R., Herrmann, A., & Landwehr, J. R. (2012). It is all in the mix: The interactive effect of music tempo and mode on in-store sales. *Marketing Letters, 23*(1), 325–337.

Kreutz, G., Bongard, S., Rohrmann, S., Hodapp, V., & Grebe, D. (2004). Effects of choir singing or listening on secretory immunoglobulin A, cortisol, and emotional state. *Journal of Behavioral Medicine, 27*(6), 623–635.

Lea, S. E. G., Tarpy, R. M., & Webley, P. (1987). *The individual in the economy*. Cambridge University Press.

Milliman, R. E. (1982). Using background music to affect the behavior of supermarket shoppers. *Journal of Marketing, 46*(3), 86–91.

Milliman, R. E. (1986). The influence of background music on the behavior of restaurant patrons. *Journal of Consumer Research, 13*(2), 286–289.

Nawijn, J. (2010). The holiday happiness curve: A preliminary investigation into mood during a holiday abroad. *International Journal of Tourism Research, 12*(3), 281–290.

Páez, D., Bilbao, M. Á., Bobowik, M., Campos, M., & Basabe, N. (2011). Merry Christmas and Happy New Year! The impact of Christmas rituals on subjective well-being and family's emotional climate. *Revista de Psicología Social, 26*(3), 373–386.

Pryor, F. L., & Graburn, N. H. (1980). The myth of reciprocity. In *Social exchange* (pp. 215–237). Springer.

Schmitt, M. T., Davies, K., Hung, M., & Wright, S. C. (2010). Identity moderates the effects of Christmas displays on mood, self-esteem, and inclusion. *Journal of Experimental Social Psychology, 46*(6), 1017–1022.

Spangenberg, E. R., Grohmann, B., & Sprott, D. E. (2005). It's beginning to smell (and sound) a lot like Christmas: The interactive effects of ambient scent and music in a retail setting. *Journal of Business Research, 58*(11), 1583–1589.

Syrek, C. J., Weigelt, O., Kühnel, J., & de Bloom, J. (2018). All I want for Christmas is recovery – changes in employee affective well-being before and after vacation. *Work & Stress, 32*(4), 313–333.

Wansink, B., Payne, C. R., & North, J. (2007). Fine as North Dakota wine: Sensory expectations and the intake of companion foods. *Physiology & Behavior, 90*(5), 712–716.

Wansink, B., Van Ittersum, K., & Painter, J. E. (2005). How descriptive food names bias sensory perceptions in restaurants. *Food Quality and Preference, 16*(5), 393–400.

Webley, P., Lea, S. E., & Portalska, R. (1983). The unacceptability of money as a gift. *Journal of Economic Psychology*, *4*(3), 223–238.

Webley, P., & Wilson, R. (1989). Social relationships and the unacceptability of money as a gift. *The Journal of Social Psychology*, *129*(1), 85–91.

Weinstein, N., & Ryan, R. M. (2010). When helping helps: Autonomous motivation for prosocial behavior and its influence on well-being for the helper and recipient. *Journal of Personality and Social Psychology*, *98*(2), 222.

Werner, C. M., Peterson-Lewis, S., & Brown, B. B. (1989). Inferences about homeowners' sociability: Impact of Christmas decorations and other cues. *Journal of Environmental Psychology*, *9*(4), 279–296.

Zhang, Y., & Epley, N. (2012). Exaggerated, mispredicted, and misplaced: When "it's the thought that counts" in gift exchanges. *Journal of Experimental Psychology: General*, *141*(4), 667.

Index

Abel, E. L. 87
absenteeism 94
abstract thinking 25, 26
accessibility 202
accommodation 23
ACTH levels 203
action games 42
ACTIVE (Advance Cognitive Training for Independent and Vital Elderly) clinical trials 43
active control groups 44
active learning 21, 28; through activities 30; as construction 22–26; definition 22; differences 30–32; Piaget's stage theory 23–26; teachers' role 27; and teaching 32–35; Vygotsky's peer learning 28–30
Adachi, M. 169
Adeimantus 2, 18
affection 45
aggression: and crimes 139–140; and video games 48–50
air freshener 103
Aknin, L. B. 195, 197
Allwood, C. M. 113
Amabile, T. M. 99
Amazon Mechanical Turk 167
Ancient Egyptians 2, 56
Ancient Greeks 2, 154
Anderson, C. A. 49
Anderson, D. E. 120
anthropomorphism 7
anti-social behaviour 48–50
anxiety 76–80, 121–122
aquarium 169
Arai, Y. C. 186
Arevalo, J. P. M. 48
Armario, A. 154
Arnold, Matthew 185
Ashbullby, K. J. 185
Ask, K. 145
assertivity 45
assimilation 22–23
asymmetrical skepticism 145
Atkinson, C. 104

attachment anxiety 121–122
attention 158–159
Attention Restoration Theory 153, 157, 173
attractiveness 138–139, 145
Attributional Style Questionnaire 96
Attrill, M. J. 65
Au, J. 44
Austin, M. E. 156
autonomy 104
Ayers, W. 32

babyfaceness 139–140, 143
backward digit span 157, 159
"Bah Humbug" syndrome 193, 204
Bain, K. 35
Ballesteros, S. 45
Balling, J. D. 168
Balmer, N. J. 74
Balodi, A. B. 48
Bandura, A. 83
Bani-Melhem, S. 99
Bannister, Roger 80
Barger, P. B. 97
Baron, R. A. 103
Baron-Cohen, Simon 6
Barr, P. S. 98
Barsade, S. G. 95–96, 106
Barton, J. 166
Barton, R. A. 63–64
Bateson, M. 8–9, 13, 15, 16
Baum, A. 155
Baumeister, R. F. 73, 79
Baxter, M. 114, 119
Beedie, Christopher 82
behaviour: anti-social 48–50; pro-social 8–10, 17, 45–47, 195; sentinel 111, 121; unobserved 15
Beilock, S. L. 80
Benedict, J. O. 101
Benfield, J. A. 158
Bentham, Jeremy 2–3
Berman, M. G. 157, 159
Berry, D. S. 140
Biden, Joe 5
Bingley, A. 170

biodiversity 186
Biophilia Hypothesis 153
Bjork, R. A. 30
black colour: in sports 62–65; vs. red colour 62
blended learning 31
Bless, H. 98
blue space: Eurocentric view 188; future 189; good and bad 188; mental health 184–185; physical health 182–184; psychological health 186–187; restorative effects 185–186; types of 187–188
Bodenhausen, G. V. 98
body language 71
Bogaard, G. 114, 115
Bond Jr, C. F. 113–114, 123
Booth, A. 155
Boston fern 101
Boudreaux, C. J. 72
Bowler, D. E. 156
brain-training games 39–41
Breaugh, J. A. 103
Breuer, J. 48
Brick, N. E. 87
Brighouse, T. 33
Bristow, Eric 78
Brown, B. B. 203
Brown, K. J. 155
Bryant, William 185
Buber, R. 166
Budé, Luc 29
Bull, R. 147
Buraimo, B. 75
Burgoon, J. K. 117
Burgoyne, C. B. 198
Burleson, W. 23
burnout 94
Bushman, B. J. 47, 49

Calhoun, J. B. 154–155
Calogiuri, G. 189
Calvo, M. G. 78
Cameron, J. 86
Caplow, T. 196

capuchin monkeys 119–120
Carder, B. 99–100
Catastrophe Theory 71
Cavior, H. 139
Cavior, N. 139
Cerankosky, B. C. 51
Chamberlain, Neville 142
Chatzisarantis, N. L. 86
cheating 122
Chen, T. W. D. 87
Chen, Y. 186
Cherney, I. D. 30
child developmental stages 23–26
Choi, W. B. 86
Christensen, M. 102
Christmas: decorations 202–203; dinner 201–202; festive season 193–195; gifts 195–199; shopping 199–201; spirit 202–204; as time of relaxation 204–205
Cilic, Marin 77
Cimprich, B. 158
city living 154
Clinton, Bill 112
Clinton, Hilary 112
cognitive anxiety 78–79
cognitive development 25
cognitive skills, and video games 40–43
collaborative reading 31
Collins, D. 188
combat sport 87
communal identity 202
compatibility 159
compensation effect 143
concrete operational stage 25
confidence 120
connectedness 194
Consciousness Processing Hypothesis 79
conservation tasks 25
constructivism 22–26
contextual anthropomorphism 7
co-operative teams 95
Cordova, D. I. 86
Corley, J. 174
Cortisol 161, 163, 186
Costi, M. 105
COVID-19 pandemic 154, 173; Ghost Games 73; watching eyes effect 11–12
Cowell, J. 155
Cox, R. 73

creativity 42, 98–99, 103
Cremades, J. G. 85
Crim, D. 104
crime reduction 10–11
Criminal Man (Lombroso) 134
criminals, spotting 122, 133–148; through eye-witness 146–147; honesty and dominance 141–142; importance 143–146; physical appearance implications 147–148; physical characteristics 136–138; self-fulfilling prophecy 142–143; stereotype 138–141; types of criminals 134–136
Crisis City 47
Crombie, W. 42
Crompton, J. L. 154
crowd effect 71, 73, 75–76, 154–155

Dangerous Decisions Theory (DDT) 145
Davis, H. L. 197
Dawson, Charles 112
DDT *see* Dangerous Decisions Theory (DDT)
Dear, K. 10
De Bell, S. 185
de Burgh, Chris 55–56
deception, detecting 111–115, 121–123; China in 1000 BC 115; drawing 125–127; eliminating visual information 117–118; group decisions 123–125; improving 123; low pitch voices 116; Tipping Point Framework 111, 120; unconscious 118–120; unexpected questions 127–129; verbal cues 115–116
Deci, E. L. 86, 104
decision-making 98–99, 120, 123–125
deeper learning 30
Dempsey, S. 184, 186
Denault, V. 118
DePaulo, B. M. 113–114
DeSchriver, M. M. 169
desensitisation effect 49–50
Deslauriers, L. 31–32
Devil's Advocate approach 128
De Vries, S. 163
Dickens, Charles 154
Dictator Game study 14
Digit Span task 157–158

direct anthropomorphism 7
discovery learning 27
Dixson, A. F. 56
Djokovic, Novak 76
Dodson, J. D. 77
Dohmen, T. J. 75
dominance 141–142
Downward, P. 75
Dowsett, A. 50
drawing, as detection tool 125–127
Dreiskaemper, D. 64
drive theory 76
Dumas, R. 144–145
Dunn, E. W. 195, 196–197
Duvall-Early, K. 101
dwarf date palm 101

economical benefits, of greenspace 165–168
Ede, A. 84
educational psychology 21
Ein-Dor, T. 121–122
Eisenberger, R. 86
Eisenbruch, A. B. 61
Ekström, M. 9
Elliot, A. J. 56–58, 60–61
Elliott, L. R. 183, 187
Ellis, B. J. 61
Elsbach, K. D. 98
emotion: cues based on 118; expressions 118, 141–142
employees/staff psychology: better performance 96–98; burnout 94; commitment to organisation 94–95; creativity 98–99; empowerment 103–104; intuition 99–106; plants in office 100–103; teamwork 95–96
Endless Ocean 47
Engle, R. W. 44
environmental psychology 153; gender differences 155; Lungs of London 154–155; phytophilic effect 156, 157–158
Epley, N. 124–125
Epstein, Y. 155
Ernest-Jones, M. 16
Estrada, C. A. 98
Etcoff, N. L. 118
extrinsic motivation 85
eyes: contact 114; power of 2–4; size 140
eyewitness 146–147
Eysenck, M. W. 78

failure 23
Falk, J. H. 168
Fang, E. S. 199
Farabee, A. M. 103
Fay, A. L. 27
Fazey, J. 77
Felsten, G. 159
Festinger, L. 86
festive seasons 193–195
fidgeting 114
Finnegan, M. C. 165
First Dates 62
Fischer, K. 73
Fischer, P. 50, 51
flexibility 43, 104
Flowe, H. D. 141–142, 146–147
fluency 43
fluid intelligence 45
Foldit game 42
food description 201–202
formal operational stage 26
Forrest, D. 75
Foucault, Michel 3
Fox, S. 95
Franceschini, S. 43
Frank, M. G. 62
Fredrickson, B. L. 99
Freud, S. 48, 113
Fried, R. I. 33
frowning 87
Furst, M. L. 81

games-based learning 28, 31–32
GAM *see* General Aggression Model (GAM)
Garrett, J. K. 184
Gascon, M. 163, 184
Gaston, K. J. 174
Gatersleben, B. 166
gaze aversion 114, 115
gender differences 50, 155
General Aggression Model (GAM) 39, 48
General Theory of Crime 138
George, Jennifer M. 95, 96, 105
George, T. R. 81
German Bundesliga 73
Ghost Games 73–74
gift-giving 195–199
Gilovich, T. 62
Gino, F. 67
Giolla, E. M. 127
giver-centric gifts 197
Glaucon 2

Global Deception Research Team 114
Goldon pothos (*Epipremnum aureum*) 101
Goldstein, A. G. 137
"Go/Leave" dog study 13–14
Goodrich, R. 101
Gottfredson, M. R. 138
Gould, D. 83
Gouldner, A. W. 198
Graburn, N. H. 198
Grandey, A. A. 97
Granhag, P. A. 113, 114, 115, 145
Granic, I. 42
Graydon, J. 76, 78
Greenlees, I. A. 65
green space 100, 153; benefits 156–159; better performance at work/school 157–159; Biophilia Hypothesis 168–169; different effects 169–170; economical benefits 165–168; effects on prisoners 159–160; evolutionary past 173; future 173–174; individual differences 170–171; longer life 156–157; mental health 161–163; physical health 163–165; social support 171–172; videos/photographs 159–160; in well-being 164–165
Gregory, C. A. 198
Greitemeyer, T. 45–47, 48, 50
Grézes, J. 120
Groenewegen, P. P. 165
group decisions 123–125
Gruehn, D. 166
Grunberg, N. E. 155
Guéguen, N. 59, 200
Gullone, E. 168–169
Gyges 2

Hackman, R. J. 104
Haeffner, M. 189
Hagger, M. S. 86
Hall, L. 104
hand-washing 11–12
Handy, C. 33
Harackiewicz, J. M. 86
Hardman, Suzanne 112
Hardy, L. 77, 83
Harrison, M. A. 116
Harrogate waters 182
Hart, P. 7
Hartig, T. 158, 160

Hartwig, M. 122–123
Haslam, S. A. 103
Haucap, J. 73–74
Hawthorne, Nathaniel 56
Hawthorne Effect 44
Hayes, S. 139
Hereford 10
Herrbach, O. 94
Herrera, V. 138
Herrmann, A. 201
Herzog, T. R. 187
high-fiving 72, 87–88
Hill, R. A. 63–64
Hinton, Martin 112
Hipp, J. A. 163
Hippocrates 154
Hirschi, T. 138
Hitler, Adolf 142
Holder, R. L. 75
holiday happiness curve 193, 204
home advantage 72–76; crowd effect 73; referee role 74–76
honesty 141–142, 143
Hong Kong 184
Honold, J. 161
Horus 2
Hougaard, A. 204
houseplants 101–102
Hudik, M. 199
Hughes, S. M. 116
Hull, C. L. 76
Hulme, C. 44
Human, L. J. 197
Humphrey, S. E. 104
Humphries, J. E. 146–147
Hunter, M. R. 186
hunter-gatherer living 168
Hutchinson, J. C. 84

indoor plants 101–102, 163, 166
innocence 144
instructional scaffolding 29
intrinsic motivation 85–86
intuition 99
involuntary attention 159

Jackson, M. 50
Jacob, C. 59
Japan, Olympic Games in 72
Jensen, E. N. 113
Jewkes, Y. 188
Jiménez Sánchez, Á. 73
job: retention 103; satisfaction 94–95, 104, 165; sharing 104

Job Affect Scale measure 99
Johnson, H. 137
Joliffe, Therese 6
Jones, M. 75
Jonides, J. 157
Joye, Y. 173
Julian, J. P. 187
Jupe, L. 122–123

Kalasountas, V. 81
Kaplan, R. 100, 156, 157, 165–166
Kaplan, S. 100, 157, 159
Kasser, T. 194–195
Kawashima's Brain Training Game 40
Kearns, R. A. 188
Keating, D. P. 26
Keeler, J. R. 203
Kelsey, C. 4
Kennion, George 182
Kestenbaum, G. I. 48
King, Billie Jean 82–83
Klatt, T. 140, 142
Klein, N. 124–125
Knight, C. 103
Kocher, M. G. 75
Kozlowski, K. 56
Kramer, R. S. 62
Kraus, M. W. 87
Kreutz, G. 203
Kruger, M. L. 87
Kühn, S. 48
Kurtzberg, R. 148
Kweon, B. S. 172

Labyrinth 5
"Lady in Red, The" 56–58
lady palm 101
Lamers 45–46
Lange, E. 166
language development 24
Larsen, L. 102–103
laughter 34
Laumann, K. 160–162
Lavín, J. M. 73
Lea, S. E. G. 198
Leach, A. M. 117–118
leadership 105–106
Leal, S. 128
Lechtzin, N. 164
Leins, D. 127
Lemmings 45–46
Lepper, M. R. 86
Lewinsky, Monica 112

Lewison, E. 147
lie detection *see* deception, detecting
Lin, Hanyu 59
Lloyd, E. A. 12
Lobo, G. J. 30
Locke, E. A. 83
Lohr, V. I. 168
Lombroso, Cesare 134–135, 138, 147
Longacre, J. J. 147
Lown, C. 145
"low stakes lies" 118
Lumosity 45
Lungs of London phrase 154–155
Luther, M. 166
Luttik, J. 166
Lyons, M. 118

Maas, J. 172
MacKerron, G. 185
MacLin, M. K. 138, 147
MacLin, O. H. 146, 147
Madjar, N. 99
Madriz, E. I. 139
Maier, M. A. 66
Makin, S. 44
Malpass, R. S. 146
Manesi, Z. 16
Mann, S. 115, 117
Maori communities 188
Marsh, H. W. 81
Martin, L. L. 98
Martorano, S. C. 26
Mayer, R. E. 27
McArthur, L. Z. 140
McCain, G. 155
McDonald, S. M. 145
Meijer, E. H. 115
Melby-Lervåg, M. 44
Melton, R. J. 97
mental health: blue space 184–185; green space 161–163
Meyer, J. K. 147
Meyer, P. 113
Millbank Prison 3
Miller, D. J. 40
Milligan, C. 170
Milliman effect 193, 200
Minecraft game 42–43
Mobekk, H. 12
Moller, A. C. 85
monetary gifts 198–199
monkey virus 42
Montepare, J. M. 139

Moore, E. O. 164
Moran, D. 159–160, 164
motivation 71, 85–86
Mourato, S. 185
Mozart 99
Mügge, D. O. 48
Mühlfeit, J. 105
Mulgrew, J. 62
Murray, Andy 76–77
music tempo 200

Nalbandian, David 77–78
Napoleon 112
natural views 158, 163
Nawijn, J. 204
Neave, N. 140
Necker Cube Pattern Control Test 158
negotiations 96
Neilands, P. 13–14
Nelson, L. R. 81
nervousness 114, 115
Nettle, D. 10, 14–15
neutral games 47
Nevill, A. M. 74, 75
NHS Acute Trust, in UK 104
Nickell Helping Attitude Scale 48
Niesta Kayser, D. 56–57, 58
Nintendo DS Lite system 40
non-anthropomorphism 7
non-verbal cues 115
Nutsford, D. 161, 184

object-based learning 28
object permanence 23
occupational psychology *see* employees/staff psychology
Oda, R. 17
Oldman, G. R. 104
Olive, R. 188
Olympic Games, Japan 72
optimism 96
originality 43
Orwell, George 4
Osswald, S. 45–47
Othello error 113
overconfidence 82–84
overcrowding 154–155
Owen, A. M. 44
oxytocin 203
Oyabu, T. 101

Páez, D. 195
Pallavicini, F. 41

Index

Palumbo, R. 104
Panagopoulos 5–6
panopticon 2–4
Park, S. H. 169
parks 154, 156; *see also* green space
part-time jobs 104
passion 33
Pazda, A. D. 56, 61, 62
PBL *see* problem-based learning (PBL)
Pearson-Mims, C. H. 168
peer learning 28–30
Pelled, L. H. 94
Perceptual Fluency theory 153, 173
performance: contingent rewards 86; happy employee 96; proof-reading 158
Perry-Paldi, A. 121
personality traits 137
Peterson-Lewis, S. 203
Petr, C. 200
Pfattheicher, Stefan 11
Philippen, P. B. 87
Photofit images 139
physical health: blue space 182–184; green space 163–165
physiological arousal 50–51, 71, 76–80
phytophilic effect 156, 157–158
Piaget, Jean 22, 24–27
Picard, R. W. 23
Piltdown Man 112
Pitt, H. 187–188
Pitt, M. 102
Pitt, William 154–156
placebo effect 81–82
plants: flowering 167, 169; in office 100–103
plastic surgery 147–148
Plato 2
pleasant smells 103
Poincare, Henri 99
Pollet, T. V. 16
Portal 2 game 42–43
Porter, S. 142–144, 145
positive and negative affect 196, 204
positive emotions 41, 96, 195
positive leadership 105–106
pre-operational stage 25
Pretty, J. 166
Prince, M. 22, 28
prison inmates, in lie detection 123
problem-based learning (PBL) 28
problem solving 25

Processing Efficiency Theory 71–72, 78
productivity, through indoor plants 102–103
pro-social behaviour 8–10, 17, 45–47, 195
Pryor, F. L. 198
psychological health 186–187
puzzles games 42
Pyle, R. M. 174

Raanaas, R. K. 165
Ragan, P. T. 99–100
Ramsden, P. 33, 35
Rana, M. P. 172
Razak, A. A. 31
Readdy, T. 86
reading development 43
reasonable doubt 144
recidivism 147–148
recreation 172, 188
red colour: confidence level 63; fashion 62; limitations 60, 66; among other species 60; "Lady in Red, The" 56–58; in sports 62–64; status and authority 61–62; universal phenomenon 58–59; *vs.* black colour 62
referee bias 74–76
Regas, J. C. 56
Regoeczi, W. C. 155
Rehabilitation for the facially disfigured (Longacre) 147
Reid, C. E. 169
relaxation 47, 156
religious experiences 194–195
Remote Association Test 100
re-offending 147–148
reputation management 1, 13–14
Resident Evil 4 47
restorative environments 100, 159
reverse order questioning 127–128
rewards 85–86
Riddick, C. C. 169
Riggs, Bobby 82–83
risk aversion theory 1, 12
Robbins, Sally 78
Roberts, D. 29
Robertson, D. P. 40
romantic red effect 55, 57–58, 60
Rossignoli-Palomeque, T. 44
Rothmann, S. 104
Routh, D. A. 198
Royer, C. E. 136, 139

Royne, M. B. 7
rubber plants 101, 103
Russell, Richard 182–183
Ryan, E. D. 85
Ryan, R. M. 104, 195

salience 15–16
Sanders, S. D. 72
satisfaction 100, 156
savannah environments 168
scents 200–201
Schaeffer, P. V. 166
Schindler, S. 123
Schmidt, H.G. 28–29
Schmitt, M. T. 203
scholarships 85
Schulman, P. 96
SDT *see* Social Defence Theory (SDT)
sea view 181–189; *see also* blue space
sea-water 182
Seijts, G. H. 104
self-belief 71, 80–82
self-conscious 79–80
self-fulfilling prophecy 142–143
self-preservation 122
Seligman, M. E. 96
Sénémeaud, Cécile 8–9
sentinel behaviour 111, 121
Serious Sam game 42–43
Shakespeare 113
Shao, R. 50
Shaw, H. 118
Sheldon, K. M. 85, 194–195
Shepherd, J. W. 139
Shields, K. 140
Shoemaker, D. J. 137
shopping 199–201
shopping malls 166–167
Simmons, R. 75
Simons, D. J. 43
Singh, S. 95, 96
singing 203
skill development 79
smiling 87, 97
Smith, A. 102
snake plants 101, 103
social approval 15
social bonding 203
Social Defence Theory (SDT) 111, 121
social interaction 185
social support 172, 195

Soga, M. 173–174
Solomon, L. Z. 165
Sorokowski, P. 63
Sors, F. 75
Spangenberg, E. R. 199
Sparks, K. V. 80
Spector, P. E. 95
Spira, M. 147
sport psychology 71; controlled physiological arousal and anxiety 76–80; high fiving teammates 87–88; home advantage 72–76; intrinsic motivation 85–86; overconfidence 82–84; self-belief 80–82; smiling 87
staff empowerment 103–104
Staw, B. M. 96–97, 106
Steinhilber, A. 73
Stillman, T. F. 140–141
Stojanoski, B. 44
Stress Recovery Theory 163
Strömwall, L. A. 115
Su, F. 33–34
Sugiyama, T. 172
Super Mario Galaxy 47
surveillance 2
suspiciousness 120
Sutter, M. 75
swimming 184
syllogistic reasoning 98
Symbol Digit Modalities Test 158
symbolic thinking 24
Syrek, C. J. 204

Takano, T. 156
Talbot, J. F. 156
task-contingent rewards 86
teaching 32–35
teamwork 31, 95
ten Brinke, L. 118–120, 125, 142, 145
Tennessen, C. M. 158
Tennstedt, S. L. 43
Testé, B. 144–145
testosterone levels 140–141
Tetris 45–46
Thoma, M. V. 185
Thompson, K. M. 148
Thornton, G. R. 136–137
Tifferet, S. 156, 169
tipping 59
Tipping Point Framework 111, 120
Torrance Test of Divergent Thinking 42

touch 87–88
Tracy, J. L. 58, 60
Trier Social Stress test 186
Trotsky, Leon 27
Trump, Donald 5
trustworthiness 141–142
truth: bias 119, 120; truth-tellers 114–116
Turner, J. 164
turnover 94
Tyler, S. 26

Ulrich, R. S. 163–164
Umbach, P. D. 32
unattractiveness 138–139
unconscious lie detector 118–120
unexpected questions 127–129
unfaithfulness 122
Unverzagt, F. W. 43

Valins, S. 155
Valla, J. M. 138
Van den Berg, A. 173
Van Dillen, S. M. 172
Van Rompay, Thomas 15
van Veldhuizen, T. S. 125
vegetation houses 166
Ventura, M. 41
verbal cues 115–116
Vert, C. 183, 187
video games 39–51; and aggression 48–50; anti-social behaviour 48–50; cautious reasoning 43–45; and cognitive skills 40–43; pro-social behaviour 45–47
videos, of green space 160–161
Vilnai-Yavetz, I. 156, 169
violence: crime 139; in games 47–48
Virenque, Richard 82
Visser, V. A. 105
visual information 117–118
Vogt, W. 82
Völker, S. 184
Vrij, A. 65, 113–116, 119, 126–128
Vygotsky, L. 21, 27, 28–30

Wagner, S. L. 85, 86
Walia, B. 72
Walker, R. J. 33
walking 156, 158, 160, 172, 182–183
Wang, Y. 50

Wansink, Brain 201–202
Wason Selection Task 26
watching eyes effect 1; avoiding risks 12–13; COVID-safe 11–12; crime reduction 10–11; historical suggestion 4–8; limitations 16–17; probability of donation 15; pro-social behaviour 8–10, 17; reputation 13–16; sensitivity 8–12
water sounds 185–186
Wawrzynski, M. R. 32
Webley, P. 197–198
Weinstein, L. 48
Weinstein, N. 48, 102, 195
Weis, R. 51
well-being 100, 185
Werner, C. M. 202–203
West Mercia police 10
Wheaton, B. 188
Whitaker, J. L. 47
White, E. V. 166
White, J. 78
White, M. 188–189
white lies 113
Williams, A. M. 74
Wilson, E. O. 168–169
Wilson, M. 78
Wilson, R. 197–198
Wolverton, B. C. 101
Wolverton, J. D. 101
women: gender differences 155; sensitivity to red colour 61
Wood, M. 33–34
Woodman, T. 83
Woods, D. 33
Woodward, Smith Arthur 112
work from home 103
workplace: burnout 94; dog in 102; flexibility 104; *see also* employees/staff psychology
Wright, T. A. 96
Wyles, K. J. 187

Xin, K. R. 94

Yerkes, R. M. 77
Yuan, Y. 186

Zebrowitz, L. A. 139–140, 143, 145
Zhou, X. 172
Zloteanu, M. 114
Zone of Proximal Development (ZPD) 21

Made in United States
North Haven, CT
13 September 2025